THE ORGANISATION OF EUROPE

Developing a Continental Market Order

D.M. Harrison

London and New York

First published 1995
by Routledge
11 New Fetter Lane, London EC4P 4EE

Simultaneously published in the USA and Canada
by Routledge
29 West 35th Street, New York, NY 10001

© 1995 D.M. Harrison

Typeset in Palatino by Florencetype Ltd, Stoodleigh, Devon

Printed and bound in Great Britain by Biddles Ltd,
Guildford and King's Lynn

British Library Cataloguing in Publication Data
A catalogue record for this book is available from the British Library

Library of Congress Cataloging in Publication Data
A catalogue record for this book has been requested

ISBN 0–415–11070–X (hbk)
ISBN 0–415–11071–8 (pbk)

For Isobel

(in the hope that one day she might read it)

The Union shall be founded on the European Communities, supplemented by the policies and forms of cooperation established by this Treaty. Its task shall be to organise, in a manner demonstrating consistency and solidarity, relations between the Member States and between their peoples.

(Article A of the Treaty on European Union, signed in Maastricht in 1992)

But this leads to a new approach to the problem of politics, for it forces us to replace the question: *Who should rule?* by the new question: *How can we so organise political institutions that bad or incompetent rulers can be prevented from doing too much damage?*

Sir Karl Popper, *The Open Society and Its Enemies*

CONTENTS

Preface		xi
Acknowledgements		xv
A note on the treaties		xvi
1	INVENTING THE EUROPEAN COMMUNITY	1
2	THE SHAPE OF THE UNION	37
3	THE PRINCIPLES OF THE SINGLE EUROPEAN MARKET	53
4	THE SINGLE MARKET IN PRACTICE	68
5	FINANCIAL EUROPE	92
6	ECONOMIC AND MONETARY UNION	104
7	AGRICULTURE	129
8	EXTERNAL RELATIONS	151
9	THE COLLAPSE OF COMMUNISM	176
10	WHAT IS EUROPEAN INTEGRATION?	194
	Notes	214
	Bibliography	220
	Index	223

PREFACE

This book started life as a series of lectures (in English) at the French business school HEC (Hautes Études Commerciales), just outside Paris, in the autumn of 1991. The bulk of it was written in Stockholm in late 1993 and early 1994. It draws on my experience in working more or less continuously on various questions connected to the European Community over a period of ten years: as a member of the British Diplomatic Service in Brussels, London and Paris; as a consultant on the French financial markets; and as a consultant to the European Bank for Reconstruction and Development. It is not an academic's view of European integration. Still less is it an inside story about Britain and Europe. It is, instead, an attempt to put into a comprehensible framework the main issues driving the European Community (or the European Union, as this entity renamed itself as I was drafting) and to render them accessible to the interested reader.

The series of lectures at HEC was entitled 'A Framework for Business in the Single European Market' and was clearly 1992-oriented. The essential points are still to be found in this book. But by 1994, with the single market programme mostly agreed, with the Maastricht Treaty ratified, with the negotiations on the next round of enlargement well under way, and – above all – with the collapse of communism becoming ever more clearly a defining moment in European history, it seemed just as important to consider the basic justification of European integration and to ask what relevance it has in today's world. It may seem that to do this is to depart from the strictly business approach to the Community (as promoted by the 1992 programme) but, as I shall explain shortly, I do not think this is so.

Like perhaps many people I have become increasingly dissatisfied with the rather simplistic terms under which questions concerning European integration are usually discussed. On the one hand, it seems beyond reasonable doubt that in a global economy the nation state can no longer be regarded as the measure of all things and that there are economic forces which make the notion of national control of the economy illusory. If that is true of large economies like the United States, then the same must apply to medium-size economies such as those of western Europe. On the other hand, the model of European integration which is often put forward in opposition (a United States of Europe, a federation, a new nation in the making) appears to contain errors which, although different, are equally important by trying to duplicate on a much larger scale what is in fact proper to a national political organisation.

Embracing the scientific method of Sir Karl Popper, I have tried to put forward a new hypothesis which better fits the facts of European integration as they can be observed, rather than trying to fit the facts into old hypotheses. I do not claim this hypothesis is perfect; merely that it is a better explanation of what is actually happening than many existing explanations. (I would direct the reader to the final chapter for my conclusions on this point.)

On the way to creating this hypothesis I have attempted to explain the background to the main events in the development of the European Community – or Union. I may have over-simplified some complicated problems in doing so, but I believe this is preferable to overloading the book with a mass of indigestible jargon and unprocessed facts. At a time when the collapse of communism removes many of the old certainties in Europe, it seemed a good moment to try to establish a few simple points which appear to have held good since the Second World War – and to consider where they might be developed next.

What is the business connection? It is that, as rather few people seem to have noticed, the principal individual behind the creation of the European Community – Jean Monnet – was schooled in the world of international business rather than political theory. As the author of a new biography of Monnet[1] points out, Monnet spent virtually the entire period after leaving the League of Nations in 1923 up to the Second World War on business in different parts of the world, principally working as an investment banker. From 1936 New York was the Monnet family home and English was his working language. Although by origin a man of the French countryside (where the family cognac business was still located), Monnet's international life – and above all his experience of living and travelling around America – impregnated him with the spirit of enterprise. As Roussel puts it: .'This citizen of the world had the mentality of a Frontiersman.'[2]

It was this can-do attitude of the New World that Monnet brought back in the post-war period to the stuffy, hidebound, hierarchical, formalistic Old World, riven by ancient conflicts and hatreds. 'The America that Jean Monnet loved was this optimistic America, generous, efficient, conscious of its responsibilities,' Roussel writes.[3] It was the America of Roosevelt and the decisive tilt against Nazism in the war. It was the America of Harry Hopkins (Roosevelt's personal envoy to Churchill, also a confidant of Monnet). And it was, after the war, the America of the Marshall Plan and the reconstruction of western Europe (which Monnet helped co-ordinate in France). Faced with the problem of post-war national redevelopment, Monnet brought a reformist zeal to lethargic French conditions under the banner 'Modernisation or Decadence'. And faced on the larger scale with the problem of France and Germany once more sliding into positions of antagonism and mistrust, Monnet put forward a scheme which struck – deliberately – at the heart of the establishment in each.

One would have had to have been living on another planet (as opposed to in another country) to be unaware when writing this book that 'Europe' as a subject has again become a matter of great political controversy. (And yet this is not simply a British phenomenon: many European political parties are also groping for a discourse which works at both the national and European level.) I doubt if anyone who has made up his or her mind about these matters will find much to change it in these pages. My aim is not to convince anyone about anything, but rather it is to explain what some of the original ideas were (and in some cases how they have been forgotten). Two important points in particular I believe tend to go by default. The first is the original idea that the Community should work in close partnership with the United States (as I have explained in Chapter 8). The second is the commitment to market-creation which underlay the Treaty of Rome (to explain which I have gone into the Spaak Report in rather more detail than usual in Chapter 1). We tend to think we have just discovered market forces, but they were alive and well in the 1950s.

No one who has studied the Community (or Union) could possibly claim that it is perfect. But to those who would say we should tear it down and start all over again, or that it is so bad that it is not worth taking part in, I would recall what Monnet said during the war to a young assistant who thought that certain passages in a plan by the French Resistance needed to be modified: 'Your ideas are perhaps good ones, perhaps better than what is written here . . . but they are only in your head. The plan, on the other hand, exists and we are going to keep to it.'[4]

I have tried to demonstrate that the Community (or Union) is really a *method* of organising relations between nations rather than a political programme. It has become overlaid by generations of differing political views but in essence it is politically neutral. It is, pretty much, what we make of it. It is certainly no utopia. It could even, perhaps, be described as the worst kind of European system – except for all those other kinds that have been tried from time to time.

ACKNOWLEDGEMENTS

I would very much like to thank the following very busy people, who have helped either in the sense of providing constructive criticism or in pointing me towards valuable material which I have needed for the book: Anthony Teasdale, Philip Ward, Jean Guyot, Stephen Fisher, John Houston, Peter Stein, Andrea Minton Beddoes, Philippe Duclos, Helen Wallace and especially and above all my wife Valerie. I would also like to thank Matthias Brinkmann, Kerstin Ljungberg and Johan Ekwall of the Stockholm office of the European Commission for helping me in some arcane researches. My agent Frances Kelly deserves a special mention for assistance beyond the call of duty in getting the book from idea to reality. It goes without saying (but I will say it anyway) that none of the aforementioned are implicated in any way in any mistakes of fact or judgement in this endeavour: they have simply helped contain the number.

A NOTE ON THE TREATIES

The main treaties of relevance to this book are: the European Coal and Steel Community Treaty (the Treaty of Paris) of 1951; the European Economic Community and European Atomic Energy Community Treaties (the Treaties of Rome) of 1957; the Single European Act of 1986; and the Treaty on European Union (the Maastricht Treaty) of 1992. (I have generally followed normal practice and referred to 'the Community', although there are still strictly three 'Communities'.)

Life has become rather more complicated since Maastricht. From the entry into force of that Treaty in 1993 the collective entity known as the European Union has been in existence, and this has become the widely used title of what was previously known as the Community. But, despite this, the European Community still exists as a part (and in fact the most important part) of the European Union; and much of this book deals with matters which in any case predate Maastricht. So as a rule of thumb I have used 'European Union' when dealing with the collective entity post-Maastricht (particularly in relation to external affairs) and 'Community' for matters pre-Maastricht and/or where it is important to be clear we are talking about Community activity. Inelegant though this may be it is current usage in the European Council, which must be presumed to know what it is doing.

Maastricht also renames the European Economic Community in the 1957 Treaty so that it becomes the 'European Community' throughout. Hence the shorthand I have used for the main treaties is: ECSC Treaty, EC Treaty, SEA and Maastricht Treaty.

1

INVENTING THE
EUROPEAN COMMUNITY

INTRODUCTION

Why do we need to know something of the origins of the European Union as it exists today? There are several reasons. One is that, as this book will demonstrate, neither the new European Union nor its core component, the old European Community, is a static organisation. The Community has always been moving, not always in the most obvious direction. To understand where it is going we have to understand a little of where it has been. Many of today's arguments about the shape and nature of both the Union and the Community have been gone over many times before, in particular in the very early days. There is something of a cyclical pattern to such issues, and old arguments often come back in a new disguise.

There is, however, an additional reason why UK readers in particular need to start with a little history. The entry of the UK into the Community was late. This breeds a certain tendency to assume that the story began on 1 January 1973, when the UK, Denmark and Ireland acceded to the EC and the Six became the Nine. But of course in reality the EC already had over twenty formative years – an entire generation – behind it by then. That period of EC history is not well understood in the UK. Yet a glance into the past helps explain much about current attitudes and assumptions. And now that the UK has been a member itself for a generation another generation is opening before us. The prospect of enlargement on a much greater scale – an EU of fifteen members and more – will inevitably lead back to references to the original guiding principles. What is the Community for? Why was it invented? Is it still necessary? Can it adapt while retaining its original essence?

1

To help clarify these questions I propose to go back to first principles, to try to explain the unique combination of politics and economics which lies at the heart of the Community and (because the story repays retelling in this post-cold war period oddly reminiscent as it is of the periods after the ends of the First and Second World Wars) to try to do some justice to the man who more than anyone else is responsible for the present organisation of Europe: Jean Monnet, who died in 1979. A brief look at both his extraordinary career and the prototype Community institution which he created and first led – the High Authority of the European Coal and Steel Community, founded in 1951 – is still rich in insights of use today.

JEAN MONNET

Monnet remains to this day an obscure figure in the UK. In A.J.P. Taylor's *English History 1914–1945* he features only in a laconic footnote on page 593 – 'French economic expert, who later devised the Common Market' – (Taylor 1975: 593). And yet in 1975 Henry Kissinger said of Monnet that in his opinion no man on earth had more marked and changed the political life of our times (quoted in *Témoignages à la mémoire de Jean Monnet* 1989: 317). After Monnet's death, former senior British civil servant Lord Plowden offered this remark in his memory:

> He [has] through imagination, concentration on a subject, perseverance and determination done more to unify Europe on a permanent basis than all the emperors, all the kings, all the generals and all the dictators since the fall of the Roman Empire.
>
> (Témoignages 1989: 399)

Who was Monnet?

Monnet pursued a wide variety of careers in both what would now be called the public and the private sectors. In private life he was (as perhaps befits someone whose ideas led to the creation of the European market) an international businessman and banker, born and raised in France but for much of his life living abroad on business; in London in his teens before the First World War, representing the interests of his family cognac firm, then later doing the same in Canada and the United States, before working with an American investment bank first in central Europe, then in

San Francisco and then for two years in China in the 1930s. He was bilingual in French and English, speaking the latter with a slight American accent. But it is Monnet's public career that is so remarkable. He was, in the period 1914–18 (from the age of 26), instrumental in organising (from London) the pooling of Allied French and British shipping which overcame the shortfall in supplies caused by German submarine attacks during the First World War. Then, from 1919 (at the age of 31), he was appointed Deputy Secretary General of the League of Nations (where he worked, among other things, on the Silesia and Saar questions left over from the war). In the period 1940–3 he was first with de Gaulle in London and then in Washington as a member of the wartime British Supply Council. There he both inspired Roosevelt's phrase that America must become the 'arsenal of democracy' and also convinced Roosevelt that the American war effort on behalf of the allies be stepped up – which, in the opinion of Keynes, perhaps helped shorten the Second World War by one year.[1] In 1946 he was the principal architect of the first post-war modernisation plan for France (largely credited with turning France from an economy which before the war had been one of the most backward and stagnant in Europe to one which became that of a major industrial power). In 1950 he was the inventor of what became known as the Schuman Plan to pool French and German coal and steel production, which was the first step towards the Community (and about which more below). In 1952, after chairing the conference which drew up the first Treaty, he was appointed first President of the High Authority of the Coal and Steel Community (the precursor of today's European Commission). And finally, in 1973 (after UK accession to the Community – which, unlike de Gaulle, he strongly supported) Monnet was the main inventor of what is known now as the European Council – the regular meeting of EC heads of government intended to consider broad strategic questions and give the EC political direction.

This brief survey of Monnet's career is necessary because it shows him playing a key part in many of the critical events of this century. When he came to suggest the method which became the foundation for the unification of western Europe he did so not on the basis of abstract ideas or theories plucked from the air, but on the basis of direct practical experience in two world wars, two post-war reconstructions, wide contacts within both the spheres of business and politics and a life already lived in the four corners of the world. Anglophone and anglophile, convinced of the need for America and Europe to work together in the joint service of democracy, convinced also of the need to eliminate the causes of successive wars in Europe by creating common French and German objectives, Monnet was the precise opposite of the caricature of the European who sees Europe purely in terms of opposition to the United States, as an extension of national interest or as a defensive fortress.

One of Monnet's guiding principles was that at birth all men are the same, but as they grow they do so within a framework and within a system of rules which then come to determine their later behaviour, and under which they seek to maintain the privileges they have gained, often by a policy of domination. The nation has itself become one such framework (although not the only one). Monnet thought that, while it may not be possible to change human nature, it *may* be possible to change the framework which determines human behaviour, and in particular to establish a new framework by creating for individuals – or nations – a new common sense of purpose and common objective. On one level this can be read as no more than the truism familiar to anyone in business that the most diverse elements can be brought together to establish mutual confidence in the pursuit of a common outcome. This is the heart of virtually any successful negotiated deal. But Monnet's originality lay in finding ways of applying such thinking in the public sphere, and in particular in the immense grey area of relations between nations, where for the first half of this century in particular practices based on domination and attempts at domination had laid waste to continental Europe. The failure of the League of Nations to maintain the peace after the First World War convinced Monnet that after the Second World War a new approach to handling international relations was needed. That approach was to aim to substitute rules of conduct between nations for the classical arbitration of differences by force; to substitute the rule of equality between both individuals and nations for attempts to achieve positions of crushing domination; and to substitute the pursuit of a common objective in the common interest for attempts to negotiate individual reciprocal advantages. These were not perhaps completely new ideas in themselves: but, in the sphere of international relations where hitherto the projection of force had been the strongest factor, their application was revolutionary.

The mechanism which in Europe put such ideas into operation grew to become the European Community. We will now look at how it was first created.

THE EUROPEAN COAL AND STEEL COMMUNITY

In his memoirs Monnet recalls how, in the spring of 1950, he left France for a two week walking trip in Switzerland, during which he reflected on the problem of the growing crisis in relations between France and Germany. Five years after the end of the Second World War tensions were building up which were strikingly similar to those which had developed after the First World War – and which themselves had contributed to the outbreak of the Second World War. The fundamental problem – as before – was how to reconcile the inevitable revival of the ravaged German economy and nation with the fears by her neighbours of renewed attempts at domination. Germany, although still under the legal authority of the victorious wartime powers, was already seeking further economic and political independence. French policy amounted at the time to no more than a rearguard attempt to block or at least delay the granting of further freedoms. In 1949 France and Germany had already disagreed over the status of the economically strategic Saar and Ruhr regions; and in early 1950 France sought to detach the Saar from Germany. While Germany was seeking to increase its steel production from eleven to fourteen million tonnes, France was opposed to such expansion. However, France could not rely on support from the other Allies, in particular a United States which was, on the contrary, keen to see the revival of the German economy and thus a reduction in the costs of its own financial contribution. Monnet predicted how, if nothing happened to change the situation, the course of events would run:

Germany growing; the dumping of German exports; calls for protection for French industry; an end to freedom of trade; a recreation of the pre-war cartels; perhaps an orientation of German production towards the east, as a prelude to political agreements; France stuck once more in the rut of limited and protected production.

(Monnet 1976: 422)

5

It was against this background that in the spring of 1950 Monnet sought a solution which would combine a political symbolism powerful enough to seize the imagination of leaders and populations with a technical content sufficiently rigorous to address the underlying problem.

Already in the period immediately following the Second World War there had been many calls for European unity. Churchill, in his great Zurich speech of September 1946, had called for 'a kind of United States of Europe' (Cannadine 1989: 311). And in March 1950 German Chancellor Adenauer had suggested a complete political and economic union of France and Germany (an idea which was in fact too bold to be well received in France). Monnet believed that Adenauer's idea contained the germ of a solution to the disputes between France and Germany, but that it came at the problem the wrong way. Rather than trying to dissolve all differences within a global union it would be better first to concentrate directly on the core difficulty.

At that time it seemed to Monnet that that core difficulty could be narrowed down to the fundamental parts of the economies of both Germany and France in times of peace and war: coal and steel production. The regions of production of these basic industries lay awkwardly situated athwart the French and German borders. The importance of these regions had increased in the industrial age – but this period had also coincided with the rise of nationalism. The frontiers which ran through these areas not only blocked trade but also had become lines of political and military demarcation. Neither side felt secure unless it possessed all the resources available – which in turn meant possessing all the relevant territory. This rivalry was then translated into war, but this could only solve the problem for a while – the time needed for the loser to prepare for revenge. As Monnet put it:

> Coal and steel were both the key to economic power and also to the arsenal where the weapons of war were forged. This double power gave them an enormous symbolic significance which we have forgotten, like that belonging to nuclear energy today.
>
> (Monnet 1976: 424).

The problems caused by what in today's terms might be called the heartland of the European military–industrial complex had long been recognised. In 1926 a Luxembourg ironmaster named Emile

Mayrisch had attempted to promote cross-border co-operation in Europe through the International Steel Cartel. But this – a purely private sector arrangement – had been recognised by its author as insufficiently strong to bind European nations themselves. Yet in the public domain the weakness of the League of Nations left the Saar problem unresolved. Churchill argued in his book *The Second World War* that, after the First World War, French occupation of the Ruhr (in an attempt to enforce reparations) had contributed to the collapse of German monetary and political stability – which in turn paved the way for the rise of Nazism (Churchill 1965: Vol I, 11).

The proposal which Monnet came up with in 1950 to break the Franco–German deadlock was radical in the extreme. It was to place the whole of both French and German production of coal and steel under an international authority with membership open to other European countries, and for this authority to have as its purpose the unification of the conditions of production leading to a gradual extension of effective co-operation in other areas.[2]

It is not necessary to give all the details here of how Monnet first persuaded the French government to adopt this plan (which became known as the Schuman Plan when it was formally put forward by the French Foreign Minister in May 1950), how it was received enthusiastically by the German government, how an international conference on the plan which opened in June refined certain aspects of it – in particular the institutional side – and how finally the Treaty on the European Coal and Steel Community was signed in Paris one year later in April 1951 between France, Germany, the Benelux countries and Italy. The details – and they are fascinating – can be found in Monnet's own *Mémoires*.

But it *is* necessary to consider the mix of politics and economics which lay at the heart of the plan, an understanding of which illuminates the development of the European Union to this day. On the broad political and strategic level both France and Germany (and, indirectly, the other signatory countries) obtained benefits. For France the plan directly addressed the fears caused by the prospect of a resurgent Germany. Chancellor Adenauer recognised this vital point when he wrote:

> The fear persisted in France of being once again attacked by a revived Germany, and it was conceivable that similar

ideas circulated in Germany. Any rearmament would first involve an increase in production of coal, iron and steel. If an organisation as envisaged was created that would allow the two participating countries to detect the signs of such a development that new possibility would contribute to an immense sense of relief in France.

(quoted in Monnet 1976: 438)

And while France gained in terms of a greater sense of strategic security, Germany, too, made political gains. Unlike after the First World War, Germany was this time to be allowed by France to develop the core of its economy on a basis of clear legal equality free from a penal burden of reparations. (In 1950 German industry was still under the formal control of the wartime Allies – whose permission in fact had to be sought before formal talks between France and Germany could begin.) And so for Germany participation in the plan was an important step forward in its reintegration into western, democratic Europe.

While the plan involved these unprecedented multiple political gains, it also broke new ground in economic and technical terms. The economic heart of the proposal was, as Article 1 of the Treaty of Paris put it, *a European coal and steel community comprising a common market, common objectives and common institutions.* And this creation of a common market for coal and steel – in other words a market which joined together the French and German national markets, as well as those of the Benelux countries and Italy – involved radical new thinking in the application of market economics. While the final objective was a liberal, market-creating one, that objective could not under the circumstances prevailing be obtained without a strong organisation – an organisation strong enough to challenge national methods of market organisation and so create a new common entity. And so, here at the outset, was one of the apparent paradoxes of the European Community – the fulfilment of liberal, market-creating objectives by a strong, independent authority. But the paradox was only apparent: the authority was strong and independent not in order to control the economy in the Soviet sense, with centralised planning of the means of production and distribution, but precisely because it had the task of breaking down the barriers to the wider market created within the member states themselves. As Monnet put it:

8

We were not aiming to substitute the responsibility of the High Authority for that of companies, but rather to create the conditions of true competition in a vast market where producers, workers and consumers would each find an advantage. It was not utopian to think that this balance would establish itself in most cases, but it would not be wise to pretend that it could endure without the interventions of the independent High Authority. The essence was to limit interventions to what was strictly necessary, to codify them and to control them openly.

(Monnet 1976: 476)

Some examples may illustrate the issues arising.

One of the most difficult problems to be resolved in drawing up the Treaty of Paris was the decartelisation of heavy German industry in the Ruhr. The excessive industrial combinations in that area had formed the industrial backbone of the Reich. After the war it was American policy to break up such concentrations, in particular the dominant monopoly controlling German coal sales, and the ownership of coal mines by steel interests. And equally in France industrialists could not be expected to operate in a market where supplies of raw materials could be closely controlled by competitors. It required Adenauer himself to accept the Allied decartelisation plans before German reservations on the anti-trust articles of the Treaty were lifted. It is interesting to note here that the relevant articles, which forbid 'all agreements between enterprises, all decisions of associations of enterprises and all concerted practices which tend, directly or indirectly, to prevent, restrict or falsify the normal play of competition in the common market', and which thus became the basis of present-day EC competition policy, were in fact drawn up at the request of Monnet by the American anti-trust expert Robert Bowie, who was adviser to the American High Commissioner in Germany. Later Bowie was to underline how important it was that in so breaking up its cartels Germany should believe that it was being treated on a basis of equality and not inferiority (*Témoignages* 1989: 81).

A second area where the new authority was given new powers was in obtaining and publishing information about the coal and steel industry on a common, European basis. This meant that hitherto jealously guarded information relating to the formation

9

of prices was now available openly. Monnet recalled how, when the High Authority was first set up, two recruits who were former officials from the respective French and German railways authorities met and confessed to each other the tariff practices they had each previously mounted against each other to distort competition. Both experts then concentrated their energies together on jointly removing national discriminatory measures in the European transport sector.

The High Authority soon encountered a third area where its competence conflicted with those of national authorities – that of taxation. Although the common market in coal opened on schedule under the terms of the Treaty in 1953, the opening of the common market for steel had to be delayed by two months when the Germans raised an unforeseen problem over the fact that French levels of turnover tax were higher than German levels. In cross-border trade should the tax of the country of origin or the country of destination apply? While majority opinion in the Authority favoured the latter, the Germans complained that this was discriminatory, and that the tax should be that of the country of origin. In the absence of any system of tax harmonisation between member states the only solution was to seek the arbitration of a committee of independent tax experts, who duly reported in favour of the majority view. The German objection was lifted and the common market in steel opened. Some years later the German finance minister admitted to Monnet that an element in the German position had been the temptation to use the fact of lower German taxes to obtain an overwhelming advantage in the market (Monnet 1976: 571).

To summarise so far; the European Coal and Steel Community was original both in the way it addressed the existing broad political and strategic problems arising in the post-war period as well as in the way it addressed new economic problems. But it was original in a third way also: it was also meant not just to be an end in itself but was clearly intended to be the first step towards a wider European unity.

The form of that unity was expressed in different ways. The 1951 Treaty of Paris itself spoke only in general terms in its preamble of how establishing an economic community would be to lay 'the basis for a broader and deeper community among peoples long divided by bloody conflicts; and to lay the foundations for institutions which will give direction to a destiny henceforward shared'. The first public statement by the French government when putting forward the plan used the now well-known formula: 'Europe will not be created all at once or in a global construction: it will be created by concrete achievements first creating a de facto solidarity' (Monnet 1976: 540). And the German response to the French plan emphasised how it 'is not made up of general formulae, but of concrete suggestions based upon equality of rights' (ibid.: 440).

However, in the draft first setting out the plan Monnet thought the following wording was the most accurate description of the objective at the time:

> By the pooling of their basic industries and the establishment of a new High Authority, whose decisions will bind France, Germany and the countries taking part, this proposal will lay down the first concrete foundations of a European federation indispensable to the preservation of peace.
>
> (Ibid. 1976: 431)

This formula, with the use of the word 'federation', placed the proposal squarely in the general trend of thought in favour of a United States of Europe which was widely popular after the war, not least through Churchill's use of the phrase in Zurich in 1946. And the question of whether or not the Community is, or should be, seen as a movement towards a federation like that of the United States of America has hung over the debate about its nature ever since. We will examine this point in more detail in Chapter 10. For the present it may be worth adding that when he came later to reflect upon the actual development of the Community, Monnet made the following point:

> I have never doubted that the process will lead us one day to a United States of Europe, but I do not attempt to imagine its political framework today, so imprecise are the words used in argument: confederation or federation. What we are preparing, through the action of the Community, *has probably no precedent.*
>
> (Ibid.: 787; emphasis mine)

So what, finally, were the institutions which underpinned this proposal which was such a unique blend of politics and economics? They were, curiously enough, not thought out completely at

11

the beginning but rather shaped through the negotiations leading up to the signature of the Treaty itself. The starting point was not so much 'how can we create the future European institutions in embryo?', but rather 'how can we best set up an organism devoted to the specific and unusual task of pooling coal and steel between six European countries?'

The institutional heart was the *High Authority*. For the plan to work at all it was essential for the High Authority to have teeth. Monnet was convinced that the pre-war mistake of a toothless League of Nations should not be repeated. Rather than the High Authority being subject to the direction of the member states (who would, almost certainly, then tend to ignore it and do as they pleased), it was vital from the outset that it have independence and legal authority, and that its decisions be binding on the member states. This point was preserved throughout the negotiations, and in Articles 46 to 67 of the final Treaty it was granted considerable powers. Among these were in particular the right to:

> Study markets and prices and draw up long-term strategies;
> publish market information (with the right to fine companies
> not providing such information);
> raise its own capital both by applying a levy on European
> coal and steel production and by contracting loans;
> assist investment programmes by providing loans and
> guarantees to companies;
> provide financial assistance to diversify employment out of
> coal and steel and into other sectors;
> take direct measures (e.g. institute production quotas) if a
> reduction in demand were to lead to a 'manifest crisis';
> define abusive pricing practices;
> if necessary set minimum and maximum prices within the
> common market;
> stop the establishment of trusts, cartels and other distortions
> of competition by member states themselves.

It was only through the discussion leading up to the Treaty that the precise form of the other institutions – Council, Parliament and Court of Justice – emerged.

The key difficulty was clearly from the start the crucial relationship between the High Authority and the governments of the member states. The Benelux states in particular wished to maintain a specific role for national governments within the institutional configuration – even to the extent of being able to issue political directives to the High Authority. The French and German representatives, on the other hand, emphasised the eminently political nature of the High Authority, and the need for it to remain independent of governments. The two points of view were reconciled by the creation of what became the *Council of Ministers*, and a conceptual division of the work of the Coal and Steel Community into two: those matters which were the responsibility of the High Authority, for which it would be given a *clear mandate written into the Treaty*, and other matters which were proper to national governments and on which they could intervene – provided they acted together. But this in turn raised a further point: how should such collective activity be organised?

Thus emerged the issue of the rules governing *majority voting in the Council*. The problem was to avoid a system where the classical rule of unanimity applied (which automatically allowed any member state, great or small, to block anything) and to devise a system which encouraged the adoption of a common view of a problem and the taking of common action. But a simple system of majority voting giving each country one vote would be unbalanced, since of the six participants the Benelux countries plus Italy produced only a quarter of the coal and steel output of France and Germany. On the other hand, a voting system weighted purely in terms of economic strength would be unbalanced in the other direction and give too many votes to Germany, thus upsetting the principle underlying the whole plan of equality of rights between France and Germany. The solution – which was again original – was to adopt a system of weighted voting rights (subsequently known as qualified majority votes) which meant that France and Germany had equal votes but that no decision could be imposed on the other four by a coalition of France and Germany alone, nor on France and Germany by the other four acting together. (We will look later at the precise voting arrangements which prevail in the Council today.)

Two episodes in setting up the Coal and Steel Community illustrated for Monnet the dangers of the classical rule of unanimity – but also the need for sensitive use of majority voting. The first was the decision on the siting of the High Authority, which was one of the last points to be resolved between the Six before the Community came into being, and which called for unanimous agreement. Negotiations dragged on in 1952 from a Tuesday morning to dawn on Thursday in what Monnet called 'the ultimate and derisory parade of the right of veto' (Monnet 1976: 540). The names of the cities of Strasbourg, Liège, The Hague, Sarrebruck, Brussels and Turin were put forward without agreement until finally it was settled that work should begin (purely on an interim basis) in Luxembourg, to allow time to reflect on what to do next. Ever since then the choice of siting EC institutions has been one of the most contentious among member states.

The second episode – the question of whether German opinion on the taxation regime for the common market in steel should be overridden, already mentioned above – showed the dangers of the opposite approach: too automatic a rejection of a minority view. As Monnet put it:

> The rule of the majority was the best way to encourage unanimous agreement because it led to decision taking and this prospect drove the minority to wisdom. But for the majority also wisdom consists in not using its power to impose its point of view, or at least only to make it prevail after a complete discussion.
>
> (Monnet 1976: 570)

The balance between stasis and action, and how and when to transform majority opinion into a firm decision, remains one of the tests of political judgement in the EU today.

The final remaining major institutional innovations in the Coal and Steel Community – the *Parliamentary Assembly* and the *Court of Justice* – were less contentious in their establishment. We shall see later how the former, now become the European Parliament, fits into the present institutional framework; and how the latter has become a major force within the EU – in fact arguably much more important than what remains of the High Authority.

Looking back over this account of the establishment of the bases of common action in the Coal and Steel Community, what conclusions can we draw that are relevant today? Four suggest themselves.

The first is that the underlying economic approach was market-oriented, even though the High Authority was given clear powers of intervention. The economic objective was explicitly to create a market, a European market which was greater than the existing national markets.

However, the second point is that the establishment of such a market was not left solely to market forces, or to the benign operation of the invisible hand. In the sensitive sectors of coal and steel, with their organic links to armaments production, and given the formidable weight of European history, it was never going to be likely that private sector operators alone would be able to get very far. A private sector initiative between the wars – the International Steel Cartel – did nothing to prevent war recurring. To break down the national barriers a strong public authority was thought to be needed.

The third point is that the economics of the matter could not be divorced from the politics; and that, ultimately, the politics were far more important. The neutralisation of a cause of military tension between France and Germany was a prize far greater than any technical benefit. The establishment of a climate of confidence in an area which had been a faultline of war not only contributed to post-war peace, it also provided the stable basis for future western European economic growth. And even beyond the economics and the politics those who were actually involved in the scheme saw another dimension to it – that of morality itself. Both Monnet and Adenauer referred to the moral aspect of what they were doing, by which they meant that they were attempting to use forces which had divided their two countries as a lever to unite them.

The fourth point is the extraordinary degree of innovation involved in the undertaking. To resolve a problem between two nations by ring-fencing it, taking it out of their jurisdiction and placing it under the control of a wholly new independent body that was nonetheless common to its members required a rare combination of lateral thinking and organisational ability. In setting up the Coal and Steel Community the founders addressed problems not previously encountered in either political theory or practice – and they did so guided by pragmatism rather than by abstract theory.

So what has happened to the European Coal and Steel Community? Coal and steel are no longer what they were. Their symbolic significance as objects of strategic contention between France and Germany has long since faded. At least since the early 1960s, when nuclear and missile technology introduced a new dimension into modern warfare and made traditional land borders meaningless, the idea of ownership of coal and steel production as a means of controlling rearmament and checking armed invasion has become largely redundant. The scenario which the architects of the Coal and Steel Community no doubt had in mind – the remorseless build up in German weapons capacity in the 1930s, and the breaching of the provisions of the Versailles Treaty – has become otiose.

On the purely economic level coal and steel have turned from being key European industries to becoming sectors of heavy industrial backwardness. The problem facing the European steel industry today is not one of closed national markets but rather one of adapting to near universal oversupply. Low prices, overcapacity and recession among customer industries have contributed to a series of crises in the industry. Plans at the European level turn on reducing total capacity rather than pooling resources.

The High Authority of the Coal and Steel Community has long since vanished. In 1967, under the terms of a Merger Treaty, the High Authority was subsumed into the European Commission, where its work is diffused around several directorate generals, notably DG III (industry) and DG IV (competition). Although the European Community retains powers in this sector which are greater than in most others, the common market for coal and steel is now only part of the general common market which was agreed between the member states in 1957 (which we will look at shortly), and of which the single European market of the 1990s is an extension.

Finally, a major new factor has now entered into the equation in Europe. Some of the additional European steel capacity now comes from former East Germany, now legally part of the Community. And some of the imports of steel disrupting the European market come from central and eastern Europe. The overthrow of Soviet communism since 1989 and the ending of the state trading apparatus of the Council for Mutual Economic Assistance (Comecon) has led to a collapse in trade within the former Soviet bloc and the switching of trade away to western Europe, and in particular to the markets of the EC. The Community is faced then with this paradox: the widening of the market-based economy in Europe has created new competition and new strains in the very industries which once formed the basis of its own integration. This is a problem unimagined by the early architects (and perhaps unimaginable in the way it has come about): but it is one facet of

16

the greater challenge now posed to the Community by the end of the cold war.

Given all these factors does this first, prototype model of integration through coal and steel continue to have any value? Much, of course, depends on what might have happened had Monnet not convinced the French government in 1950 to use it as a means of abandoning a policy towards Germany based on attempted domination. Perhaps in retrospect the fears of international tension after the war were exaggerated; perhaps the more enlightened economic and political policies which boosted general western European growth would have sufficed to keep the peace. But certainly this was not obvious at the time. And it must be doubtful whether the process of international market building which has continued to this day in western Europe could have begun without a kernel of integration in the first most sensitive markets of all. In that sense, at least, the Coal and Steel Community appears to have fulfilled its purpose. New problems may be faced today, but only because some difficult old problems have effectively been surmounted.

BUT WHERE WERE THE BRITISH?

Before leaving the Coal and Steel Community it is necessary to say a word about the British position at the time of its creation.

Although in 1952 the UK was the first country to send a goodwill message to the newly established High Authority in Luxembourg (observing that it supported the objectives of the Community and would seek the 'closest possible' relationship with the High Authority itself), the UK was conspicuously absent from the negotiations leading up to the creation of the High Authority. It was not until 1973 – over twenty years later – that the UK joined what by then was the European Community, which included what remained of the High Authority. Why was this?

Much has been said about this period in terms of a missed opportunity. Immediately after the war Britain was the dominant power of western Europe, with vast reserves of moral authority derived from the defeat of Hitler. Churchill's 1946 speech in Zurich, calling for European unity and observing that the 'first step in the re-creation of the European family must be a partnership between France and Germany' (Cannadine 1989: 312) was literally inspirational to many who heard it. When British Foreign Secretary Ernest Bevin said in the House of Commons in 1948 that 'the free nations of Western Europe must now draw closely together . . .. I believe the time is ripe for a consolidation of Western Europe' he was credited at least by Belgian Foreign Minister Paul-Henri Spaak as having been 'the Foreign Minister who gave the European movement its initial impulse' (Spaak 1971: 145; emphasis in original).

So what happened? Why did a Britain which was clearly in favour of the general strategic objective of European unity, if for no other reason than that a strong western Europe was needed as a bulwark against a threatening Soviet Union, not participate in the creation of the first mechanism to establish it? In the first volume of *The Second World War* (first published in 1948) Churchill wrote:

> To me the aim of ending the thousand-year strife between France and Germany seemed a supreme object. If we could only weave Gaul and Teuton so closely together economically, socially and morally as to prevent the occasion of new quarrels, and make old antagonisms die in the realisation of mutual prosperity and interdependence, Europe would rise again. It seemed to me that the supreme interest of the British people in Europe lay in the assuagement of the Franco-German feud, and that they had no other interests comparable or contrary to that. *That is still my view today.*
>
> (Churchill 1965: Vol. I, 26; emphasis mine)

And yet, as Spaak later put it, although in 1948 it seemed obvious that Britain would be the leader of a future united Europe, by 1951 it was evident to him that 'any attempt to unite Europe could only succeed if Britain took no part in it' (Spaak 1971: 221).

These rather harsh words arose from Belgian disappointment that Britain was not prepared to make the same commitment to the Coal and Steel Community as the other European countries, and thus act as a political counterweight to France and Germany. Monnet was more dispassionate. He regretted British non-participation at the outset but predicted – accurately – that Britain would join once the Community was up and running and seen to work.

The philosophical difference was this. As has been made clear, the essential point of the Coal and Steel Community – and what rendered it completely novel in the field of international relations – was a deliberate pooling of national power (or 'sovereignty') in a clearly defined area, and the placing of that power under the clear control of an entity which was common to the member states but nonetheless legally independent. As we have seen, both France and Germany could in fact obtain direct advantages from such an approach, which made such a high price well worth paying (France because it removed the fear of a resurgent Germany; Germany because it allowed it to rejoin western Europe on a basis of equality). The other four participants (Benelux plus Italy) were minor producers of coal and steel compared to France and Germany, but would gain from any arrangement which allowed them a say in the economic development of their larger neighbours.

The British starting point was wholly different. Unlike each of the Six, Britain had not been invaded during the war. British capital stock emerged from the war battered but largely intact (and indeed its growing antiquity was later to become a problem in itself). The political debate immediately after the war in Britain was not so much to do with modernisation or reconstruction (at least not in the acute sense that such words applied in both France and Germany) as with the transfer of the ownership of key parts of the economy from the private to the public sectors. In the period 1947 to 1949 the coal and steel industries, the railways, electricity and gas were all nationalised in Britain and therefore placed under the control of the state. It was perhaps asking too much for the state then to hand over rights won after the political battles of that stormy period to an untried international entity. Lord Plowden, who held official discussions with Monnet on Franco–British co-operation in the 1940s, observed later that 'there was not the slightest chance that a Labour government of the time would agree to join the Community on the terms fixed by Jean Monnet'. He added: 'I do not think either that the Conservative government would have acted differently' (*Témoignages* 1989: 401). To confirm the latter point, it is worth recalling Harold Macmillan's words about the Schuman Plan to the Council of Europe in 1950:

At all events, one fact is certain, and we had better face it frankly. Our people will not hand over to a supra-national authority the right to close down our pits and steelworks.

19

We shall not permit a supra-national authority to reduce a large section of our fellow citizens in Durham, the Midlands, South Wales and Scotland to unemployment. *These fears may be imaginary*, but their existence is a fact, and a fact, moreover, which no British Government can afford to ignore.

(quoted in Spaak 1971: 216; emphasis mine)

A second difference was that although Britain was genuinely keen to see a unified western Europe and – as Churchill wished – a reconciled France and Germany, it was not envisaged that this would involve a sole or exclusive British commitment. In the period after the war Britain had many remaining global commitments – not least to the countries of the Empire and the Commonwealth which had helped win the war. Although it was Churchill who popularised the idea of 'a kind of United States of Europe', it was *not* Churchill's intention that Britain should be one such state. Instead, in the concluding words of his 1946 Zurich speech he recalled that France and Germany should provide the lead and that:

Great Britain, the British Commonwealth of Nations, mighty America, and I trust Soviet Russia – for then indeed all would be well – must be *friends and sponsors* of the new Europe and must champion its right to live and shine.

(Cannadine 1989: 314; emphasis mine)

A third difference in starting points was perhaps grasped in an intuitive way by Monnet. He recorded in his memoirs how he felt at the time that behind the formal discussions with the British there lay a lack of confidence in the future of continental Europe, and uncertainty whether it could (in this period at the height of the cold war) resist a possible Soviet invasion. He suspected that the British felt that if the continent was occupied they would – as during the war – have to keep their independence and fall back on a separate alliance with the United States. In fact, the record shows that he seems to have been right. Official papers from 1949 show an important point of principle *was* adopted by the British government at this time; in the prevailing uncertainty there was a consensus that Britain should not commit itself to Europe so far that it lost independent viability. If Europe collapsed, Britain must be able to survive, and rebuild

20

with American and Commonwealth support (mentioned in Young 1984: 122).

And all this leads on to one further major difference of perspective. For Britain, by 1950, five years after the end of hostilities, *Germany was no longer the main European problem*. Unlike France, for whom the direct experience of invasion ensured that foreign policy was dominated by the German question, Britain after the war switched its preoccupations to the threat posed to Europe by an expansionist Soviet Union. British energies became concentrated on the need to check Stalin. When it became clear that this could not be done alone, Britain – and in particular Foreign Secretary Bevin – was instrumental in ensuring a US commitment to continental security through the creation of Nato. Although in 1950 France was worried about a resurgent Germany, Britain was not, or at least not as much; it was more keen (as was the United States) to see Germany back on its feet to counterbalance the Soviet Union. And when, the same year, discussions began on the (aborted) European Defence Community, French and British starting points again were different. For France the EDC was primarily a way to address the problem of the rearmament of Germany by placing it in the context of the creation of a European army. For Britain the EDC was a means to another end: the creation of a European force, including Germany, which could, along with Nato, defend Europe against the Soviet Union. When the EDC project collapsed in 1954 (through non-ratification of the treaty in the French National Assembly) Britain swiftly moved to put in place arrangements which ended the Allied occupation of Germany and provided for direct German membership of Nato.

For all these reasons, then, Britain came to the creation of the Coal and Steel Community with a different viewpoint from that of the two principal partners, France and Germany. And indeed, once the Schuman Plan was announced, Monnet records how there was a flurry of diplomatic exchanges between Paris and London in an effort to clarify what it and the conference to be held to create the High Authority were meant to be all about. He wrote that it took 'ten days, eleven notes, four thousand words' to define the respective French and British positions (Monnet 1976: 450). In the end the difference was this: Britain in 1950 was prepared to take part in the discussions, but not on the basis of a prior commitment to pool resources and institute a High

Authority with sovereign powers. Monnet, fearful that too vague a commitment at the outset would dilute the project (in particular in Germany), insisted on the UK taking part on the same basis as everyone else. On this point the exchanges finally broke down. The UK did not participate.

It will be a theme of this book that in many ways the European Community can be seen as a pact whereby those who take part expect to obtain benefits which are greater than those given up with the loss of independence. In this sense it shares one of the characteristics of other alliances or pacts; joint action can obtain better results than single action. Although there is an important difference from other organisations, in that the Community has refined to a much higher degree the *mechanics* of organising such joint action, it remains the case that those who take part do so on the basis of a rational expectation of gaining more than they lose. When in a different sphere the UK in 1954 was prepared to pay the price of committing armed forces to European defence, it did so because this was clearly necessary if others were to do the same, and this price thus bought a greater benefit.

When in 1950 the UK was not ultimately prepared to pay the price of ceding powers (or 'sovereignty') in a major economic area it was because, in the final analysis, what was on offer did not seem at the time worth that price. The general objectives of European unity and German economic and military regeneration could be obtained without British participation, the Coal and Steel Community had little direct bearing on the threat from the Soviet Union, the domestic economic and political argument was about the state ownership of industry and British trade was still geared to countries outside Europe.

Although it is possible, in retrospect, to regret that Britain did not take part in the formative European institution that was the Coal and Steel Community the decision not to do so is at least explicable in rational terms.

TOWARDS A COMMON MARKET

Following the collapse of the European Defence Community project in 1954 (which would have used machinery similar to that of the Coal and Steel Community to create a European army as a means of rearming Germany), the Six were plunged into one of the crises of identity which have become subsequently a familiar feature of Community life. This was resolved by agreement among the foreign ministers of the Six at a conference at Messina in Italy in 1955 to relaunch the Community, and to do so by taking further steps together in the economic sphere. The Six also agreed on a procedural step which was to be used again in the future; a group of experts was mandated to review all the relevant technical issues and prepare the ground for drawing up a legal treaty.

It is sometimes said that the creation of the common market involved a Franco–German deal whereby Germany was granted access for its industrial products in exchange for EC assistance for French agriculture. This is not strictly accurate. In fact the original trade-off was this: the common market was seen as a way of rallying the Germans to a further scheme – the creation of an institution, modelled on the High Authority, to oversee the peaceful development of nuclear energy in Europe. Monnet (who was not as directly involved in drawing up the Treaty of Rome as the Treaty of Paris, but who nonetheless contributed to a memorandum submitted to the Messina conference) saw nuclear energy as being the natural sector for European development after coal and steel, the more so as in 1954 the US had relaxed legislation restricting the transfer of nuclear technology.

And so a report was produced by the committee of experts mandated by the Messina conference which became known as the *Spaak Report* after its chairman (although Spaak freely admitted that he did little of the detailed drafting, but confined himself to directing the work of three technical experts, in particular that of French economist Pierre Uri).[3] This report became the basis of the Treaty of Rome and contained distinct sections on first the establishment of the common market and second the setting up of an Atomic Energy Community (Euratom). It also had a short third section on some specific areas requiring separate action, like air transport and posts and telecommunications.

This *Spaak Report*, tabled in April 1956, remains a key document. It reviews the issues which were felt in the 1950s to need addressing in creating a genuine common market (going beyond the sectors of coal and steel) between the original six member states of the Coal and Steel Community. It thus is the main philosophical antecedent of the approach to economic integration which has been prevalent in the Community ever since – including the development of the single European market and the economic aspects of the Maastricht Treaty. For this reason (and since it is scarcely known today) it is worth considering in some detail.

The report opens by describing a common market in terms of a *merger of the existing separate national markets*. This is to allow a greater division of labour, a reduction in the waste of resources and increased security of supply which will make production cheaper. Such a merger of markets opens the way to much greater use of modern production techniques, constrained by the small size of national markets which tend to create de facto monopolies. A wider market can combine both mass production and the absence of monopolies. Companies in that market will be put under a permanent pressure to invest, develop production, improve quality and modernise. They will have to run to stand still.

Such a common market requires a fixed timetable to achieve it, collective means to make the necessary changes, the end of practices distorting competition between producers, and co-operation between participating states to ensure monetary stability, economic expansion and social progress. While in theory there is no reason why complete freedom of trade should not exist on a world scale, a true common market is only achievable between a limited group of states – although it is desirable that that group be as large as possible. And although a common market can only be regional it is not meant to be opposed to the rest of the world or disturb the international division of labour. It should, on the contrary, *reduce protection in its own area and contribute to a general lowering of tariff barriers around the world*. Given the pervasive and distorting nature of state activity in the market sector, a common market is, however, not conceivable without common rules, common action and a system of institutions to oversee it.

The body of the report refines these general principles. For example, it is made clear early on that a common market will imply free circulation not only of products and services but also of the factors of production: capital and labour. And the obstacles to trade are seen as consisting not only of customs duties, quotas and monopoly importers, but also restrictions in foreign currency transfers, discriminatory transport tariffs and also internal national regulations, in particular in the services and agriculture sectors. (We can note in passing that this theme will be rehearsed once again in the single market programme over thirty years later.)

Given the fundamental changes required in creating a common market a *long transition period* will be needed to accomplish it. The report suggests a maximum of fifteen years: three stages of four years each, with a possible three year additional period. At the end of that period all the mechanisms of the common market should be in place – in other words the ending of internal tariff barriers and quotas, the creation of a common external tariff, the ending of national market regulation (and, if necessary, the establishment of common regulation or organisation), free movement of capital and labour, the ending of national derogations and the adoption of tax or social legislation in specific areas.

The report also reviews the difference between a *customs union* (which is to form the basis of the common market) and a *free trade area*. There are two important points. The first is practical: a free trade area (under Gatt rules) allows participating countries to continue having different national tariffs and thus negotiate separate tariff agreements with third countries. However, between countries having common borders, such as in continental Europe, this would create virtually insurmountable problems, since differing tariff regimes would distort trade with third countries (which would naturally flow in line with the differing tariffs) and thus require limiting the free circulation of goods to those from the member states – which would itself entail continuing frontier controls. The second point is economic: in allowing differing commercial and customs policies towards third countries a free trade area would allow the maintenance of differing exchange rates towards them, which in itself could disturb the balance and nature of trade within the common market. (It will be recalled that in 1956 the Bretton Woods semi-fixed exchange rate system was in operation.)

Although for these reasons a customs union is preferable, the report makes clear that this will be *compatible with Gatt rules*. In particular, it will be compatible with the Gatt requirement that the general level of common tariff should be no greater than the separate tariffs it replaces. 'By its nature, the common market will be equipped against the risk of constituting a zone of high external protection, tending to isolate it from the rest of the world or distort trade flows. *A high protection is excluded a priori'* (*Rapport des chefs de délégation aux ministres des affaires etrangères* 1956: 22; emphasis mine). (It should be noted that the levels of protection introduced later for agriculture departed spectacularly from this

25

principle – but also that agriculture was not at the time subject to Gatt rules.) In addition, the report suggests the possibility of adding to the common market a free trade zone with neighbouring countries, provided the existence of differing tariff arrangements does not distort trade.

The report recognises that it is impossible to specify in advance all the measures needed to set up the common market in a treaty. Therefore, the treaty should include institutions and procedures which have a certain latitude in establishing the common market in the light of developments as they occur. It is hard to see (as in the Coal and Steel Community) how the oversight of commitments undertaken or the administration of safeguard procedures could be left up to the member states themselves; a rule of unanimity would allow a veto by anyone and majority voting would allow a coalition of interests rather than the objective recognition of the truth. *The creation of a body with its own authority and a common responsibility is indispensable.* And thus are born the European Community institutions proper: a Council of Ministers (where member states are consulted and common decisions are taken); the Commission (responsible for administering the Treaty and watching over the functioning and development of the common market); the Court (to consider Treaty violations etc.); and an Assembly to exercise parliamentary oversight.

The report makes a number of detailed points about the creation of the common market which continue to be pertinent. It recognises, for example, that the *service sector*, in all its manifestations (transport, financial services, distribution, liberal professions, etc.), is particularly awkward to handle, since the obstacles to trade lie not so much in duties or tariffs as in national regulations. No one formula can apply. One principle should be that priority should be given to deregulating services directly affecting the common market in goods. But, in any case, by the end of the transitional period, regulation in the service sector should be on a common basis, except in agreed exceptional areas. (This proved to be wildly over-ambitious.)

Agriculture is another special case. It would be impossible to conceive of a common market without the agricultural sector. But the peculiar nature of agriculture is that many countries intervene heavily in the market for a wide variety of reasons, including to ensure food security and to avoid massive price fluctuations. Thus it will be necessary to adopt a common approach to this market intervention as the counterpart to creating free trade in agricultural goods. The precise mechanisms for doing so (which will differ from product to product) will need further study, and should be in place by the end of the transition period. (We will look at agriculture and what actually happened in more detail in a later chapter. For the moment the important point is this – agriculture was from the outset not to be regulated for its own sake, but because it was an important part of the common market. The means of organisation was left completely open. The report in fact includes the following uncannily prophetic words: 'Precautions must doubtless be taken against the risk that measures to organise the whole of the market, in substituting for national regulations, tend to create a vast whole protected against the exterior and aligning its prices on marginal internal exploitation' (*Rapport* 1956: 51). It would be hard to find a more succinct description of what in fact came to pass.)

The report also goes in detail into the various kinds of *market regulation* needed in a common market. Thus it sketches out the need for a *competition policy* to avoid discriminatory practices, the need for means to address *monopoly practices* which threaten to disturb the common market, and the need for clear rules concerning distorting *state aids* to industry (which should in principle be banned except in certain specified cases).

It also looks at the problems arising from differing national *legislative and regulatory practices* in the economic sphere. Here it argues that although there may be differing costs (for example in terms of public expenditure and social security charges) between member states, these do not necessarily distort competition because of differing terms of trade between them, in particular exchange rates. And rather than seeking, for example, to equalise factors such as salaries and interest rate charges on companies at the outset, these will progressively tend to equalise themselves as the free circulation of the factors of production increases. Indeed the report makes here what is an important general economic statement:

> It is not possible to try to modify as if by decree the fundamental conditions of an economy such as result from natural resources, the level of productivity or the weight of public costs. One part of what is usually termed harmonisation will therefore be the result of the very functioning of the market,

the economic forces that it sets in play and the contacts it leads to between parties.

(*Rapport* 1956: 61)

So where *is* action needed? The report suggests this should be in the limited number of areas where specific distortions affect certain branches of activity. And even here it has to be recognised that some distortions (e.g. tax distortions) exist *within* national markets, about which nothing much can be done. It suggests as a rule of thumb that distortions should be investigated when an industry bears differing costs from the average of the economy where it is located, and it recommends that the Commission proceed cautiously in this area with a judicious mixture of safeguard measures for discriminated industries and proposals to governments to eliminate distortions where they are serious.

The report adds that in certain cases the best way of eliminating distortions could be to bring the legal arrangements in the differing countries closer together, but that the impact of such changes on the cost/price structure has to be borne in mind. A unified system of *tax and social security costs*, although not an absolute condition of a common market, would eliminate some important distortions and the Commission should make recommendations here (which, however, can only be adopted unanimously). The report looks at the area of *conditions of work*, and suggests that, while it is difficult to imagine conditions seriously diverging within a common market, it will be the 'spontaneous tendency of harmonisation' of social systems and salary levels, including via trade union action, which will bring about alignment. In fact, the report specifically warns against trying to regulate such problems directly ('A shortening of the legal or normal length of the working week, for example, amounts in fact to an increase in salary' (*Rapport* 1956: 65).) It suggests that procedures should be found which take into account the diversity of the economic conditions of working traditions and policies to raise employee living standards. But it suggests also that a special effort be made to harmonise regimes progressively in the particular areas of equality of male and female salaries, overtime terms and conditions and paid holidays. (This whole debate would again be rehearsed many years later under the umbrella of 'Social Europe'.)

The report addresses further broad *macroeconomic issues* in a section entitled 'The Balance of Payments'. Here, it foresees that the progressive adoption of the rules of the common market will provide an incentive to reach equilibrium in the general application of monetary policy. The creation of the common market, and the changes in trade resulting from it, might change in an unpredictable manner the conditions of balance of payments between countries, and thus lead to exchange rate adjustments. While from a theoretical point of view this might seem desirable, one important objective of the common market is to allow adjustments to take place *through the structure of production and costs* rather than through sudden shifts in the external value of currencies. In particular, the risk of devaluations with the sole aim of obtaining a competitive advantage is such that safeguard action may be needed to protect member states affected by unilateral action. As well as this, a system of mutual support between member states should be developed, including the possible provision of credits to countries in particular difficulty. Balance of payments problems with third countries will also become matters of common concern: as trade increases within the common market there will tend in any case to be a convergence of the economic fundamentals determining monetary conditions.

A final section of this part of the report concerns the *free movement of workers* and the *free movement of capital*. Both are held to be necessary within the common market, and the Commission is asked to make the relevant proposals. The report concludes its observations on the common market by recognising that the degree of economic integration resulting from the free movement of goods, services, persons and capital will only be partial, since it does not involve a renunciation of autonomy in the areas of budgetary, financial or social policies, or the adoption of a single currency. But it adds that that degree of integration should, in itself, have enough force to maintain sufficient convergence between those policies and to ensure that the movement once begun does not come to a halt.

When, thirty-two years later in 1988, the European Commission wanted to give publicity to the benefits of the single European market, it published the Cecchini Report. That report spoke in glowing terms of the positive effects of the 'supply-side shock' to the European economy, to be produced by the removal of barriers to European trade. Although the term would have been unknown as far back as 1956, it can be seen that the Spaak Report, in the way it proposed the abolition of national market

29

restrictions and the creation of a single large market for all goods, services, capital and people, was in itself the initial exercise in European supply-side economics.

The Spaak Report *did* envisage two expenditure programmes: the establishment of a European Investment Fund to help finance cross-border projects, assist less developed areas and help industrial conversion (most of the finance of which was to come from the market); and a Retraining Fund, based on pooling part of member states' social security funds, which would be aimed at providing new skills for the unemployed throughout the Community. But these, and indeed all the intervention policies which were envisaged at a Community level, were means to arrive at the main objective, which was quite literally the establishment of an international market where the division of labour – Adam Smith's term for the basis of commercial society – would be increased.

Was it successful? In one sense it was. The Spaak Report was considered by foreign ministers of the Six at a conference in May 1956, and according to Spaak himself (1971: 240) it was agreed unanimously to constitute the basis of discussions in less than two hours. Although in later negotiations there was more hard bargaining (for example over a French demand to include a link with its overseas countries and territories), the essence of the Spaak Report *was* in fact translated into legal form in the Treaty which established the common market, signed in Rome in March 1957, and which entered into force in January 1958.

THE TREATY OF ROME

Under the terms of the Treaty of Rome the common market was to be progressively established over a transition period of twelve years, divided into three periods of four years each – in other words it was to be established by 1970 at the latest. The areas for action were set out in Article 3 of the Treaty, as follows:

1 the elimination of all customs duties and quantitative restrictions on trade between the member states;
2 the establishment of a common customs tariff and a common commercial policy towards third countries;
3 the abolition of obstacles to the free circulation of people, services and capital between the member states;

4 the creation of a common policy for agriculture;

5 the creation of a common policy for transport;

6 the establishment of a regime to ensure competition is not distorted in the common market;

7 procedures allowing the co-ordination of economic policies in the member states and safeguarding against disequilibria in the balance of payments;

8 the approximation of national legislation where needed for the functioning of the common market;

9 the creation of a European Social Fund, to help employment and raise living standards;

10 the creation of a European Investment Bank, to help economic expansion;

11 the association of overseas countries and territories, so as to increase trade and pursue economic and social development.

What happened to these ideas in practice? Customs tariffs between the Six were phased out ahead of schedule and a customs union was created in the summer of 1968. This event was little noticed at the time, overshadowed as it was by student demonstrations in Paris and the Soviet invasion of Prague. But was this creation of a customs union the same as the creation of a true common market as envisaged? The answer to this is no: the whole point of the much later single market programme was to *complete* the construction of this very same market by doing away with the barriers to trade which still remained – notably in the large service sector, which even in the 1950s was responsible for over a third of Community GDP – right up to the 1990s. And so the common market was only partly built in 1968. Indeed the single market programme – which we will look at in more detail – acknowledged that not everything would be accomplished even by 1 January 1993. And to this day there has been no common policy for transport to match that for agriculture. *In this and other ways the member states are still living in a Europe where economic integration, as originally envisaged in the Spaak Report and programmed in the Treaty of Rome, is not yet complete.*

Nonetheless, the Treaty of Rome *does* appear to have encouraged substantial economic progress. The partial construction of the common market, in particular for traded goods, coincided with a period of strong continental economic activity. In the first four years trade between the Six grew by over 60 per cent (and in the period 1958 to 1986 it was to grow more than twenty fold in Ecu terms). Between 1958 and 1967 the average annual per capita GNP growth among the Six, at 1963 exchange rates and prices, was a brisk 4 per cent, compared with an average annual rate in the UK of 2.5 per cent. Average income per employed person rose in real terms in the Six over the period 1958 to 1969 by 76 per cent (compared with 39 per cent in the UK).[4]

It may, of course, be argued that the period from 1958 was only the culmination of a general post-war boom in western Europe, which included the German economic miracle starting with the Erhard monetary reforms of 1948, as well as the 'trente glorieuses' of steady French economic growth. Yet all these developments added together to form part of the same picture of renewed domestic and international confidence. Monnet, at least (responsible for both the internal plans for French economic modernisation which in effect laid the basis for post-war growth and also, as we have seen, for the basic structures of the Community), saw both domestic and European economic development as two sides of the same coin. A continuous philosophical link *can* in fact be traced from the Marshall Plan assistance of 1947, which helped put post-war Europe back on its feet, through the Franco–German reconciliation of the Coal and Steel Community, and to the ambitious plans for the creation of the common market. This link is the rebuilding and then the expansion of the market economy in Europe, first on a national and then on an international scale.

In addition to the common market, a parallel Treaty signed also in Rome in March 1957 created the *European Atomic Energy Community* (known as 'Euratom'). This too went ahead on the basis of the recommendations of the Spaak Report. The premise of Euratom was that development of the nascent nuclear energy sector was essential to the growth of the European economy, but that it would only be by pooling separate national efforts that one could be built up. Thus, in an extension of institutional thinking owing something to the original High Authority, it was proposed that Euratom take an organisational role in co-ordinating European civil nuclear research. It was to be involved in ensuring the distribution of technical know-how; in drawing up security norms for workers and the population at large; in helping make investments; in ensuring equal access to supplies; and in enlarging market outlets and maximising technical capacity by merging national markets for specialised material and equipment, as well as by allowing the free movement of experts.

However, Euratom never became what its founders had hoped. The nuclear energy sector did not succeed the heavy industries of coal and steel as the natural economic integrator of Europe. (One is reminded of Monnet's remark that coal and steel had a symbolic significance 'like that belonging to nuclear energy today'.) The later separate development of civil nuclear energy programmes in the various member states – including both France and Germany – illustrated that at least in this sensitive sector the national framework would remain predominant. Even apart from such political considerations, continuing economic doubts about nuclear energy have removed the certainty that it could be at the forefront of the European economy. This particular avenue of European integration proved to be something of a dead end.

The *British* (although they took a non-committal interest in the proceedings) did not sign the two Treaties of Rome. Various explanations have been put forward for the continued British aloofness. Official papers from 1955 suggest that, despite the experience with the Coal and Steel Community, it was still felt in London that the common market would not get off the ground and that, even if it did succeed, Britain would be better off staying out, mainly because of its continuing wider international interests. Four 'decisive considerations' against membership of the prospective common market were put forward in the key policy paper of 1955: first, that membership would weaken economic and political links with the Commonwealth (still then responsible for half UK external trade); second, that a European common market would be incompatible with worldwide free trade and payments (although the Spaak Report in fact argued otherwise); third, that participation would in practice gradually lead to an unacceptable degree of political integration (which point we shall return to in the final chapter); and fourth that membership would involve *removing* protection for British industry against European competition. (The nationalised industries were employing some two million people and accounting for some 11 per cent of UK GDP. And even until the 1960s the bulk of British exports went to the protected markets of the old Empire and of the Commonwealth, which did little to encourage the development of industry that would be competitive by European standards.)

The above analysis draws on a review of the 1955 official papers by Burgess and Edwards (1988). The authors conclude with the observation that 'However momentous the events of this period might seem in retrospect, it is the matter-of-factness and the continuity of contemporary British attitudes which are so striking. The decision not to join the Six largely took itself' (1988: 413). It is, however, worth adding that, whatever reservations of principle were held in London during the drawing up of the Treaties, they were clearly overcome quite rapidly. It was only three years after the entry into force of the Treaty of Rome (in 1961) that the first British application to join the Community was made – or, in other words, while the first phase of the transition period leading to the expected creation of the common market was still under way. The subsequent two vetoes to British entry by de Gaulle, in 1963 and 1967, meant that entry did not take place until 1973 (and this meant also that, because of the transition arrangements for the UK, the full application of the rules of the common market did not take place until 1978). By the mid-1970s the long post-war boom of the European economy had run out and the impact of the oil price shocks was felt throughout Europe. Britain had in fact joined the Community at one of its lowest points.

CONCLUSION

This brief survey of the early years of the Community illustrates how political and economic forces were combined from the outset. The Coal and Steel Community was *meant* to be a shock to the system, a deliberate affront to national traditions, a breach in the wall of national sovereignty. The object of the exercise was to create a new form of institution with strong powers in an explicitly sensitive sector, at a time after the war when history was still fluid. The economic means of doing so – the creation of a unified market for coal and steel – were secondary to this main purpose. However, the next major step of Community development – the creation of the common market – took this economic process much further. It envisaged a total merging of the existing national markets and the creation of one large European market, with common rules and procedures governing that market. Where there was intervention at a European level it was meant to be market-correcting; and the greatest powers were thought to be needed *to counteract the effects of existing state intervention.* This process of market building proved in fact to be much more difficult than first thought; and it is still a continuing factor in today's Europe.

The early years also show some subtle shifts in the institutional framework. It is clear that the first intentions were to concentrate maximum powers in the High Authority, since it was thought that only a dramatic new initiative concentrated in this area could change the pattern of events. It seems likely that, in fact, Monnet at first saw the High Authority operating much as had the French Modernisation Commission – more by the power of persuasion of national public authorities based on a common assessment of economic data than by direct edict. Early on, however, it became necessary to formalise the relationship between the High Authority and the member states, and so the bases of the array of today's European institutions were laid.

In fact, the function of those institutions has also subtly changed. The two explicit attempts to clone institutions direct from the original High Authority – the European Defence Community and Euratom – were not particularly successful. The European Commission – as it was conceived for the common market – was given much broader and vaguer powers than the High Authority, and the member states also had a clearer role in making the common market work.

Despite such differences in approach, Monnet saw fundamental continuity. His later definition of the underlying Community dynamic is still relevant:

> To create progressively between the people of Europe the greatest common interest managed by common democratic institutions to which is delegated the necessary sovereignty.
>
> (Monnet 1976: 786)

Yet this definition, and indeed the very success of the Community in its early years, raises further questions which will be looked at in the course of this book. One broad set of questions concern the relationship – both political and economic – between the Community, its institutions and the member states. It remains an issue because it concerns that vital grey area where national economies overlap but national jurisdictions do not. A second broad set of questions concerns the relationship between the Community and the world beyond: a world which itself is rapidly turning into a global market, of which Europe is but a region. The collapse of communism as a credible alternative to a market order emphasises the importance of that change.

The word 'sovereignty' in Monnet's description, affecting as it does both these internal and external questions, will bear further examination. We shall return to it in Chapter 10. Next we must look more closely at the present day European Union.

2

THE SHAPE OF THE
UNION

INTRODUCTION

From the entry into force of the Treaties of Rome in 1958 to the
present day the key events in the history of European integration
can be summarised as in Box 1. Such a survey illustrates an

Box 1   Key dates

1961	The first UK accession application (with Ireland and Denmark). But vetoed by France in 1963.
1965	Merger of the institutions created by the Treaties of Paris and Rome.
1965–6	Following a crisis with France over voting on agricultural questions, adoption of the 'Luxembourg compromise'. This was a delicate political understanding which meant that, notwithstanding the terms of the Treaty, unanimity should be the basis of decision-taking where 'very important' national interests are at stake.
1967	The second accession application by the UK, Denmark and Ireland and the second veto by France.
1968	The phased abolition of tariffs between the Six accomplished, and a customs union thereby created.
1970	The eventual opening of accession negotiations with the UK, Denmark, Ireland and Norway. The first three acceded in 1973; Norway decided not to join after a referendum.
1974	EC leaders decided to allow direct elections to the European Parliament. The first were held in 1979.
1975	Greece applied to join the EC and eventually did so in 1981.
1977	Spain and Portugal applied to join the EC and did so in 1986.
1979	The European Monetary System was established.

1983	A Solemn Declaration on European Union was adopted by EC leaders.
1984	The UK budgetary contribution problem was resolved by EC leaders.
1985	The Commission put forward its White Paper on completing the internal market.
1985	An Inter-Governmental Conference to revise the Treaty was opened.
1986	The outcome was the Single European Act which increased majority voting, gave impetus to the single market and also a legal basis to the practice of Political Co-operation. The SEA entered into force after ratification in 1987.
1987	Turkey applied to join the EC.
1988	EC leaders mandated a committee of Governors of Central Banks to look into economic and monetary union (Emu).
1989	Their report proposed a three stage path towards a single EC currency.
1989	Austria applied to join the EC followed by Sweden, Switzerland, Finland, Norway, Malta and Cyprus.
1990	Two parallel Inter-Governmental Conferences opened, considering the questions of both Emu and Political Union.
1991	The outcome was the Maastricht Treaty (formally signed in 1992) which both created a legal framework for Emu and also instituted a raft of other diverse measures (see below).
1991	The EC agreed to create a European Economic Area (EEA) with the seven European Free Trade Area countries. Association agreements were also signed with Poland, Czechoslovakia and Hungary.
1992	Accession negotiations opened with Austria, Sweden, Finland and Norway. Following referenda in each the first three were due to join in 1995. Norway again voted against.
1993	Target date for completion of the single market programme. Entry into force of the Maastricht Treaty following lengthy ratification difficulties (including two Danish referenda). As a result of Maastricht the formal title of the EC became the European Union, which included the traditional EC plus some new policies.
1994	Entry into force of the EEA. Hungary and Poland applied to join the EU.

important point. The fast growing complexity of life in what has been formally known since 1993 as the European Union, both in quantitative terms (more members) and also qualitative terms (more policy issues). Between 1973 and 1986 the Community

doubled the size of its membership, and this process of enlargement looks set to continue. (So far, only Greenland, as a part of
Denmark, has actually left the Community.) As well as this, the
Community has continued to evolve in its basic nature, partly as
a consequence of the shifting political and economic views
among the member states, partly as a consequence of external
events and partly as a consequence of the slow incremental inter-
play of its institutions. Although the bedrock of the Community
remains economic integration through the process of market-
building (and this applies to the core parts of both the Single
European Act as well as to the Maastricht Treaty), the political
consequences of integration have themselves had effects at
both European and member state level. Completely new areas
of activity have been launched under the umbrella of the
Community, such as monetary and foreign policy co-operation.
Finally, and perhaps most significantly, the political background
in Europe has changed completely with the dramatic collapse of
Soviet-led communism. This has altered the internal dynamics
of the Community through the effects of German unification
and also has placed it in a new and unforeseen position in
relation to the volatile emerging market economies to the east of
the continent.

How does the European Union of today attempt to cope with
this explosion of activity? How do its institutions measure up to
such changing circumstances?

THE EU INSTITUTIONS

The rather peculiar configuration of the European Union institutions reflects the functional origins of the Community and the
incremental, not to say haphazard, way in which powers have
developed. There does not exist a single European constitution
against which the institutions can be compared, or towards
which they can be said to be progressing. Although there have
been several attempts to draw up such a constitution, and there
have circulated several draft blueprints for the institutional
future of the Community/Union, none has so far achieved consensus. One reason is that the prime component parts of the
Union – the member states – each have differing constitutional
backgrounds, traditions and internal political arrangements.
Some are republics, some kingdoms, some have centralised

systems, some decentralised systems, and so forth. A common conceptual language on the most desirable arrangements at a European level has not so far been found. This difficulty complicates the debate on political union, which means that the steps forward tend to be those of the lowest common denominator.

Because of this fundamental inability to construct an agreed model, the Community institutions have developed piecemeal, almost as it were in the interstices of the national constitutions. The Maastricht Treaty has attempted to rationalise these developments by use of what is generally known as the 'pillars' approach. The European Union is defined as including the traditional European Communities (pillar one), plus a common foreign and security policy (pillar two), plus co-operation between the member states in the fields of justice and home affairs (pillar three). In addition, Maastricht made yet further piecemeal changes to some of the existing institutions.

The institutional starting point remains the *European Commission*, the successor to the High Authority. In the EC Treaty, the Commission was given four distinct functions, explicitly linked to the operation and development of the common market. The first was to watch over the application of the Treaty, including by the Community institutions themselves. This is its so-called 'guardian of the Treaties' role. The second was to put forward recommendations or opinions on matters covered by the Treaty – its role as proposer of legislation. The third was to take decisions in areas specified by the Treaty (its management role). And the fourth was to take action in areas where the Council itself confers its responsibility.

In hierarchical terms the Commission is broken down into two segments. There is the 'college' of commissioners, of roughly ministerial rank, appointed by the member states for a four year mandate. (Under Maastricht this term was increased to five years.) They are required to be fully independent of the member states and to act in the general interest of the Community. Then there are the 13,000 permanent staff who work to them, mostly based in Brussels, broken down into twenty-three departments (or Directorates-General). Examples of important Directorates-General are DG I (covering External Relations), DG III (Internal Market), DG IV (Competition), DG VI (Agriculture), DG VIII (Development) and DG XVI (Regional Policy).

The *Council of Ministers* is the EU institution which directly represents the member states, and one member from each member state attends its meetings, which are usually held in Brussels. Under the EC Treaty the Council was set up to ensure the co-ordination of the general economic policies of the member states, to act as a decision-making body and to define the general management operations of the Commission. The Council is thus the main decision-making body on most major issues; and it takes such decisions in most cases on the basis of Commission proposals. (Box 2 gives further details of the actual decision-taking mechanisms.) In theory the Council is meant to be indivisible. In practice it is split according to function (foreign affairs, finance, agriculture, internal market, etc.) with the relevant minister going to the meeting in Brussels from his national capital. Much preparatory work is done by officials at a lower level before business actually gets to the Council, with a committee of Permanent Representatives of member states (at Ambassadorial level) overseeing the work of countless expert official working groups, some permanent, some ad hoc.

The working methods of the Council have changed over time. Until the Single European Act its practice on most questions in the twenty years since 1966 (the final stage of the transition period establishing the customs union) had been to take decisions on a unanimous basis, even on subjects where the Treaty specified voting. Since the Single European Act voting has, however, been used much more to adopt single market legislation. (We shall look into this more in Chapter 3.)

In the 1970s it was felt that, in order to correct the tendency of the Council of Ministers to be a forum for the exclusive bargaining over narrow or specific national interests, a new high level political authority should be set up which would inject broad political vision into the debate. Monnet had at first proposed that the institution be styled the 'Provisional European Government'. His idea had been to replace the situation whereby ministers in the Council acted on the basis of national instructions, welling up exclusively from within each national administration, with one where they receive instructions from a common source – a body composed of their political seniors. (This was a typical example of Monnet lateral thinking.) In the event, the title 'European Council' was chosen, and this body, comprising European heads of state or government, met for the first time in 1975. Since then it has provided broad political impetus to

41

the EC, and set strategic work programmes for specific Councils of Ministers to concentrate on. The Single European Act specified that the European Council should meet at least twice a year, and the Maastricht Treaty formalised the role of the European Council by stating that it should provide the European Union 'with the necessary impetus for its development' and 'define the general political guidelines thereof' (Maastricht Treaty Article D).

The administration of the entire gamut of the Council of Ministers, from lowliest working group to the European Council itself, is the responsibility of the member state holding the six month revolving Presidency, and which chairs meetings, sets agendas and fixes the six monthly calendar of work.

Box 2 Decision taking in the European Union

1 There are four broad classes of Community (i.e. Maastricht 'pillar one') legislation:

- *Regulations*, which have general application and are directly applicable in all member states. They do not have to be confirmed by national parliaments in order to have binding legal effect. If there is a conflict between a Regulation and existing national law, the Regulation prevails.
- *Directives* are binding on member states as to the result to be achieved within a stated period, but leave the method of implementation to national governments. In the UK this generally involves either primary or secondary legislation.
- *Decisions* are binding in their entirety on those to whom they are addressed, whether member states, companies or individuals.
- *Recommendations and Opinions* have no binding force, but simply state Community views.

2 The right of proposal of legislation lies with the Commission, but the Council might, for example, ask the Commission to make a proposal in a specific area. Once a proposal is on the table it then depends on the precise Treaty legal basis as to whether (i) the proposal is subject to *unanimity, simple majority voting* or *qualified majority voting* and (ii) the European Parliament needs simply to be consulted (non-binding) by the Council or, as is now the case in a wide body of legislation connected to the single market, whether the more complicated *co-decision procedure* (explained in Box 3) comes into effect.

3 If a proposal is subject to voting in the Council this is normally by *qualified majority*, which means that the votes of each member state are weighted as follows:

42

Germany, France, Italy, UK	10 votes each
Spain	8 votes
Belgium, Greece, Netherlands, Portugal	5 votes each
Denmark, Ireland	3 votes each
Luxembourg	2 votes
Total	76 votes

4   In general *fifty-four votes in favour* are needed to adopt a proposal.[1]

The Strasbourg-based *European Parliament* has a slightly odd role among the EU institutions. Although since 1979 the 518 MEPs (subsequently increased to 567 to take into account German unification) have been directly elected, they have historically had few real powers, apart from some say in the EC budget, the right to censure and thus dismiss the entire Commission (never used) and the right to issue opinions on EC activity. Real legislative and decision-taking authority has been elsewhere – shared between the Council and the Commission. It is interesting, for example, that when in 1992 the French Constitutional Council looked at the question of the increase in powers of the European Parliament under the Maastricht Treaty, it discovered no particular constitutional difficulty on this point, since in its opinion the European Parliament 'does not constitute a sovereign assembly with general powers tending to compete with the exercise of national sovereignty'.[2] Nonetheless, the European Parliament – whose policy objective since direct elections has been to share the power to enact legislation with the Council – *has* clawed some powers to it in recent years. Both the Single European Act and, more significantly, the Maastricht Treaty gave the Parliament real if limited powers governing certain types of EC legislation – powers which, according to Commissioner Sir Leon Brittan, 'amount to an effective veto' (Brittan 1994: 235). A rather complicated *co-decision procedure* (see Box 3) ensures that the Parliament has a say in draft legislation transmitted by the Commission to the Council, and can both propose amendments which the Council has to take into account and also block legislation if a sufficient majority in the Parliament is against it. The Maastricht Treaty also gave the Parliament the right to approve or reject the appointment of the President of the Commission by the member states, and also to approve international agreements and the accession of new member states to the EU. It also added further detailed

---

Box 3 The co-decision procedure with the European Parliament

1 Under the Maastricht Treaty a wide range of legislation subject to qualified majority vote in the Council (covering single market issues, services, the free movement of workers, the right of establishment, research and environmental programmes, education and cultural issues) is now also subject to a greater say by the European Parliament (EP). Two broad sets of circumstances can arise:

- The Council might adopt a common position on the proposed legislation which the EP then rejects (by an absolute majority of its members). In this case a *Conciliation Committee* between the Council and the EP is formed, to try to agree on a joint text. If in the final analysis this is not possible the EP, again by absolute majority, can block adoption of the text.
- The EP might instead propose amendments to the common position reached by the Council (again by an absolute majority of its members). The Council then can either approve all EP amendments by qualified majority vote or reject them (in which case the Conciliation Committee comes into effect, as above).

2 This procedure means that in theory either the Council or the EP could block approval of a proposal. How this will change the actual dynamics of decision taking remains to be seen (and will not be clear until the new EP elected after the 1994 elections establishes a working routine with the other institutions). The need for the EP to muster absolute majorities to affect legislation will itself affect the way in which political parties in the EP work with each other.

---

provisions: the right of any individual to petition the European Parliament, the right of the Parliament to set up Committees of Inquiry to investigate alleged maladministration, and the right of the Parliament to appoint an Ombudsman to investigate complaints.

The *European Court of Justice* (thirteen judges, based in Luxembourg) has grown to become an extremely important member of the family of EU institutions since it acts as the final arbiter of Community law, deciding on matters where there is dispute between the Commission and the member states. The gradual development of a body of European law and interpretative jurisprudence by the Court was not planned or obvious when the Treaties were first drawn up, and that development well illustrates the evolutionary, almost organic nature of the Union. It would not be misleading to suggest that while economic integration has been the dominant overt theme since the birth of the Community, it has been the application of European law which has in reality proved the most significant institutional innovation. There could have been no development of the common market – and certainly no single market – without the growth of a corpus of common European law, becoming an accepted part of national jurisdictions. While it may have been difficult for political leaders to agree on the precise codified political or constitutional shape of the future Community and Union, there has been no parallel difficulty in living with the alignment after the event of national law with European law. It has been precisely because the EU member states, through their varying national constitutions, each consider themselves subject to the rule of law that the law has become such a powerful unifying force between them. It has been a strictly peaceful process: the Court possesses no coercive institution with which to enforce its rulings.

Three key findings of the Court are worth a particular mention here. As early as 1963 the Court ruled that EC law has *direct effect* in member states. This means that it applies not only to the governments of the member states (the classical arrangement in international treaties), but also to the individuals and companies within those member states. As a corollary it has also meant that individuals and companies could invoke EC law in national courts – which has become important in single market cases.

In 1964 the Court made the landmark ruling that where there is a conflict between national law and EC law (a point not clarified in the Treaty) EC law has *primacy over national law*. In doing so it observed the following:

In creating a Community of an indeterminate duration, with its own institutions, with its own personality, with legal capability, with the capability of international representation and, most particularly, with real powers resulting from a limitation of authority or a transfer of attributes from states to the Community, the states have limited their sovereign prerogatives, although in restricted areas, and have

45

thus created a legal corpus binding their nationals as well as themselves.

(Quoted in Mattera 1990: 644)

In 1979 the Court handed down the famous *'Cassis de Dijon'* ruling, which the Commission later used as the cornerstone of a new and fruitful legislative approach to completing the single market (as we shall see in the next chapter). The 1979 judgement turned on the specific legal point that German laws concerning alcohol strength should not constitute a trade barrier to imports from France. But from this and similar case law over this period the concept of 'mutual recognition' of national standards was derived. This principle, vital to the extension of the common market into the services sector, could not have been developed without prior Court jurisprudence.

It will be seen that if, as Monnet had originally envisaged, the Community can be conceived as a network of rules – laws – cutting across the national boundaries of the member states and prohibiting them from doing things agreed to be against the common interest, then the Court must have a vital role in clarifying and reviewing those rules and considering how they apply to events in the real world. In its day to day interpretation of the broad swathe of European law, and its comparison of national law with European law, the Court has – within its sphere of operations – a direct authority less spectacular but perhaps comparable in its way to the independence and power of the original High Authority.

What exactly is its sphere of operations? The Treaty of Rome specified that the Court is competent to pronounce on the interpretation of the Treaty, on the validity and interpretation of acts of the Community institutions and, where they allow, on the interpretation of the statutes of bodies created by the Council. In other words, the powers of the Court are clearly Treaty-based: it has no general powers to pronounce on questions falling beyond it. The Maastricht Treaty, in providing the legal basis for the new institution the European Central Bank, added that the Court would also have jurisdiction concerning the validity and interpretation of its acts (a point which could prove vital if and when a single monetary policy comes into being). At the same time, however, the Maastricht Treaty also specified (Article L) that the Court would *not* have jurisdiction in the new areas of common foreign and security policy and co-operation on justice and home affairs matters (for example police questions). Thus, it should be emphasised, the Court of Justice is explicitly *not* concerned with the wider questions of criminal and civil justice within the European Union: only with the doings of the Community and its institutions.

The Single European Act also established a Court of First Instance, intended to deal with more routine legal matters and disputes and leave the major cases for the Court of Justice. The Maastricht Treaty in addition gave the Court of Justice the power to impose fines on member states disobeying Community laws.

Apart from these main institutions, the EU includes a host of other *minor institutions*, which have specific, mostly self-explanatory, functions. Examples are the *European Investment Bank*, the *Court of Auditors* and the *Economic and Social Committee* (which comprises representatives of various categories of economic and social activity, and has an advisory role). The Maastricht Treaty has added a new advisory body in the shape of the *Committee of the Regions*. Finally, Maastricht has also made provision for the creation of the major new institutions of the *European Monetary Institute* and the *European Central Bank*, the role of which will be explored further in Chapter 6.

POLICIES OF THE UNION

Although we shall be looking in greater detail at certain important aspects of the European Union, now may be a good moment to survey briefly the overall nature of the post-Maastricht ensemble as it stands in the 1990s.

The dominant theme of economic integration through the merging of national markets has continued to provide the core of activity. That theme was present from the outset in the establishment of the post-war Coal and Steel Community; it was broadened when the common market was set up; the single European market refined and updated it; and economic and monetary union, as defined in the Maastricht Treaty, can be viewed as simply one more (and possibly the ultimate) step in this economic integration. At each stage the creation of a market order on a European scale, joining together national markets, has itself then required the creation of institutions concerned with the organisation of that market order: the High Authority, the European Commission, the

Court of Justice – and even the future European Central Bank, which is intended to oversee the functioning of a future European monetary order.

Around this market-creating core a number of subsidiary activities have developed, resulting sometimes from the tension between national and EC institutions, sometimes from clear acts of political will to integrate national activities and sometimes from attempts to carry out explicitly market-correcting or interventionist policies at a European level. As well as the common market, the EC Treaty itself made provision for common policies to be developed in the areas of agriculture and transport, and also for the creation of a European Social Fund to help the labour market. In the 1970s leaders of Community member states asked the Commission to develop new policies at a European level in areas such as economic and monetary union, regional development (including the creation of a Regional Development Fund), science and technology, the environment and energy. The Single European Act formalised such extensions of Community activity by amending the EC Treaty to include general provisions in these areas. The Maastricht Treaty added to this list by including within the activities of the Community matters such as the strengthening of the competitiveness of industry, the development of 'trans-European networks', contributions to a high level of health protection and to education, training and 'the flowering of the cultures' of the member states, contributions to strengthening consumer protection and measures in the spheres of energy, civil protection and tourism.

Of course in many of these areas member states already pursue their own national policies. And this brings us to our next point: the shifting borderline between national and European policies.

In its purest form Community activity replaces national activity. This was, explicitly, the purpose in setting up the Coal and Steel Community. In a limited number of other cases – agriculture is one, the common commercial policy another – the member states have simply handed over legal powers to the Community, with the Commission acting as its effective management agent. But virtually from the outset there have been attempts to develop new forms of co-operation and common action based on the political premise that joint or common activity by the member states is likely to have more impact than individual behaviour. Such joint action has by no means been confined to areas specified in the Treaties. The creation of the European Monetary System and the system of foreign policy co-ordination known as political co-operation are two examples of such innovation. (Both were later written into the Treaty, but only *after* they had been created.) And there is a host of examples of activity involving *both* national and Community authorities – on environmental questions, for example, on social policy, or on technological development. Finally, the Maastricht Treaty has, as we have seen, created a completely new legal category by enshrining the concept of the 'European Union'. This is based on the European Communities *plus* 'the policies and forms of cooperation established by this Treaty' (that is, a common foreign and security policy and co-operation between member states in the fields of justice and home affairs).

Maastricht thus brings together the many diverse forms of common or joint activity by both member states and the Community at a European level and puts them under the umbrella title of 'European Union'. The European Union has been given as its primary task 'to organise, in a manner demonstrating consistency and solidarity, relations between the Member States and between their peoples' (Article A). The prime authority in the European Union is the European Council, which (as we have seen) is to 'provide the Union with the necessary impetus for its development and shall define the general political guidelines thereof' (Article D).

In an explicit sense, therefore, the European Union is conceived as the next political step forward in the creation of an 'ever closer union' between the peoples of Europe – a step beyond the economic forms of integration characterised by the Community itself. And, indeed, Maastricht introduces the concept of *citizenship* of the Union (and provides for some modest new political rights by allowing member states' nationals to vote and participate in one another's local and European, but *not* national, elections).

It will be evident from the above that the European Union as it emerges from the Maastricht Treaty is in fact a highly complex political and economic entity, combining as it does Community-level action, national-level action and indeed action which is a mixture of the two. It also, to complicate matters still further, brings into the picture for the first time *regional-level* action through the creation of the advisory Committee of the Regions.

One attempt to clarify at what level decisions should be taken in this complex whole has been to introduce the concept of *subsidiarity* into the debate. Thus, according to a new provision introduced in Maastricht:

> In areas which do not fall within its exclusive competence, the Community shall take action, in accordance with the principle of subsidiarity, *only if and in so far as the objectives of the proposed action cannot be sufficiently achieved by the Member States and can, therefore, by reason of the scale or effects of the proposed action, be better achieved by the Community.*
> (Maastricht Treaty Article G B (5); emphasis mine)

And, to reinforce this point, Article A of Maastricht specifies that 'decisions are taken as closely as possible to the citizen'.

Useful though these principles may prove to be, they do not at present provide clear guidance over where the dividing line between European and national action lies – and indeed may not do so until Court jurisprudence has been created on the basis of concrete examples. However, there is room for doubt about the ease of arriving at a clear agreed demarcation line on this point, if for no other reason than different member states have different views about their own authority.

We must consider the modern European Union as a complex legal and political entity which, unlike any other organisation in the world, groups together democratic nations within a framework of binding common rules, and which has as its chief economic motor the development of an ever better market. It does not, as such, greatly resemble a state as we commonly think of a state. One way to put this into context is to consider Union activity in terms of *expenditure policies*. The budget of the European Union in 1993 was some Ecu 68 billion (about £52 billion). (A breakdown is in Box 4). This figure may seem high (and to the finance ministries of the member states it no doubt is too high). However, it nonetheless represents only about 1.2 per cent of total EU GDP; and it represents only about 2.4 per cent of the total public expenditure of the member states. In other words, over 97 per cent of public expenditure within the Union is still directly controlled by the member states – including all the major blocks of expenditure on social welfare, on defence, on education, on infrastructure and so on. Although the population of the Union, following German unification, is currently some

---

Box 4   The EU budget
(1993: main expenditure items)

Total   68 billion Ecu

Agriculture   35 billion Ecu
Regional and social expenditure   22 billion Ecu
Research   3 billion Ecu
Other internal policies   2 billion Ecu
Aid for developing countries and post-
   communist Europe   4 billion Ecu

---

340 million (compared with a US population of 250 million) central EU expenditure remains small compared to the 18 per cent of GDP which the US government spends.

It may of course be pointed out that public expenditure *does* take place on a large scale within the Union, for which European institutions cannot substitute, and this is correct. But the really significant public expenditure programmes in Europe, on say social welfare costs (now exceeding 30 per cent of GDP in several EU countries), take place *within* each member state, not across national borders. About half the EU budget is devoted to the special case of running the Common Agricultural Policy (CAP). We shall look further at this later, but it is clear that the farm price support mechanisms financed through the CAP are not *intended* to transfer resources from one country to another, in a redistributional manner. If, therefore, within the remainder of the 1993 budget, funds for regional and social programmes (Ecu 22 billion) are added to research funds (Ecu 3 billion) and funds for miscellaneous internal European policies (transport, education, energy, industry and so on) (Ecu 2 billion), and if all these together (Ecu 27 billion) are considered very roughly as the sum total of EU expenditure on redistributional policies, transferring funds across borders, this figure would still amount to less than a third of the gross public sector transfers from west to east Germany in 1993.[3] It is true that EU budget expenditure is set to rise by about a fifth by the end of this century, but this is at least partly to be offset by the expected accession of the comparatively wealthy EFTA countries to the EU.

The overall picture therefore emerges of the European Union today as a perhaps unexpected entity: institutionally rather strong when it comes to market creation, with an array of independent

51

bodies as powerful, or even more powerful, than the constituent member states, and backed by the force of law. Yet it is institutionally rather weak when it comes to spending policies, with little central authority over European public expenditure as a whole.

It is against this general background that we shall consider in the chapters ahead some of the policy issues facing the EU.

3

THE PRINCIPLES OF THE SINGLE EUROPEAN MARKET

INTRODUCTION

In the 1970s and early 1980s it was widely felt that the European Community was running out of steam. Despite the completion of the customs union in 1968, which meant that customs duties and quantitative restrictions on intra-Community trade had been formally abolished, non-tariff barriers distorting trade between the member states remained and indeed proliferated as the recession and oil price shocks in the 1970s signalled the end of the long period of post-war European growth. Protectionism among the member states took the further form of growing public expenditure subsidies to national industries which could not otherwise compete. Free trade in the enormous services sector (contributing by now over half of value added in the EC economy) continued to be fragmented. Differing national standards and practices continued to distort the market. EC decision-taking itself was hobbled by the habit of consensus that had developed since 1966 (it has been estimated that in the entire period 1966 to 1979 only forty to forty-five votes were taken, including routine ones on the annual budget).[1] The enlargement of the Community (from six to twelve members between 1973 and 1986), rather than strengthening common disciplines, seemed instead to contribute to a sense of paralysis of purpose and blockage of movement. *Eurosclerosis* was in vogue.

In 1985 the European Commission, headed by former French Finance Minister Jacques Delors, chose the completion of the internal market in Europe as the one major forward-looking theme most likely to rally both political and economic support across the Community. The same year the Commission published its White Paper on the same subject. In 1986 the Single European

Act amended the EC Treaty to write into it the goal of aiming by the end of 1992 at the creation of 'an area without internal frontiers in which the free movement of goods, persons, services and capital is ensured' (SEA: Article 13). The programme of single market legislation was launched, an in-depth study of its economic benefits was published, companies across Europe began positioning themselves for its arrival, cross-border mergers and acquisitions boomed, the remaining western European countries of EFTA sought to become part of this great market and – to cap the process of market-building – full economic and monetary union was adopted as the next target stage for the Community, and was itself written into the 1992 Maastricht Treaty.

While not denying the motivating power of the single market programme (or 'Project 1992' as *The Economist* magazine put it), and its enormous success in rallying support among both business and political leaders in a Community that was now double its original size, it is worth recalling that the thrust of that programme was in fact implicit in the Community from the outset. Some commentators have suggested that the definition of the internal market in the Single European Act as 'an area without internal frontiers' is a slight step further than the earlier conception of a simple common market, on the grounds that the latter may include certain residual internal frontiers (Mattera 1990: 15). It is true that the original EC Treaty does not itself provide a clear definition of a common market. But Court of Justice jurisprudence had in 1973 already found that the EC customs union 'must be so complete that any barrier whatever, financial, administrative or any other, is abandoned so as to establish a unity of market between the member states' (quoted in Mattera 1990: 25).

As we have seen in Chapter 1, a reading of the text of the 1956 Spaak Committee Report, on which the Treaty of Rome was based, makes it clear that the intention at the outset was to merge national markets and to create one single market, within which the better division of labour could function. As the Spaak Report put it:

> Obstacles to trade do not only take the form of customs duties, quotas or import monopolies, but also restrictions in allocating currency, discriminations in transport tariffs depending on the country of origin or destination, even internal regulations, in particular affecting services and

54

agriculture, which lead in practice to the elimination or regulation at will of foreign competition.

(*Rapport* 1956: 16)

So the objective from the beginning was to arrive at a situation whereby, by the end of the initial transitional period, not only would formal internal customs duties and tariffs be abolished but there would be the 'suppression of separate regulation of the markets' and 'the creation, where necessary, of a common regulation or organisation' (*Rapport* 1956: 20).

What in fact happened was that the difficulties which the Spaak Report accurately foresaw in establishing a true common market, in particular in the services sector, were simply not overcome by the time the customs union was created in 1968. Whereas in agriculture (recognised also as a difficult area) the fundamental problem of the prior existence of national market regulation *was* addressed by the setting up of the Common Agricultural Policy in the 1960s, no comparable effort was made to deal with other existing national market regulations which – in particular in the much larger services sector – continued to distort the market. Article 63 of the EC Treaty – which should have led to the adoption during the transitional period of a general programme to abolish restrictions on trade in services – remained a dead letter.

The 1992 internal market programme may thus be thought of as a delayed attempt to put right problems which strictly speaking should have been addressed by 1968. While, as we shall see, some of the policy tools used were new, the underlying fact that distortions of the common market would arise from the very existence of national market regulations and intervention had already been diagnosed over thirty years before. What was missing for many years was not so much an understanding of the issues but rather the collective political will to address them.

THE SINGLE MARKET PROGRAMME

The focus of this renewed attempt at market development was the *Commission White Paper of 1985*. It was that document which spelled out the programme and the timetable to achieve the goal of completing a fully unified internal market by 1992. This political goal was agreed by the Council and written into the Treaty when in 1986 the Single European Act was signed.

The White Paper argued that there remained essentially *three different types of barrier* to the completion of the internal market. The first category came under the heading of 'physical barriers' and the most obvious example of these were customs posts and other controls at frontiers between EC member states. The White Paper argued that such physical barriers were means not ends – they existed mainly because there also existed two other types of barrier between member states, which could be described as 'technical' (such as differing national standards for goods and services) and 'fiscal' (such as differing VAT regimes). Once these latter barriers were removed, and once alternative ways had been found of dealing with other relevant problems like public security, immigration and drug controls, the reasons for the continued existence of the physical barriers would have been eliminated.

The White Paper was nothing if not bold in its approach. Under the heading of *physical barriers* it stated flatly that the objective 'is not merely to simplify existing procedures, but to do away with internal frontier controls in their entirety' (White Paper 1985: 9). It proposed a programme of measures to do this, including reforms in the means of dealing with the transit of both goods and individuals at borders. For goods, border checks arising from commercial and economic requirements should be phased out; checks arising from health protection (eg of plants and animals) should be moved away from the border to the place either of departure or destination (with a tougher common supervisory regime); checks on national transport policy grounds should be either abolished or carried out within member states; and checks purely for statistical purposes should also be phased out. For individuals, the use of border controls for police purposes should be phased out in line with greater co-operation between national authorities and the adoption of a common approach to matters such as third country nationals travelling within the Community.

Under the heading of *technical barriers* the White Paper, faced with the continued proliferation of effective non-tariff barriers to a common market embedded within national practices and regulations, called for a radical change of attitude. What was involved can be explained as follows. When dealing with differing national standards or procedures between member states, affecting any type of tradable good or service within the common market, existing Community practice had been to try to 'harmonise' such standards or procedures on a common basis. This approach was not only conceptually difficult, given the variety of national rules and regulations and the immense number of objects potentially involved. It also was immensely time-consuming and labour intensive and – the height of absurdity – had produced cases that took so long to agree between the member states that new technology had in the meantime made the good or service in question redundant.

This attempt to replace all national regulations by Community regulations was now to be abandoned. Instead, the Commission proposed a much simpler solution: the general principle (subject to certain important constraints) that *if a product is lawfully manufactured and marketed in one member state, there should be no reason why it should not be sold freely throughout the Community.* This would hold true for goods, for services and indeed for the economic activities of people themselves:

> If a Community citizen or a company meets the requirements for its activity in one member state, there should be no valid reason why those citizens or companies should not exercise their economic activities also in other parts of the Community.
>
> (White Paper 1985: 17)

The significance of this seemingly simple idea – known technically as 'mutual recognition' – is in fact quite great, as a moment's reflection will suggest. Inspired by the *'Cassis de Dijon'* Court of Justice ruling of 1979, mentioned in the previous chapter, it implies a 'light' method of Community lawmaking, one that is better suited to modern, mobile industries, such as financial services, than the old 'heavy' forms of regulation, which were applied to basic industries such as coal and steel and taken to extreme lengths in agriculture (as we shall see in Chapter 7). It allows for the continued existence of national differences and variations – as long as those do not become legal impediments to trade. In this way it encourages market forces to do some of the legislative harmonisation on behalf of the Community (as in fact the Spaak Report had originally suggested).

Apparently simple though this idea of mutual recognition is, it rests upon a number of assumptions. One is that the basic objectives of market regulation within each member state, such

57

as the protection of human health, life and the environment, are more or less shared by all, even though the means of achieving them may differ. This in turn implies a deeper assumption – that, by and large, despite their obvious differences, the member states of the Community are fundamentally similar, in terms of economic and political outlook. It implies also a degree of mutual trust and goodwill, since, for mutual recognition to work, different national administrations must also work side by side. And it implies lastly a functioning and credible legal system to ensure that the rules are not abused, and also to adjudicate on hard cases. So, though the idea may now seem self-evident (and it is a fertile concept which may yet have wider application), there is room for doubt as to whether it could in practice have worked had the Community not progressed to a particular stage of political and economic development. Indeed, it is questionable whether it would have been feasible in the decade just after the Second World War.

As the White Paper makes clear, mutual recognition is not meant to be a free for all. It rests upon continued essential minimum rules, for example for health and safety, which may still have to be harmonised on a Community basis. Indeed, the key to the legislative programme in the technical barriers area of the single market is the case by case identification of what irreducibly must be harmonised and what can be left to the free play of economic forces.

Under technical barriers the White Paper also addressed a number of specific sectors where distortions to the internal market were particularly serious and required action. One such was the area of procurement of goods and services by the national authorities of the member states (a huge market still largely dominated by national protection). Another was the obstacles to the free movement of both the self-employed and employees, where there were problems concerning the recognition of professional qualifications. Another was the entire service sector itself:

> In the Commission's view, it is no exaggeration to see the establishment of a common market in services as one of the main preconditions for a return to economic prosperity.
>
> (White Paper 1985: 26)

The White Paper noted how, despite the fact that in 1982 market services and non-market services accounted for 57 per cent of

58

value added to the EC economy (while industry accounted for less than 26 per cent) and despite the fact that in theory the freedom to provide services had existed since the end of the transitional period (1968), in practice there was much less freedom than in the area of goods. Priority areas of action were the traditional services such as banking, insurance and transport, but also new service industries such as broadcasting and information technology, with linked industries like electronic banking and payments systems. To accompany the liberalisation of financial services, greater liberalisation of capital movements in the Community would also be required (which we will look at in more detail in Chapter 5).

As well as measures designed to liberate parts of the market, the White Paper also recommended action to improve cross-border industrial co-operation (such as by reforms in the legal environment for setting up companies and creating links between them, and also simplifying the company taxation regime). It also recommended strengthening the application of EC law in its relation to the market, particularly in the areas of competition policy and state aids to industry (which we will look at in more detail in the next chapter).

Finally, under the third heading of *fiscal barriers*, the White Paper argued that national systems of levying indirect taxes among the member states (like value added tax on goods and services and excise duties on spirits and tobacco) themselves created barriers within the market, since member states used frontier controls to collect national tax revenue due to them. To fulfil the objective of removing frontier controls it proposed firstly treating the taxation of cross-border trade in the same way as if it were internal trade within any member state (with VAT applied on sales and deductible on purchases); secondly introducing an EC 'Clearing House System' to ensure that VAT collected in the exporting member state and deducted in the importing member state was reimbursed to the latter; and thirdly reducing the wide disparities between national indirect taxation rates so as to reduce price distortions and scope for cross-border tax fraud within the single market. On this last point the White Paper argued that tax levels would not have to be exactly the same ('harmonised'), but rather that they should not diverge too far from a central mean ('approximation'). Drawing on experience from the United States, it suggested that, for VAT, differences of up to 5 per cent were tolerable at national borders, which meant that a margin of plus or minus 2.5 per cent either side of a target or central rate could be allowed.

Although apparently fairly straightforward in principle, in practice this approach entailed juggling with a number of important variables and differing interests between the member states. One variable was the differing take from indirect taxes as a proportion of GDP among the member states (ranging from 9 per cent of GDP in Germany to 17 per cent of GDP in Ireland); the second was the differing *bases* of goods and services to which indirect taxes were applied among the member states; and the third was the differing *rates* of taxation which were actually applied in each case. As often in the Community, the real complexities thus arose not so much from trying to establish common market rules for the private sector, but rather trying to make national administrative and public sector practices – developed separately within each member state – compatible with one another. We will see in the next chapter how successful this approach to the removal of fiscal barriers has been.

This brief survey of the White Paper – and the physical, technical and fiscal barriers it identified – illustrates how heterogeneous was its subject matter. Although its overall policy objective could be stated quite readily – the completion of a fully unified internal market in the Community by 1992 – the action involved to achieve this, even assuming the abandonment of total harmonisation in favour of mutual recognition, in practice involved a myriad small-scale or technical reforms to impediments to the market. And so the legislative programme which the White Paper heralded ran to more than 280 detailed proposals, from directives on jams and fruit juices to the liberalisation of long-term capital and the elimination of customs formalities at borders. There was, though, a common factor: in essence the single market programme amounted to an attempted final assault on the accumulated obstructions to the market – for the most part due to the actions of the national authorities of the member states themselves – in place already or even added since the signature of the Treaty of Rome.

THE PROMISE OF GROWTH

The first year in which the single market was supposed to operate, 1993, was a year of particularly dismal economic performance in the Community, with low growth, an exchange rate crisis and mounting unemployment. It may seem incongruous in retrospect, but the single market was of course supposed to usher in a new era of European prosperity. And, in fact, along with its legislative programme, the Commission also undertook a detailed economic study of the expected future benefits of the single market, and had published the results in 1988.

The *Cecchini Report*, as it was known, may appear on the face of it to be wildly over-optimistic. It suggested that the economic integration resulting from the completion of the single market – the 'supply-side shock to the Community economy as a whole' (Cecchini 1988: xix) – could 'in the space of a few years' put between *four and seven percentage points* on the Community's domestic product. Alternatively, according to a different method of doing the calculations, it could reduce costs and thus produce potential economic benefits worth over Ecu 200 billion. The report was quite categorical about the chances of enhanced European growth: 'This vista is not a tantalising chimera. On the contrary, it is a firm prospect' (Cecchini 1988: xvii).

Was the Cecchini Report a misleading public relations exercise designed to sell the single market programme, with its arithmetical conclusions only 'of frankly dubious worth' (Colchester and Buchan 1990: 33)? Like all such attempts at complex economic modelling the results of course depended upon the assumptions underlying it. The main macroeconomic assumption underlying Cecchini was that the single market programme would engender a virtuous circle whereby the removal of barriers to the market would force costs down, leading to falling prices stimulating additional demand and allowing companies to increase their output. Public sector deficits would be eased as a consequence of open public procurement and better economic growth. And there would be a positive medium-term impact of market integration on employment:

> With its injection of inflation-free growth, coupled with a loosening of the constraints on public exchequers in the Community's member states, the European home market of the 1990s raises the prospect, for the first time since the early 1970s, of very substantial job creation.
>
> (Cecchini 1988: xix)

We shall return to the overall macroeconomic policies of the

61

Community in the chapter on economic and monetary union – and in particular at the unforeseen shock to the system caused by the effects of German unification. But at this stage a number of comments on Cecchini may be worth making.

The main one is of course that the extra growth and the virtuous circle arising from the single market were never expected to be immediate. Cecchini talks about the 'progressive impact' of market integration, of what would follow 'in the space of a few years' (1988: xvii), and of the positive 'medium term impact' (1988: xix) on employment creation. In 1993, even had the Community not been affected by worldwide poor growth in general and the impact of German unification in particular, it would have been too soon for most of the positive effects of the single market to have worked through. (Although it may not have been too soon for the short-term *negative* effects to be felt, as uncompetitive industries shed labour and squeezed costs: and for these negative effects to be made even worse in the poor economic climate.)

So the *potential* for growth may nonetheless still exist. The encouragement to trade between the member states and thus to increased economic activity which resulted from the original development of the common market in the 1950s remains a valid example. Between 1958 and 1986 trade between the original six member states grew from around Ecu 20 billion to over Ecu 460 billion, and the share of the trade of each within the Community grew from around 33 per cent to over 50 per cent (Mattera 1990: 4). The effective dismantling of the remaining barriers to trade within the EU – including in the large service sector – should, all other things being equal, have some comparable effect. (Although whether the law of diminishing returns will allow a return to the fast growth rates of the past – the average 4 per cent per annum between 1958 and 1967 – may be a different proposition.)

While we may remain sceptical about its precise quantification, it is also worth recalling where exactly Cecchini thought the growth was going to come from. The Report approached the problem of measuring such growth backwards – it first considered the economic costs of the barriers to the single market which remained in place (which it called the 'cost of non Europe' (1988: xviii)) and it then proposed two different models to measure the gains resulting from the lifting of such barriers. The Cecchini survey of the costs of barriers to the market provided a mass of detailed evidence of specific examples of economic disbenefits within the Community. A survey of European businesses, for example, found that they believed that administrative barriers to cross-border trade (like customs procedures) were their number one problem. A study of cross-border trade among six member states suggested that firms were actually paying around Ecu 8 billion in terms of costs and delays arising from frontier customs controls (equivalent to 2 per cent of the value of sales) and were also foregoing a large volume of business (put at between Ecu 4.5 and 15 billion). Differing technical standards continued to impose costs, such as the Ecu 286 million of additional costs reckoned necessary to develop a volume passenger car to meet the differing European specifications. And closed national markets, such as in telecommunications equipment, were adding costs of up to 25 per cent because of national procurement rules and differing national standards (and this in a market worth some $17.5 billion).

The two ways by which Cecchini attempted to quantify the gains from the removal of such barriers were first by an 'economic welfare', microeconomic, approach and second by a broader macroeconomic approach. A summary of the results of the economic welfare approach is in Box 5. The step by step logic which leads to the final result (an average increase in economic welfare gains worth Ecu 216 billion, or 5.3 per cent of EC GDP) is as follows: step one is a quantification of the benefits of the removal of barriers which directly affect intra-EC trade (essentially customs formalities and related delays); step two concerns the removal of barriers to production itself – barriers which 'hinder foreign market entrants and thus the free play of competition' (Cecchini 1988: 83) such as protective public procurement, divergent national standards and regulations and restrictions on services and manufacturing; step three represents the cost reductions achieved by businesses exploiting more fully potential economies of scale such as increases in production in a larger market cutting fixed investment costs; step four represents other gains in efficiency due to intensified pressures of competition, such as the reduction of monopoly profits. It should also be mentioned that this summary excludes what Cecchini thought would be *further* dynamic effects from market integration resulting from new business strategies and technical innovation.

Box 5   Economic welfare gains arising from completion of the single market

Step 1	Ecu billion	% of GDP
Gains from removal of barriers		
affecting trade	8–9	0.2–0.3
Step 2		
Gains from removal of barriers		
affecting overall production	57–71	2.0–2.4
Gains from removing barriers (subtotal)	65–80	2.2–2.7
Step 3		
Gains from exploiting economies of		
scale more fully	61	2.1
Step 4		
Gains from intensified competition		
reducing business inefficiencies		
and monopoly profits	46	1.6
Gains from market integration(subtotal)	62–107	2.1–3.7
Total		
for 7 member states at 1985 prices	122–187	4.3–6.4
for 12 member states at 1985 prices	174–258	4.3–6.4
mid-point of above	216	5.3

(*Source*: Cecchini 1988: 84)

Box 6 summarises the alternative, *macroeconomic* approach to measuring the benefits of market integration through the 'supply-side shock' to be given to the European economy by the removal of customs barriers, the opening up of procurement markets, the liberalisation of financial services and the formulation of new business strategies. It assumes that four major constraints on overall European growth will be significantly loosened as a result (public finances, external trade, inflation and unemployment) 'even if, in the case of employment, the gains – and considerable gains they are by any measure – will come in the medium term' (Cecchini 1988: 92). (It is also worth mentioning here that Cecchini argues that even greater benefits could arise from collective adjustments of the European economic policy mix.)

What further comments can we make about Cecchini and its promises of growth? The first is that both sets of calculations rest upon something very close to a perfectly integrated European

---

Box 6   Medium-term macroeconomic effects of the single market

Relative changes (%)	1	2	3	4	Total Average	Spread
GDP	0.4	0.5	1.5	2.1	4.5	(3.2–5.7)
Consumer prices	–1.0	–1.4	–1.4	–2.3	–6.1	(–4.5––7.7)
Absolute changes						
Employment (millions)	200	350	400	850	1800	(1300–2300)
Budgetary balance (% of GDP)	0.2	0.3	1.1	0.6	2.2	(1.5–3.0)
External balance (% of GDP)	0.2	0.1	0.3	0.4	1.0	(0.7–1.3)

Notes: 1 = customs formalities; 2 = public procurement; 3 = financial services; 4 = supply-side effects
Source: Cecchini (1988: 98)

---

market developing, as a result of which economic operators experience virtually no perceptible difference between one member state and the next. Now, it may be that such a market *will* develop from the single market legislative programme, but we are clearly not there yet – either in terms of the effects of the legislation or even in some cases in terms of its legal implementation (see the next chapter). The single European market – as rigorously defined by Cecchini – *has not yet been established*. There even arises a further question of whether a market like this *can* ever be completed – or whether its improvement will be a permanent process as unforeseen new products and techniques and new national differences emerge.

Second, it is striking how such optimistic macroeconomic hypotheses can be blown off course by external events. The assumption that budgetary constraints will be *relaxed* has for example been overshadowed by the serious deterioration in public finances in many EU member states, exacerbated by the general economic recession and the mismatch between tax revenue and public expenditure: a problem which in turn has meant that the next step in market integration, in terms of economic and monetary union, looks more problematic.

Third, neither of the two points above necessarily invalidates the main proposition that major economic benefits *should* flow from market building, as they have in the past. What they will be, and when they will arrive, and who exactly will benefit, might have to remain the subject of attempts at economic modelling as successful (or unsuccessful) as attempts to forecast national economic trends. (The Spaak Report wisely made no attempt to quantify the benefits from the common market in 1956, and, had it done so, would probably have been hopelessly wrong, given all the variables involved).

AGREEMENT TO GO FORWARD

The Single European Act of 1986 both defined the internal market and also endorsed the target date for establishing it (31 December 1992). It also amended the EC Treaty by adding a new article (100A) which specifically provided that EC measures which involved the drawing together ('approximation') of national rules and regulations concerning the internal market should be adopted in the Council by a *qualified majority* (subject also to new co-operation arrangements with the European Parliament). It should be noted here, however, that this arrangement excluded decisions on fiscal (tax) provisions, those relating to the free movement of persons and those relating to the rights and interests of employed persons.

The Single European Act thus reinstituted the practice of *voting* by the member states in a central area of Community policy, and in this way reversed the trend towards consensus (or unanimous) decision taking which had developed among the member states since 1966, when the third and final stage of the transitional period to the customs union came into force, and when according to the Treaty the use of majority voting should in fact have been increased.

It may be recalled that the Spaak Report had at the outset addressed the problem of differing legislative and regulatory practices among the member states, and how this might affect the future common market. As we saw in Chapter 1, it was distinctly cool about harmonisation of legislation for the sake of harmonisation ('It is not possible to try to modify as if by decree the fundamental conditions of an economy' (Rapport 1956: 61)) and recommended that the future Commission proceed cautiously in the area of national regulation, concentrating on specific market distortions as they affected industry. But Spaak had also assumed that the common market would from the outset include services, even though in most cases the barriers lay not in customs duties but rather in internal national regulations; and it proposed that by the end of the transitional period regulation of the service sector should be on a common basis, subject to any agreed derogations. It also proposed that, after the end of the transitional period, action either to modify existing regulations or to establish a common regime for services *should be on a qualified majority basis.* And so, important though the move towards increased majority voting in the Single European Act was, it could well be argued that, since it concerned an area where action had already been delayed for many years, it too was essentially part of a catching-up process to completing the market.

Qualified majority voting on single market legislation (or, to be more accurate, on the approximation of national legislation and regulation which blocked the single market) proved to be a great success in making progress on the 282 draft directives which comprised the single market programme (although not all of them were based on article 100A). In the space of five years over 90 per cent of these directives had been adopted in the Council, and Commission statistics in 1990 suggested that, since the entry into force of the Single European Act, an average of only 18 months was required to adopt such legislation (compared with, for example, five-and-a-half years needed before the Single European Act to adopt a directive on electromagnetic compatibility and eight years for a directive on the mutual recognition of diplomas).[2] This proliferation of EC legislation had its impact on the member states too: according to an estimate by one French official *more than half* of the legislative work carried out in France in 1988 and 1989 resulted from the adoption of EC laws into French law.[3] And this astonishing statistic, it can be assumed, was more or less duplicated in other member states.

In the next chapter we shall consider some of the results so far of this great legislative programme.

4

THE SINGLE MARKET IN PRACTICE

INTRODUCTION

Strictly speaking the Community missed the 1992 deadline, as defined in the Single European Act. By 31 December 1992 not only had the internal market not been fully established (in the sense that one large market had not really and effectively replaced all the existing national markets), not even all the necessary Community legislation had been agreed. And, of what had been agreed, not all had been fully implemented in all the member states.

In September 1993 a Commission survey showed that 95 per cent of the legislative programme had been adopted by the Council (264 of the 282 detailed legislative proposals in the White Paper). Of these, 219 measures needed 'transposition' in the national laws of the member states (which meant that they were the type of EC legislation needing national implementation of the detail – see Box 2); and of these 219 only 106 measures *had* actually been transposed into the national law of all twelve member states. In other words, several months after the December 1992 deadline 5 per cent of the single market programme had not yet been agreed and about a third of the programme, although agreed, had not yet been fully put into effect. There was a further dimension too, in that not all the legislation was even supposed to come into effect by the end of 1992. In a number of cases, such as in the insurance and transport sectors, it had always been envisaged that the legislation should only come into effect over a period of years, or that some member states would have longer lead times than others to put it into place. Finally, quite apart from the legislation itself, there still remained the need for the establishment of one market to work its way into the habits and

68

behaviour of both economic operators and consumers. A survey quoted by the Internal Market Commissioner in November 1993 found, perhaps not surprisingly, that so far as the internal market was concerned 61 per cent of Community citizens had noticed no difference since the beginning of the year.

Although it is important to understand the point that one market did not, on 31 December 1992, actually spring into being to replace all twelve national markets (and we shall return to this general problem later), it must still be recognised that a great deal of substantial progress *was* made. Most national administrations would be content to see most of their legislative programme or manifesto adopted more or less on schedule – 95 per cent achievement would widely be regarded as a success. The success at Community level appears even more impressive since it involved the agreement of not just one national administration but twelve.

By 1993, although the Commission still identified gaps in the programme, it could also point to some notable achievements. Of the four types of freedom of movement mentioned in the Single European Act (goods, persons, services and capital) frontier controls had at least in theory been eliminated for three: goods, services and capital. Surveys showed that national administrations had become increasingly willing to accept each other's safety and standards requirements for products (vital to the working of mutual recognition). A majority of small businesses reported reduced cross-border transport costs (even though full transport liberalisation will take many years). And even though frontier controls on the freedom of movement of persons had not been fully abolished some real improvements had been made in this area: the official presence at frontiers had been much reduced overall, and in certain cases abolished completely.

One way to analyse the situation after the 1992 deadline is in terms of the three types of barrier originally identified in the 1985 White Paper: physical, technical and fiscal.

PHYSICAL BARRIERS

It will be remembered that the White Paper objective was to do away with internal frontier controls in their entirety, and that it argued that this should become possible by eliminating the reasons for their continued existence. But by this standard, at least, the member states did not fulfil the programme. The Commission reported in November 1993 that in general 'most of the physical frontier infrastructures remain in place'. Even though improvements had been made, in terms of the introduction of blue EU channels in airports and the emptying of roadside border control offices, the paraphernalia of traffic lanes, frontier markers and chicanes 'give the impression to the Community citizen that the change which has been announced is not imminent'.[1]

The detailed picture of the remaining physical barriers in 1993 was however quite a complicated one and – as the Commission pointed out – varied at different points along a frontier, including for the same country. On the whole customs formalities had been cut and delays reduced. But health and veterinary checks continued to be a source of delay, and companies continued to have some recourse to customs authorities for statistical and VAT purposes. The major lacuna remained, however, the widespread continuation of identity checks on individuals, essentially maintained by the authorities of member states for police purposes and therefore tending to perpetuate border controls and infrastructure. The Commission strategy on solving this question post-1993 appears to be twofold: to await the much-delayed implementation of the separate Schengen Agreement between nine continental member states which is intended to eliminate controls between them, and to use that agreement (which is not Community legislation) as a lever to make further EU-wide progress; and also to rely on the increased police and home affairs co-operation between member states proposed under the Maastricht Treaty as a means of helping move controls away from frontiers.

TECHNICAL BARRIERS

Under technical barriers the White Paper had grouped a diverse range of non-tariff barriers to the market, to be found not at borders as such but within the administrative arrangements and practices of the member states themselves.

Nine months into 1993 there remained eighteen measures in this area still to be adopted by the Council, of which thirteen were considered a high priority. They included matters such as agreement on a Community trademark, adoption of a statute for an EU company, as well as a range of other detailed company law directives affecting matters such as cross-border takeover bids and company liability and tax questions, and legislation on food irradiation and the taxation arrangements for second-hand goods and small businesses.

In addition, there remained a broad range of legislation which had been agreed by the Council but where transposition into the national legislation of the individual member states was behind schedule. Important cases included measures concerning veterinary and plant health controls, the liberalisation of public sector procurement, trade in pharmaceuticals, the free movement of labour and the professions, insurance services and a number of company law and intellectual and industrial property measures. Where appropriate the Commission was pursuing laggard member states in the Court of Justice.

At the same time, however, it should be recognised that by 1993 a large number of technical barriers to the market *had* been addressed, legislation agreed and (where necessary) actually transposed by the member states. Half the White Paper measures needing transposition *had* been transposed into the legislations of all the member states: and 84 per cent of the total number of necessary transposition measures *had* been taken. Good progress had been made in particular in the areas of free movement of capital, in financial services (excluding insurance) and in technical barriers other than pharmaceuticals.

However, a Commission survey of small and medium businesses in 1993 found, again perhaps not surprisingly, that it was clearly early days so far as the real effects of the single market were concerned. The improvements in frontier formalities and cross-border transport arrangements were welcome, as well as better mutual recognition of safety and standards requirements by the differing national authorities. But, on the debit side, the need for an effective EU trademark system was strongly felt, the supposed liberalisation of public sector procurement had yet to produce any tangible effects at all and a large majority of small businesses still felt they were in a disadvantageous position if they tried to pursue legal claims in the courts of foreign member states.

FISCAL BARRIERS

Under the heading of fiscal barriers the basic *objective* of the original White Paper (the abolition of controls at borders for tax reasons) *was* actually met on schedule at the beginning of 1993. But the Council did not, in the end, go along with the Commission's *method* of achieving that objective (which was to seek the alignment – or approximation – of all national indirect tax rates on goods and services around a central mean, plus the creation of a Community Clearing House for the reimbursement of cross-border VAT).

Instead, the principles behind the arrangement which has been in place from the beginning of 1993 are as follows. First, the idea of the Community Clearing House for VAT has been dropped as unworkable: instead VAT on most cross-border sales is (under transitional arrangements in operation until 1997) to be levied at the point of purchase *within the country of destination of the goods*, rather than being levied at the frontier between the exporting and importing country. This in turn means that exporters must know the VAT registration number of their importers so that they can exempt VAT on their exports (which will be helped by the introduction of a VAT Information Exchange System) and also that, from a VAT point of view, the importer treats the transaction as if it were a domestic transaction.

Second, a political agreement between EC finance ministers has superseded the fruitless search for approximation of all *rates* of national sales taxes. Instead, it has been agreed that the system should be a more flexible one of a general VAT flat rate of at least 15 per cent plus, as the member states require it, one or two reduced VAT rates of at least 5 per cent and transitional arrangements for highly reduced rates and zero rates. A plan to unify excise duties on spirits and tobacco (which vary greatly from member state to member state) has been dropped in favour of a more flexible system based on minimum rates. Details of the new system (which it should be noted is subject to further change in 1997) are contained in Box 7.

A digression may be worthwhile. Although highly technical, the general problem of 'fiscal barriers' and the impediments they pose to trade within the single market raises some interesting issues of principle. Faced with a jungle of differing national administrative practices in the field of indirect taxation – themselves the consequence of thousands of incremental decisions arising from differing domestic economies, differing fiscal requirements and differing tax treatments and traditions – the urge to produce order out of chaos on a European level is perhaps an understandable one, particularly if such differing fiscal practices do in fact constitute a real impediment to market development. And yet an attempt at wholesale reform and rationalisation may not only be impractical, it may also be conceptually flawed if it extends beyond an attempt to solve the immediate problem – which is essentially that of cross-border trade between member states. National taxation arrangements usually represent important political agreements between governments and electorates, which cannot be lightly overturned. On the other hand, to adopt the position that national tax systems are uniquely a matter of national concern – in other words to camp on the argument of 'sovereignty' – goes to the other extreme by ignoring the need to encourage cross-border trade and indeed the international division of labour itself.

Box 7   VAT in the single market

1   Since 1 January 1993 transitional arrangements have been in effect. It is intended to move to a definitive regime from 1997.
2   Under the transitional regime, cross-frontier sales between most business operators are taxed at the point of purchase. Under the definitive regime sales will be taxed at the point of sale. Three basic types of cross-border transaction can be considered:

- Sales from *business to business*. Here VAT-registered sellers exempt sales to VAT-registered purchasers in other member states, who themselves handle such purchases as part of their normal domestic VAT declarations. The VAT Information Exchange System allows national authorities, and through them traders, access to each others VAT registers.
- Sales to *operators not liable for VAT on their sales*. These are either VAT-exempt businesses like insurance companies and banks or non-taxable entities like public authorities. In either case a VAT number will be issued if intra-Community purchases are above a certain minimum level.
- Sales to *individuals*. Individuals travelling from one member state to another pay VAT where they buy the goods, at the local rate, and are not liable to VAT on return home. Tax-free sales will continue at ports and airports for intra-Community travel until 1999, subject to the same limits as are applied to travellers from non-Community countries.

Source: Commission paper *Guide to VAT in 1993* (1992)

FURTHER MARKET MEASURES

So far in this chapter we have considered the single market mainly in terms of the abolition of barriers to trade, and it is these which form the heart of the process. But at the same time as this market deepening there have also been refined or developed a number of what might be termed *market reinforcement measures*.

Perhaps most important has been a strengthening of *competition policy*. The White Paper underlined the need to ensure that 'anti-competitive practices do not engender new forms of local protectionism which would only lead to a re-partitioning of the market'. (p. 39) It warned in particular about the need for tough action on state aid (or subsidies) to industry, to which we shall turn in a moment.

The EC Treaty itself contains a whole chapter of strict rules concerning competition in the common market, including those affecting companies themselves, the practice of dumping within the market and also the use of state aid. The spirit (and indeed much of the language) of the articles which address competition between companies can be traced to the earlier Coal and Steel Community Treaty (which, as we saw in Chapter 1, in turn owed much to the Allied – and in particular the US – wish to break up pre-war German heavy industry cartels).

The formal rules for businesses in the common market are in principle quite clear. Article 85 of the EC Treaty forbids 'agreements or other practices which distort competition and which are liable to affect trade between member states.' And Article 86 forbids one or more companies exploiting in an abusive fashion 'a dominant position in the common market or in a substantial part of it'. The practical application of such principles to real economic activity is, on the other hand, rather more complicated. The Treaty allows some leeway for activities which have wider economic benefits and the Commission has the role of assessing how the rules should apply in particular cases. Box 8 is a summary of how the Commission approaches the general problem.

Given such existing Treaty powers what strengthening of competition policy has taken place? In the first place the Commission has taken a more activist approach to applying the rules. It has made more use of its direct powers to fine companies up to 10 per cent of their turnover. In the period 1986 to 1988, for

---

Box 8   EC competition policy

1   The following summary checklist indicates what the Commission looks for when considering commercial activity under Article 85:

- An agreement (formal or otherwise) to align companies' activities;
- More than one company is involved;
- There is noticeable restraint upon competition;
- The agreement has a perceptible effect, actual or potential, on trade between member states.

2   The Commission considers the following to fall *outside* the scope of Article 85:
- Agreements of minor importance (defined as less than 5 per cent of the market of the agreement, and where total annual turnover of the undertakings is less than Ecu 200 million);
- Relationships like that of principal/commercial agent, or parent company/subsidiary;
- Joint co-operation arrangements between companies (e.g. to share services) and subcontracting arrangements.

3   The Commission may grant *exemptions* from Article 85 if the agreement:

- Contributes to 'clear objective advantages' in economic terms in the EC *and*;
- Will pass on benefits to consumers *and*;
- Involves indispensable restrictions to competition *and*;
- Allows competition for a 'substantial part' of the goods or services in question.

4   If an agreement is found to be prohibited it is (i) null and void from the outset and (ii) subject to fines up to Ecu 1 million or 10 per cent of turnover (whichever is the greater).

Source: Commission publication *EEC Competition Policy in the Single Market* (1989)

---

example, the Commission imposed fines on companies for abuses of competition to the total of some Ecu 150 million[2] (Colchester and Buchan 1990: 157). In 1991 the Commission imposed a record fine of Ecu 75 million for one abuse of competition. Many fines have been imposed on companies operating cartels in the public sector (such as telecommunications, energy and air transport), a special area of difficulty we shall turn to shortly.

In the second place the increase in cross-border commercial

activity encouraged by the prospect of the single market has meant that new rules have had to be drawn up concerning *large-scale company mergers*. The number of company mergers and acquisitions in the EC (including with non-EC firms) where the combined company turnover exceeded Ecu 1 billion in value more than doubled from 108 a year in 1985/6 to 268 in 1987/8. This then created the problem of whether it falls to the authorities of the member states or to the Commission itself to judge the competition policy implications of such mergers.

The division of responsibility was finally agreed in the 1989 *Merger Control Regulation* (entry into force 1990) which, in essence, specifies that the Commission has the power to regulate company mergers in the EU with a combined turnover of at least Ecu 5 billion, of which at least Ecu 250 million must be within the EU. However, if each company derives two-thirds of its business from the same member state, then the power to regulate competition reverts to that member state. The criterion for considering the desirability or otherwise of a merger is solely whether it impedes competition in the European market. In other words, the commercial or industrial strategy behind the merger remains outside Community jurisdiction. The Commission has already indicated that when the regulation is reviewed it would like the threshold for it to consider the competition implications to be lowered.

The White Paper was particularly emphatic about the need for a rigorous EC policy on the type of anti-competitive practice represented by *state aid to industry*. 'There are tendencies to spend large amounts of public funds on state aids to uncompetitive industries and enterprises. Often, they not only distort competition but also in the long run undermine efforts to increase European competitiveness' (White Paper 1985: 39). Once again, the EC Treaty already provides quite clear guidance on the principles. Article 92 says:

> Save as otherwise provided in this Treaty, any aid granted by a member state or through state resources *in any form whatsoever* which distorts or threatens to distort competition by favouring certain companies or the production of certain goods shall, in so far as it affects trade between member states, be incompatible with the common market.
>
> (emphasis mine)

When considering what might or might not be a state aid the

76

Commission (supported by Court of Justice jurisprudence) has taken 'any form whatsoever' quite literally:

The concept of 'aid' is a good deal wider than just government grants, cheap loans and interest subsidies, where the gratuitous element is immediately obvious. It also covers such forms of support as tax concessions, public guarantees of corporate borrowing from banks or the capital market, provision of goods and services on preferential terms, and, in some circumstances, the acquisition of public shareholdings in businesses. Any other measure having an equivalent effect will also fall within the definition.

(Commission document *EEC Competition Policy in the single market* 1989)

The scale of the policy problem represented by state aid to industry, as thus defined, may now start to emerge. It was illustrated by a Commission survey of state aid in ten EC member states (excluding Spain and Portugal) over the period 1981 to 1986. This survey found that an annual average of Ecu 82 billion was being spent during these years by these member states together on subsidies to their own industries. Such a figure is equivalent to about 3 per cent of their collective GDP. It is also, as a matter of general interest, about double the entire EC annual budget at that time. The main economic sectors receiving national subsidies were agriculture, transport and coal (notwithstanding the existence of the Common Agricultural Policy and the existence since the 1950s of the common market for coal and steel). Among the member states Italy turned out to be by far the greatest subsidiser, transferring as much as 5.7 per cent of national GDP to its industries.

Expenditure on this scale within the single market (which appears to be continuing; subsequent surveys suggest aid levels of Ecu 80 to 90 billion a year throughout the late 1980s) raises a number of important economic and political issues. In the first place it raises questions about the public expenditure policies of the member states themselves, and whether such levels of expenditure can be at all compatible with the tight convergence criteria for the 1990s demanded by economic and monetary union (see Chapter 6). (Italy, a major subsidiser, has a major public sector deficit problem.) But second, the *object* of such expenditure may also complicate the achievement of wider EU economic objectives (such as improving general competitiveness, stimulating new industry and creating jobs). Such national transfers (which, as we have seen, dwarf the central EU budget) tend not to be in new industries or technologies but rather to be concentrated in declining, non-job creating sectors, which are the least competitive. (Indeed, if one adds the central EU budget itself, the bulk of which is devoted to agricultural support, the picture becomes worse.) A third problem also arises in relation to central and eastern Europe. The collapse of communism has led to a dismantling of state subsidies to industry there and – as we shall see in Chapter 9 – a switch in trade away from the former CMEA area and towards western Europe. But eastern European exports in the basic industries like steel, textiles and agriculture (which are the legacy of communism) then run into western European restrictions designed to protect such 'sensitive' (or, rather, backward) sectors.

Of immediate concern, however, is the relationship between pervasive state aid and the single market. In the White Paper the Commission undertook to 'see to it that a rigorous policy is pursued in regard to state aids so that public resources are not used to confer artificial advantage to some firms over others' (p. 39). This has, in fact, essentially entailed the Commission making more rigorous use of its existing Treaty powers to approve or disallow state aid. Already in 1983 the Commission had warned that it would use powers confirmed by the Court of Justice to order repayments of illegitimate state aid. In 1987 it added that the argument put forward by some firms which had received state subsidies that they had done so in good faith was no longer acceptable, since they should have been aware of EC law. In 1988 the Commission further toughened its stance by stating that it needed to approve every state aid grant worth Ecu 12 million or more. Specific examples of the tough Commission approach have included ordering the British government to reduce a debt write off (equivalent to a subsidy) when selling state-owned Rover cars to British Aerospace; and making a French government aid injection into the carmaker Renault subject to a reduction in the productive capacity of the firm plus a change in the legal status of the company.

The fact that the Commission has, under the Treaty, a locus in determining the legality of financial transfers from member states to their own industries has an evident bearing on the position of *nationalised industries* within the single market. The EC Treaty does not forbid nationalised industries as such, but it does require under Article 90 that the member states do not apply to them measures contrary to the Treaty – including the rules concerning competition policy. In addition, the Commission, with the support of the Court of Justice, has evolved an important doctrine governing state sector shareholdings in companies which requires that financial transfers from the state to such companies, if they are not to be viewed as state aid (and thus potentially illegitimate), *must be similar in nature to those which a private investor would make.* The Court put it this way in a state aid finding in 1986:

> In the case of a company whose capital is held by the public authorities it should be ascertained whether, in similar circumstances, a private partner, taking account of foreseeable profit potential and removing all considerations of a social character or of regional or sectoral policy, would have extended such capital support.
>
> (Mattera 1990: 66)

This approach – added to the fact that nationalised industries are also subject to general EC competition law – can be seen to have significant long-term implications for the future of public sector industries in the single market (in 1991 still responsible for 11 per cent of the labour force in Europe, for 12 per cent of value added and 18 per cent of company investment in the non-agricultural market sector).[2] It means that, unless they fall into one of the categories of *allowable* state aid (see below), financial transfers by the state to nationalised industries must resemble capital increases which could otherwise be raised on the financial markets. In other words, it is a working presumption that the financial relationship between the state and the nationalised industry is the same as that between a private company and the market. It so happens that on wider economic grounds, and also to reduce national budgetary burdens, privatisation programmes have become widespread in Europe; but irrespective of these factors *the deepening of the European market would in any case tend to circumscribe the power of the individual state to intervene in the national economy.*

Not all state aid is illegitimate. Box 9 lists the areas where aid might be permitted under the Treaty, and it can be seen that in

---

Box 9 Allowable state aid

1 Under Article 92.2 of the EC Treaty the following are compatible with the common market:

- Aid of a social character granted to individual consumers (provided they are not linked to discrimination of product origin);
- Aid to compensate for natural disasters or other extraordinary events;
- Aid for certain regions of Germany affected by its division.

2 Under Article 92.3 the following *might* be compatible with the common market:

- Aid to develop regions where the standard of living is abnormally low or there is serious under-employment;
- Aid to allow the development of a project of major European interest, or to remedy a serious disturbance in the economy of a member state;
- Aid to develop certain activities or economic regions which do not affect trading conditions contrary to the common interest.
- Other types of aid determined by EC decision.

---

some important cases – such as aid to a region where the standard of living is very low, or where there is high under-employment, or where an important project of common European interest is at stake – there is wide scope for assistance. Nonetheless, even in these areas a major general principle should be noted, which is that the Commission must be notified about plans and must agree that such assistance is compatible with the common market. In other words, *in virtually any significant transfer of public funds from a member state to business (or indeed any other equivalent form of assistance) the Commission has the right to interpose itself between state and recipient.*

Under the heading of competition policy a final word should be said here about the specific case of *monopolies* in the single market. It may be recalled from Chapter 1 that in 1956 the Spaak Report identified a link between the fragmented national markets and the existence of monopolies. Only by creating a wider European market could the problem be overcome of national monopolies each tending to dominate its own small market: 'The power of a great market is to reconcile mass production and the absence of monopoly' (*Rapport* 1956: 13).

The EC Treaty does not in fact forbid national monopolies as such, but it does, in Article 37, require the member states to ensure that no national monopoly of a commercial nature makes any discrimination whatever among nationals of the member states so far as its supplies or outlets are concerned. Subsequent jurisprudence in the Court of Justice has established that this Article does not in itself affect the existence of monopolies, but rather that the existence of monopolies should not be allowed to infringe the principle of the free circulation of goods *between* the member states – including goods similar to those controlled by monopolies.

So far as the single market is concerned this approach has been translated into a series of measures designed to liberalise national monopoly practices in key economic sectors such as air transport, telecommunications and energy. However, although stimulated by the single market timetable, this process is in fact a much longer-term one (restrictions on air transport, for example, will only fall in 1997). It is only moving gradually in step with national legislation as the member states erode the privileged position of their monopolies. Towards the end of 1993, for example, the French government announced plans to abolish the monopoly rights of the large public utilities Electricité de France and Gaz de France in both electricity production and cross-border energy sales.

INDUSTRIAL CO-OPERATION

One area where state aid *may* be permitted is in the promotion of an important project of common European interest (although note it is for the Commission, not the state, to decide what actually *is* in the European interest). This leads on to the general question of industrial co-operation and its relationship to the single market.

The White Paper argued that removing barriers to trade in goods and services were necessary but not sufficient steps in themselves:

Community action must go further and create an environment or conditions likely to favour the development of cooperation between undertakings. Such cooperation will strengthen the industrial and commercial fabric of the internal market especially in the case of small and medium sized enterprises.

(White Paper 1985: 34)

In policy terms it may be seen that here a new and different philosophical note has been struck. So far we have looked at measures which have essentially been designed to remove obstacles to economic operators within the European market (obstacles which have in fact, for the most part, been created by the member states themselves). The promotion of industrial co-operation takes us into new and more controversial territory – one which borders on market intervention. Taken to its limits such a policy could shade into an industrial policy at a European level (or even, as some have suggested, the creation of a European public sector).[3] For these reasons it may be worth clarifying briefly what the current position is.

The first point is that in the White Paper the Commission was clearly talking about creating an 'environment or conditions' favourable to industrial co-operation rather than taking direct charge of the operation itself. And the mention of small and medium-sized industries reinforces this: it is companies of this size (rather than large firms) which have, for many practical reasons, the greatest difficulty in adjusting their horizons from the national to the European market and they may therefore need special assistance to adjust. This in turn may provide a justification for, say, a greater Commission single market information and promotion exercise than might otherwise be the case.

The second point is that industrial co-operation comprises a diverse range of measures which in fact differ widely in intent and effect. It can include, for example, a better *legal framework for cross-border co-operation between companies*. Under this heading a large number of company law measures have been adopted by the Community over the years, designed to overcome the problems caused by the fact that differing member states have differing legal requirements for creating and running companies, which can themselves impede cross-border activity. Examples are directives establishing common rules on matters such as company accounts, registers, auditors and minimum capital (all of which have been adopted). By contrast, it should be noted that so far it has not been possible to reach agreement on common measures governing *company takeovers*, largely because of widely differing views within the member states about the benefits of takeovers, and also differences over the proper relationship between shareholders and management. Nor has agreement yet been reached on a long-standing idea (predating the single market programme) to create an optional *Statute for a European Company* which companies, faced with conflicting national company law requirements, could choose to adopt. Some of the benefits of this, for example in the simplification of some company taxation matters, may yet however be achieved by other means.

Industrial co-operation can also extend, as the White Paper suggests, to better use of some areas of the various Community expenditure programmes. The Regional Fund is one such, but more significant are the various *Community Research and Technological Development programmes*, in particular in areas of new technology. The Single European Act added the following to the Treaty objectives of the Community: 'to strengthen the scientific and technological basis of European industry and to encourage it to become more competitive at international level'. Community research and development programmes have acquired funds to contribute to the costs of 'pre-competitive' research by companies, universities or national laboratories, targeted in particular at the information technology and telecommunications fields. The Commission has suggested building on this to develop 'Trans-European Networks' which interconnect the various national transport, telecommunications and energy infrastructures of the member states (and this policy aim has now in fact been introduced into the Maastricht Treaty at Article 129b).

It is, on the other hand, important to keep matters in perspective. Community action in these areas of industrial co-operation is intended to complement, not replace, action by both private firms and the public authorities of the member states. Central Community expenditure, although not negligible (some Ecu 2.6 billion in 1993), remains only a small part of total research and development expenditure throughout Europe. And the proposed European action to ensure inter-operability of national technical standards might well prove to be as important as any expenditure in the area of 'Trans-European Networks'.

Behind all these examples of ways of promoting industrial co-operation there clearly lies a fundamental policy question. This is: *how far should the Community go in attempting to direct the economic agents in the market which it is creating?* It may well be that on a general level of policy debate this is a question which will never be laid to rest so long as there are differing political views within the member states and so long as new problems and issues arise which test the border between public authorities and the market. It is impossible to disentangle the theoretical question from national political practice.

Within the Treaties as drawn up, however, the legal framework is in fact comparatively straightforward. The Maastricht Treaty amended the EC Treaty to include a new Title XIII and an Article 130 entitled 'Industry'. Paragraph 1 of this reads:

> The Community and the Member States shall ensure that the conditions necessary for the competitiveness of the Community's industries exist.
>
> For that purpose, *in accordance with a system of open and competitive markets,* their action shall be aimed at:
> - speeding up the adjustment of industry to structural changes;
> - encouraging an environment favourable to initiative and to the development of undertakings throughout the Community, particularly small and medium-sized undertakings;
> - encouraging an environment favourable to cooperation between undertakings;
> - fostering better exploitation of the industrial potential of policies of innovation, research and technological development.
>
> (emphasis mine)

This entire Title is rounded off with the following words: '*This Title shall not provide the basis for the introduction by the Community of any measure which could lead to a distortion of competition.*' Which brings us to a general observation on this subject. *Within the single market the principle of co-operation is subordinate to the principle of competition.* Competition policy *does* allow for co-operation between companies (or between companies and public authorities) in specific, well-defined areas. Under Article 85 of the EC Treaty the Commission has even drawn up a working list of co-operation activities between companies which are permissible because they are by their nature not anti-competitive (and this includes joint implementation of research and development contracts). Also under Article 85 are set out the grounds whereby the Commission (not the member states) has the power to waive the requirements of competition law if an agreement will provide clear economic advantages (and provided a number of strict criteria are all met). Equally, state aid to industry is permissible (if approved by the Commission) under Article 92 in economically backward regions, to promote important projects of common European interest, to remedy serious economic disturbances and to promote other economic activity which does not adversely affect trading conditions. In every case, however, these are *exceptions* to the general requirements of competition policy and the general prohibition on agreements or other practices which distort competition and affect trade between member states; and it is the Commission, on behalf of the Community (if need be supported by the Court of Justice) which has to allow such exceptions.

A moment's reflection might suggest why this competitive principle has to be so strong. It is because the underlying process is, in the words of the Spaak Report, *the merging of separate markets*. This means abolishing impediments, physical or otherwise, to the development of one large market; and also cutting back restrictions to trade put in place by both private and public sectors. To do this the Community requires legal instruments at least as strong as the strongest economic forces within its geographical area. Co-operation in specific areas of economic activity may certainly be permissible, so long as it is compatible with the general functioning of the market, *but if co-operation rather than competition were the general rule it would tend to freeze economic development – and freeze each national economy within its own national boundary since it is there that the major cartels, the most restrictive practices and the greatest subsidies by the state to industry are to be found.* In other words, the Community as an economic entity would scarcely be possible at all.

SOCIAL EUROPE

Although not strictly part of the single market programme, this may be the place to say a word about 'Social Europe' – the renewed emphasis on social (labour market) questions within the single market.

It may be recalled from Chapter 1 that the Spaak Report had

assumed that it would be the 'spontaneous tendency of harmonisation' of social systems and salary levels, including through the action of trade unions, which would tend to bring about alignment of working conditions within the common market. This was in line with its general view that it would be impossible to equalise all factors bearing on company costs at the outset, but rather that the effect of the market itself would be levelling: 'It is not possible to try to modify as if by decree the fundamental conditions of an economy such as result from natural resources, the level of productivity or the weight of public costs' (*Rapport* 1956: 61). Nonetheless, Spaak *did* suggest that special efforts should be made progressively to harmonise factors such as equality of male and female salaries, overtime terms and conditions and paid holidays and that, if it could be created, a unified system of tax and social security costs would eliminate some important economic distortions within the common market.

The EC Treaty rehearsed in Article 117 the belief that progress would be made both through the operation of the market and also by the impact of aligning national legal, regulatory and administrative systems. It called in particular in Article 118 for close collaboration between the member states in matters concerning employment, working conditions, training, social security, accidents at work and work-related illnesses, health at work and trade union and collective bargaining rights. It also (in Article 119) established the principle of male and female equality of remuneration for the same work (and defined remuneration widely to include any form of benefit).

The Single European Act added two new treaty provisions in this area: that the member states should set as their objective the harmonisation of conditions of health and safety of workers (Article 118A); and also that the Commission should 'endeavour to develop the dialogue between management and labour at European level which could, if the two sides consider it desirable, lead to relations based on agreement' (Article 118B).

The Maastricht Treaty has added a completely new element. Eleven member states (excluding the United Kingdom) have signed a separate *Protocol on Social Policy* which commits them to continue down the path of the 1989 Social Charter (see Box 10) and which authorises them to have recourse to 'the institutions, procedures and mechanisms of the Treaty' (Article 1) to do this. The Eleven agree among themselves that Community action shall 'support and complement' the activities of the member states in the areas of improving the working environment, working conditions, the information and consultation of workers, male and female equality and the integration of persons excluded from the labour market. To do this the Council may adopt, by qualified majority, directives setting 'minimum requirements for gradual implementation' (which must not add administrative, financial or legal constraints to small and medium-sized businesses) (Agreement annexed to Social Protocol: Article 2). Unanimity is retained for decisions in such areas as social security and social protection, representation and the collective defence of the interests of both workers and employers, the position of third-country nationals and financial contributions for promoting employment and job creation. Questions of pay, the right of association, the right to strike and the right to impose lock-outs are not affected by any of the foregoing. In addition, the Commission is given the task of 'promoting the consultation of management and labour at Community level' and – should both sides so desire – 'the dialogue between them at Community level may lead to contractual relations, including agreements' (Agreement annexed to Social Protocol: Articles 3 and 4).

Box 10 The 1989 Social Charter

1 The right to freedom of movement;
2 The right to employment and remuneration;
3 The right to improved living and working conditions;
4 The right to social protection;
5 The right to freedom of association and collective bargaining;
6 The right to vocational training;
7 The right of men and women to equal treatment;
8 The right to worker information, consultation and participation;
9 The right to health and safety protection at the workplace;
10 The right to protection of children and adolescents;
11 The rights of elderly persons;
12 The rights of disabled persons.

Note: The Social Charter is a political declaration. It was adopted by eleven heads of state and government at the Strasbourg European Council in 1989, who at the same time asked the Commission to follow it up with an action programme and set of legal instruments implementing it. The UK did not sign, primarily on the grounds that it believed that some of these questions were matters of national, and not EC, competence.

What is one to make of the Protocol on Social Policy in the Maastricht Treaty? Is it a brilliant procedural innovation which reconciles differing views among the member states and which, by allowing eleven member states to go further in one policy area, establishes a valuable precedent for variable geometry in a wider European Union? Or is it a testament of collective failure by the EU to arrive at a sensible common policy position? The truth will no doubt emerge as the Protocol is put into effect and if, for example, the Court of Justice has to rule on questions arising under it. It must be said that the Protocol has a whiff of the midnight oil about it, and reads (in sharp distinction to the clarity of language of the early Treaties) rather like the late night compromise it no doubt was. For example, it is confusing in that it mixes up matters for the Eleven and matters already in the Treaty. In this respect it suffers from what might be described as the recurring vice of the Maastricht Treaty – the tendency to include too much detail where a statement of policy principle would suffice.

Matters of presentation and legal form to one side, what is the substantive policy issue at stake here? It is in reality the integration of the labour markets of the member states: or, in other words, it is but one aspect of the wider process of economic integration resulting from the original plan to establish a common market.

Even the briefest survey of the labour markets in each member state suggests one overwhelming fact: their extreme diversity. In the United Kingdom there is a patchwork of very many trade unions, organised on both horizontal and vertical lines; wage negotiations take place at several different levels; trade union membership, although steeply falling, is high by European standards. In France there is a very low level of trade union membership; wage agreements tend to be individual rather than collective; employee representation within companies is widespread through works councils; there is a minimum wage; profit-sharing schemes are widespread. In Germany there are powerful industry-specific trade unions; wage regulation tends to be on a regional basis; works councils substitute for some of the wage bargaining roles of trade unions; the thirteenth monthly wage is often considered a bonus for salaried employees. And so on and so forth, through variations in each member state. [4]

Although complicated enough, this is by no means the whole

picture. To obtain a proper appreciation of the labour markets in each member state it would be necessary also to take into account tax and social security levels (levied on both employee and employer), the length of the working week, paid holidays, overtime, welfare and unemployment benefits, savings schemes, pension schemes, the position of the self-employed and so on. The fact of the extreme complexity of the labour markets in Europe leads to one fairly obvious policy conclusion: that it is neither possible nor desirable to harmonise everything at a European level (and indeed this has long since been recognised – hence the absence of attempts to unify, say, national social security systems). *However, neither is retaining the status quo a valid policy option.* The creation of the single market, with its mobility of the factors of production, including labour, entails an increasing inter-penetration of the national labour markets and this in turn creates its own pressure to modify individual systems.

It would be a pity, therefore, if the debate on Social Europe is to rest solely on which 'model' of social organisation should be the European model. *Because there is no existing model*, there are simply markets, some more effective than others. And this suggests a way forward from the rather sterile level of debate so far, which Maastricht only crystallised. Rather than attempting to establish a European social model at which to aim (which, rather like attempts at harmonising technical standards, may end up missing its target completely), it would be better to try to establish a regime in the single market where *best practice* can prevail and be encouraged. What is 'best practice'? That need not necessarily be defined: it can vary from place to place and from sector to sector. It is frequently self-evident. (Popper once remarked that those who suffer can judge for themselves, and the others can hardly deny that they would not like to change places (Popper 1971: 159)). No member state has the monopoly of wisdom when it comes to organising the labour market: each has its defects and each has something to learn from the experience of the others. And collectively the member states need urgently to establish a best practice for the European market as a whole if they are to surmount the challenges of rising unemployment and global competitiveness.

It might be objected that a 'best practice' approach (rather than one based on harmonisation round a social model) might lead to social dumping if companies undercut each other in offering wage levels, or locate in parts of the Community with the lowest social or other charges. To which the answer is that best practice does not itself imply undercutting and that company location is affected by many factors, of which social costs are only one. And if indeed it can be established that differing social welfare charges are having a measurable effect on company decisions that may be a problem for *competition policy*, not social policy, to address.

CONCLUSIONS

A rapid survey of the single market in practice, such as this, leads to one simple conclusion. *The single market was not established, even less 'completed', at the beginning of 1993.* As if to illustrate this, at the end of 1993 the Commission published a new strategic programme for the internal market which included measures for agreeing and enforcing measures contained in the original programme, but which also set out new goals for the European Union in the years ahead in this area: goals such as a definitive VAT system, the elimination of double taxation of companies, better legal protection for companies operating in different member states and so forth. In fact, if one steps back and considers the process over the long term, the single market can perhaps best be considered as a renewed burst of the market-creating activity which can be traced back to the Spaak Report in 1956 and which shows no sign yet of coming to an end. Every barrier that falls seems to reveal a new barrier. Even though visible obstacles may be removed, invisible obstacles, embedded within the national fabric of each member state, remain real. Indeed it is quite easy to think of potential difficulties for future generations of activist EU legislators to ponder: differing cultural habits between the member states, differing linguistic habits, differing roles for capital and labour within society, reflected by differing taxation regimes – and even differing driving habits.

While it may certainly be the case that the single market is a good *approximation* of a real unified market – and is also much better than what existed before – we should be cautious of attempts to present it as an accomplished fact. In particular, policies that assume that it has been created – rather than that it is still being built – should be treated very carefully. It is worth recalling that many of the benign Cecchini Report effects mentioned in the previous chapter rest upon assumptions of market liberalisation – such as in financial services, or in opening up public sector procurement markets – which the evidence suggests have scarcely yet come into play.

Yet the single market programme *has* changed things. The *anticipation* of a unified market, and the sense of movement towards it, has stimulated investments, company takeovers and repositioning within Europe, and has drawn the EFTA countries into the creation of the European Economic Area as a first step towards membership. The Commission believes that in the second half of the 1980s both EC investments and growth benefited from such anticipatory effects, and that an extra 10 million jobs were created.

The single market programme has also attracted high levels of investment from the rest of the world into Europe. Although global recession has caused some tapering off, it has been estimated that in the early 1990s EU countries have still been attracting around \$65–70 billion worth of new annual investment from beyond their boundaries, of which United States companies have been accounting for more than half. The United Kingdom has in fact been the main investment location, receiving about one-third of all inward investment into the EU and, by 1993, acting as home for 37 per cent of all non-EU companies operating within the single market. According to business location experts it is proximity to the market which is the most important determinant of company location, added to a complex matrix of other factors including local labour costs, availability of skills, infrastructure and productivity.[5]

Despite recession, and despite growing rivalry from other regions of the world, the building of this Community market of 340 million inhabitants (effectively enlarged to 370 million inhabitants through the extension of the European Economic Area to EFTA countries – see Chapter 8) remains an astonishingly constructive programme, continuing to unite as it has countries with widely differing traditions and economies. We shall look in the following chapters at certain aspects of this market: at the links between financial integration and economic and monetary integration, at the problem of agriculture and at the impact of the collapse of communism (which changes the background in a radical way). But what has been achieved so far – in a direct line from the period of post-war reconstruction – bears ample witness to the fruitfulness of the Community method.

5

FINANCIAL EUROPE

INTRODUCTION

Why is it worth considering as a special case the integration of the financial services sector in the EU? The first reason is that it is an important element in the European economy in its own right. It accounts for about 7 per cent of GDP of the EU (which makes it more than twice as important as agriculture) and provides for over 3 million jobs (about 2 per cent of the total). A major part of the macroeconomic benefits which the Cecchini Report expects to flow from the single market arises specifically from the liberalisation of financial services (see for example Box 6 in Chapter 3).

A second reason is that the financial services sector provides the bridge, as it were, between the single market programme and the subject of the next chapter – economic and monetary union. Monetary union, at least as conceived in the Delors Report and reflected in the Maastricht Treaty, will rely upon integrated European financial markets to provide the 'efficient allocation of resources' (Article G 105 of Maastricht). Indeed, one of the four basic tasks of the European System of Central Banks, according to the same Maastricht Article, will be 'to promote the smooth operation of payment systems' (or in other words mechanisms for transferring money around Europe).

A third reason for looking at the financial services sector is that it represents the opposite end of the economic spectrum from the heavy industries whose integration marked the post-war genesis of the Community. In the 1950s coal and steel were already old, basic industries, closely linked to the war-making capacities of Germany and France. Their integration through the creation of a common market for coal and steel involved, as we saw in

Chapter 1, radical new steps in market institutions. But it is hard to think of an industry which is more different from coal and steel than financial services, whose products are mobile, fast-moving and invisible, and clearly not susceptible to regulation in the same way. The financial services sector also poses in an acute form the problem of dealing on a European level with an industry that is already global in its nature – and one moreover with volumes of transactions often far in excess of traditional physical forms of trade.

In fact, it could be argued that economic integration in Europe has actually been working backwards, and that rather than starting with the mobile sectors of the economy like finance, which have always been highly international, and building on those, integration has in fact started with the least mobile heavy industries and only slowly, through the current implementation of the single market programme, begun to make inroads in the more mobile sectors. A few statistics will illustrate this point.

A DIVIDED MARKET

Although the European Union contains within its borders a major world capital market (London) and also some of the most advanced industrial economies in the world, the traditional feature of the financial services sector has been its pronounced *compartmentalisation*. A Commission study as late as 1983 suggested that, although total gross savings in the EC in 1980 were actually greater than in the United States (Ecu 430 billion against Ecu 340 billion), a much smaller part of those savings were intermediated through national financial markets. The volume of securities issued in the top five EC national markets together (Germany, France, Italy, the Netherlands and the UK) was much lower than securities issued on the US market (Ecu 142 billion against Ecu 212 billion). In terms of risk capital the EC had only 40 per cent of the volume of the United States. Capital flows between EC member states were dwarfed by the circulation of goods within the common market: the Commission estimated that long-term capital movements between the member states represented only about one-twentieth the volume of trade in goods.

Yet the 1980s was the decade of worldwide financial deregulation. Foreign exchange transactions ballooned in particular. By

1993 global turnover in foreign exchange (including derivatives) was thought by the IMF to be running at about US $1,000 billion *per day*. The Community was not immune from this global deregulation (and we shall see in the next chapter what has happened in the monetary sphere), but nor did its effects permeate to all levels of the European economy. Instead, a complicated pattern combining varying wholesale and retail liberalisation has emerged, reflecting differing national backgrounds, traditions and investment needs.

The main factor behind the compartmentalisation of the European financial markets was the existence until relatively recently of *national capital controls* – which in turn reflected the existence of differing currencies and monetary policies among the member states. Although by the early 1980s both the UK and Germany had abolished national restrictions on capital movements, it was not until 1986 and 1988 that two directives were adopted lifting general capital controls on an EC basis (for both long-term and short-term capital). The background to these controls lay not so much in a view of the usefulness or otherwise of financial markets within the market economy as in general macroeconomic policy. It may be recalled from Chapter 1 that the Spaak Report suggested that the free movement of capital was a necessary feature of the common market. But although Spaak provided a number of strong arguments in favour of capital liberalisation (including the fact that once the common market was in place the free movement of goods and services would in any case probably permit capital to move regardless of national controls), it also admitted the maintenance of safeguard measures on capital movements arising from the existence of continuing differing monetary policies of the member states and the possibility that speculative capital movements could create balance of payments problems. It should be recalled also that the Spaak Report, written at a time of near-stable exchange rates under the Bretton Woods system, envisaged that the common market would force the member states to move onto a virtuous path whereby economic adjustments arising from competition would take place through the structure of production and costs rather than through sudden shifts in the external value of their currencies – a very important point which we shall come back to in the next chapter.

In the event the EC Treaty, although it called on the member states in Article 67 to abolish restrictions on the movement of capital belonging to residents, added the phrase 'in so far as is necessary to the proper functioning of the common market' and this was taken to mean (as the Court of Justice in fact later confirmed) that an element of judgement could be applied to such liberalisation, taking into account the advantages and risks to the common market and also the degree of integration attained in other related areas. Article 69 specified that it was for the Council to decide on this matter. And, in addition, Articles 70, 73, 108 and 109 provided a number of safeguard clauses for member states affected by balance of payments problems or capital markets disturbances.

The consequence of this cautious Treaty language was that after two initial directives of 1960 and 1962, which provided for limited liberalisation of certain types of capital movement (for the most part those directly linked to the free movement of goods, services and people within the common market), no further progress was made at all in this area until the mid-1980s and the single market programme. Even then, it is interesting in retrospect to note that the 1985 White Paper on the single market spoke only of 'greater liberalisation' of capital movements rather than complete liberalisation. Although the Single European Act of 1986 specified that the free movement of services and capital was essential to the internal market, the Commission in a communication of 1986 was still referring to a regime 'as liberal as possible'. It was not until 1987 that a proposal was put forward for the *complete* liberalisation of capital movements in the Community. By then, however, the separate effects of the global financial deregulation of the 1980s were already making themselves felt throughout the Community. Several member states had already abolished exchange controls, others had renounced the use of safeguard clauses, and new financial and monetary markets were mushrooming, in France and Italy in particular but also in Spain, Greece and Portugal.

FINANCIAL INTEGRATION

The single market programme in financial services has, therefore, in certain ways come after the event: after the establishment of freedom of movement of goods in Europe but also after the development of global wholesale financial markets, with 24-hour trading in some specialised financial products. The various instruments for the integration of financial markets in the EU can be thought of as means of allowing liberalised wholesale capital to permeate through the many different types of economic activity now taking place in both the member states and in the single market as a whole. The complexity of the financial services sector means that there are, however, rather many detailed instruments (now well over forty) either adopted or in view. Nonetheless, a few basic principles underlie most of the programme. Apart from the essential requirement of the liberalisation of capital movements, the key to progress has been the harmonisation of the basic standards applied by the different authorities of the member states for the supervision of the various financial institutions and the protection of investors, depositors and consumers. Also important has been the *mutual recognition* by those supervisory authorities of the way in which each applies those standards. This in turn has allowed an important conceptual breakthrough: the creation of a *single licence* (or 'passport') which, when granted to a financial institution by the authorities of one member state (usually the one where the institution is based), allows it to market its services in the other member states; in competition with companies based in those states, *without having to seek authorisation again in each member state.*

It may be easiest to look at the issues arising in three broad categories of financial services (even though in practice they increasingly blur into one another): *banking, securities transactions* and *insurance.*

BANKING

Banking is the largest sector of the financial services industry in the EU, with over Ecu 5,000 billion worth of assets in 1988. There are of course very many banks located in the different member states. However – apart from some specialised areas of activity – one striking feature of banking is how it is still very much divided into national markets. Cross-border competition for many (if not most) banking services remains at a rudimentary level. Although some basic problems of defining what constitutes a bank were dealt with in a directive of 1977, the *Second Banking Coordination Directive* of 1988 (adopted in 1989; entry into force only in 1993) was the milestone piece of legislation for banking in the single market (and indeed for financial services generally).

This directive broke new ground in three main ways. First, it set out the regime of a *single banking licence*, valid throughout the Community, which allowed a bank obtaining it from its home member state to operate anywhere, either through branches or directly, without having to obtain a new licence in each member state, without being subject to discriminatory treatment against foreign banks and without having to meet new and differing capital requirements in each member state. Second, the directive defined a bank more precisely by laying down a *minimum capital requirement* of Ecu 5 million and, perhaps more importantly, by establishing a *wide list of allowable banking activities*. This includes not only familiar retail functions like deposit-taking and lending, but also merchant banking activities like share issuing and company capital business, and even more esoteric capital markets activities like trading in securities and futures and options. Third, the directive established a regime for the delicate matter of *third country banks* operating in the Community (such as the many US or Japanese banks) by requiring member states to keep the Commission informed about authorisations given to such firms. In addition, the Commission was empowered to assess periodically whether third countries were granting 'effective market access' comparable to that granted by the Community in this sector, and if need be to seek negotiating powers (including a possible freeze on new arrivals). (This clause was important because it became the model in both the securities and insurance sectors.)

Although the Second Banking Coordination Directive was the core piece of legislation, the importance of banking to the financial systems of the member states has meant that a number of subsidiary directives have also been adopted or put forward, including rules for the protection of depositors, rules limiting the size of risks which banks can assume and a directive aimed at combating money laundering. Perhaps most important have been directives setting rules for the *levels of capital* which a bank must maintain through its commercial operations (which in turn means establishing common rules for the risks of various operations and thus the minimum capital needed for each). Here the Community has followed rules on capital adequacy first set for all major banks by the Bank of International Settlements in 1988, and has adopted these as the minimum requirements for banks seeking the single licence under the Second Banking Coordination Directive.

Under the general heading of banking, special mention could be made of the problem of *cross-border payments* (a problem linked to economic and monetary union). The continued fragmentation of the banking sector in the Community, and the absence (so far) of any real pan-European retail banking market, and thus of competition for cross-border business, has led to a situation where extremely high prices continue to be charged for the processing of routine payments from one country to another. A good deal of research has shown that the ideal, where businesses and individuals can transfer money as rapidly, reliably and cheaply from one part of the Community to another as they can within their own member state, is still remote. In 1993 a survey on behalf of the Commission found that, for example, of 280 bank branches studied throughout the Community, 68 per cent of them provided no written information to their customers on their cross-border money transfer services; and fewer than 4 per cent had specific written information on both transfer services *and* their prices. The performance of cross-border payments was also fairly dismal. An experiment in the same survey, involving around 1,000 credit transfers of Ecu 100 each between 34 banks in all the member states, found that the average sender fee was just over 20 per cent, and that in a high proportion (43 per cent) of cases there was double charging by both sender and recipient bank (despite instructions to charge only the sender). The average time taken for a transfer was 4.6 working days (although in one case a transfer took 70 working days and in three cases the transfer did not arrive at all).[1]

The implications for the smooth functioning of commerce within the single market (and in particular for that of individuals and small businesses) is evident. According to the Commission, in 1990 the estimated annual volume of retail cross-border payments in the EC (those below Ecu 2,500) was more than 200 million payments. It must be presumed that this order of volume of transactions will increase as the single market effects deepen. Despite this, there clearly is not yet any reliable and cheap banking network for transferring normal small-scale retail payments around Europe (although there exist some excellent payments systems *within* individual member states).

The Commission has said that the results of the 1993 survey 'call for urgent answers' and has proposed Community legislation to tighten up banks' performance. However, although simple to describe, the problem may be less simple to resolve. Faced with accusations of exorbitant charges for cross-border trade, banks usually respond along the lines that these are small-scale, high-cost transactions which still only represent a small part of their business (and which, of course, usually involve operating in at least two different currencies). Is this a problem which will resolve itself as the competitive effects of the new Second Banking Directive come into play? Or is large-scale action needed to interconnect, say, member states' individual bank clearing networks? Whatever the answer, it will also have repercussions for monetary union and the question of a single European currency, which is also intended to promote ease of cross-border transfers.

SECURITIES TRANSACTIONS

Although some minimal progress on EC rules concerning the various member states' stock exchanges had been made by the early 1980s, it was not really until the single market programme that the Commission began to pursue in earnest the creation of a unified securities market. The aim was that issuers (companies) could raise capital on a Community-wide basis, intermediaries could offer services anywhere and investors could choose from a wide range of competing investment products. In 1985, two directives were adopted, liberalising the EC market in 'Undertakings for Collective Investment in Transferable Securities' – better known as unit trusts. These came into effect in 1989 and represented a first major step forward by allowing the retailing anywhere in the Community of approved collective investment vehicles, which group together savings for investment in particular types of securities. (It is interesting to note, however, that cross-border activity in this area took off only slowly, largely on the grounds that companies which usually sell unit trusts, such as banks and insurance firms, tend to dominate existing national networks.)

It was not until as late as 1993 that the Council adopted the analogue instrument in the securities field to the Second Banking Coordination Directive in the shape of the *Investment Services Directive*: and this will not actually come into force until 1996. The *Investment Services Directive* creates the regime for the single licence for securities firms (such as stockbrokers) *which are not banks* and allows them to offer their services anywhere in the Community, provided they are properly authorised by their home state. (It may be remembered that banks are already authorised to deal in securities on a cross-border basis under the Second Banking Directive.) Although the Commission put forward the text for the Investment Services Directive in 1989, it was held up for a long while in the Council because of differing views among the member states over the most desirable type of stock exchange structure. Specifically views differed over whether or not dealing in securities should be confined to formally recognised (or 'regulated') markets, partly on the grounds of the need to protect investors and partly because of differing dealing practices. The outcome is a complex piece of legislation ('highly interventionist, if still worthwhile', as the Commissioner responsible, Sir Leon Brittan, put it (Brittan 1994:9)) which allows firms trading in one member state to become members of the stock market of another, and which also allows member states the option of insisting that trading takes place on a regulated market, but also allows them the option of authorising large or professional investors to deal off-market.

To accompany the Investment Services Directive is an (even more complicated) instrument known as the *Capital Adequacy Directive*. This sets rules for the minimum levels of capital which firms must hold in order to take part in cross-border activity. This it does by matching capital levels to the level of risk calculated for each type of activity. A number of ancillary measures have also been adopted or are in the pipeline in this area, such as a 1989 *Insider Dealing Directive* (which requires the member states to apply similar rules against insider dealing) and a proposed *Investor Compensation Directive*, which provides for minimum uniform rules to safeguard the funds of investors using firms authorised under the Investment Services Directive.

INSURANCE

Of the three major areas of financial services the insurance sector is perhaps the least homogeneous. This is because there are so many different types of insurance activity (life assurance, motor insurance, property insurance, commercial insurance, re-insurance and so on) and most of these are closely interlinked with national habits and customs, making it comparatively more difficult to draw up European rules. Nonetheless, as in other areas, the single market programme has been a spur to activity. Since the 1960s the re-insurance market (the wholesale market where insurers cover their own risks) has been liberalised, and a raft of more recent legislation has attempted to do the same for the market in the normal forms of insurance used by both individuals and companies. In 1986 the Court of Justice ruled that so-called mass consumers of insurance (individuals) needed a greater degree of protection than large policy-holders (commercial operators). As a consequence, a directive liberalising large policy-holder activity in the non-life area (industrial, commercial and transport risks) was adopted in 1988, and in 1989 directives were adopted providing greater cross-border freedoms for both life assurance and motor insurance. It was not until 1990 and 1991, however, that major (third generation) directives in the life and non-life areas respectively were both put forward. These, like the parallel directives in the banking and investment services sectors, provide for the single licence for insurance companies and allow them, provided they are duly authorised in one member state and fulfil common rules (such as on the assets they hold), to offer services on a Europe-wide basis. These last two instruments did not enter into force until 1994.

CONCLUSIONS

In 1992 the Commission concluded its publication *Towards a single market in Financial Services* with the following words:

> The Community is aiming to establish a single market in financial services as part of the wider single European market due to be in place by 1993, allowing banks to offer the full range of their services throughout the entire Community and to set up branches in other Member States as easily as in their own, enabling customers to buy insurance providing cover throughout the Twelve on the most reasonable terms, and ensuring that the market for securities and capital is of a size sufficient to meet the financing needs of European industry and to attract investors from all over the world.
>
> (p. 13)

In most cases, however, the single market legislative programme is only the beginning, not the end, of this process. It will clearly take some time before this industry – the fastest, most mobile industry there is – assumes a European shape. For example, in the area of pension funds (which own some 30 per cent of the UK stock market), there have still not (at the time of writing) been agreed rules for the cross-border investment of funds. In many other areas, cross-border activity remains the exception rather than the rule. Indeed, following the European recession in the early 1990s, the volume of cross-border retail banking has reduced rather than increased, as banks try to save costs.

But what of the more long-term picture? Will the financial Europe that emerges from the single market process resemble a unified market – possibly a more unified market than in the US, with its own restrictions on inter-state banking? Or will it, on the contrary, come to resemble a multi-polar system, with differing national financial markets competing to offer products and services to both national and international firms and investors? Forces are pushing in both directions at the same time. On the one hand increased market liberalisation – partly as a consequence of the single market programme – is encouraging the development of financial markets and techniques in countries with hitherto underdeveloped sectors (and the emergence of new markets in the post-communist countries of eastern Europe can be viewed as an extension of this process). Having set up national markets to meet national needs, it seems unlikely that individual countries will want to lose them again. But on the other hand, the wider forces of internationalisation, and in particular competition from US and Japanese financial firms, seems to be encouraging a concentration of activity in the major markets, and in particular in London. It may be that two levels of activity will emerge. On one level will be an international service for large European firms, which will want to raise capital direct on the international markets and which will therefore require specialised financial services (which may possibly be located in London, but with branches in other centres like Paris and Frankfurt). On another level will be a more localised bank-loan type service for a much larger volume of smaller firms and individuals, which may be provided in any member state by increasingly competing retail banks and other types of financial firms.

However, there are so many variables in the equation that it is very hard to predict developments. (One unknown, for example, is how far large-scale pension funds will develop in Europe as a consequence of changes in social security systems.) The very fact that European financial services integration is either very recent or is still incomplete (for banking from 1993; for insurance from 1994; for securities from 1996), and also that partly as a consequence payments systems remain fragmented along national lines, means that it may be some while before the common market for invisibles is as established as that for goods – let alone for coal and steel.

6

ECONOMIC AND
MONETARY UNION

INTRODUCTION

Although it is at the heart of the 1992 Maastricht Treaty on
European Union, economic and monetary union (Emu) has in
reality been a long-standing Community objective. The 1985
Single European Act introduced an ambiguous formula which
referred to 'Cooperation in Economic and Monetary policy
(economic and monetary union)'. But long before that, in 1969
(immediately after the establishment of the customs union in
1968), the European Council agreed that a plan should be drawn
up with a view to the creation, in stages, of an economic and
monetary union. In 1970, the resultant Werner Report proposed
a three stage move to union over the period 1971 to 1980. And
in 1971 member states duly expressed 'their political will to
establish an economic and monetary union'.

According to Werner, Monnet told him in 1970 that 'monetary
union is at present the most important question on the European
level' (*Témoignages* 1989: 603). As far back as 1956 the Spaak
Report had concluded its analysis of the future common market
by saying that, while the free movement of goods, services,
persons and capital would only amount to partial economic
integration since it did not include giving up member states'
autonomy in budgetary, financial or social policy, or the creation
of a single currency, it nonetheless was 'sufficiently powerful to
maintain the necessary degree of convergence between these
policies' (*Rapport* 1956: 96). The EC Treaty itself committed each
member state to practise an economic policy which would maintain confidence in its own currency (Article 104) and also to treat
its exchange rate policy as a matter of common interest, un-
authorised alterations of which could provoke counter measures

by other member states if competitive conditions were seriously affected (Article 107). What has happened to change the situation since the early days of the Community, when monetary union appeared to be an objective within grasp after the establishment of the common market?

Three major factors have to be borne in mind. The first is that the world monetary order has changed utterly. The foundation of the Community took place against the background of the 1944 Bretton Woods system of semi-fixed exchange rates, dominated by the US dollar. The economic area of Europe, which became as it were the greenfield site for the common market (the separate national economies of the original Six) was itself a region of comparative exchange rate stability. The main European monetary problems of the 1950s were those of rendering currencies convertible under the Bretton Woods system. The American-led ending of the Bretton Woods arrangements in 1971 brought in today's era of floating currencies around the world (and, coincidentally, put paid to the Werner plan for monetary union). Attempts to restrict currency floating within the Community (first the 'snake' in 1972 and then, rather more successfully, the European Monetary System (EMS) in 1979) were aimed essentially at returning to a Bretton Woods-like regime within the European area (with the Deutschemark rather than the dollar becoming the pole currency). And so, unlike when the common market was first conceived, the initial conceptual step in monetary union became not one of establishing a single currency for use in one market where there was already a relatively high degree of currency stability. It became instead the problem of how to recreate currency stability before going on to create a single currency. That remains the essential problem today.

The second major factor has been the enormous change in the world financial markets under this regime of floating currencies. The volume of currencies now traded on the integrated global electronic markets – put at some $1,000 billion per day by the IMF in 1993 (three times what it was only in 1986) – far exceeds the resources available to individual governments to defend their currencies. Currencies whose values are deemed by the markets (rightly or wrongly) to be misaligned – such as sterling against the DM in 1992 and the French franc against the DM in 1993 – can only be defended at enormous cost to official reserves, if at all. (It is estimated that the UK spent £16 billion and France twice that sum in trying to defend the parities of their respective currencies in these crises). It is no longer practical politics for any European government to operate an exchange rate policy where the 'official' value of the currency differs markedly from the 'market' value (which will in practice be determined by a host of factors, including the market view of the prospects for the real economy of the country in question). In 1992 speculative attacks led to sterling and the Italian lira being suspended from the Exchange Rate Mechanism of the EMS. In 1993 these attacks led to the effective suspension of the Exchange Rate Mechanism itself. Such attacks are an unavoidable element of modern financial life, whose potential cannot be ignored so long as markets remain global and vast amounts of capital can be moved swiftly from country to country. It is sometimes suggested that the removal of EC capital controls as part of the single market programme – see the previous chapter – led to, or encouraged, the exchange rate turbulence in Europe in 1992 and 1993. But this argument seems weak. There have been no capital controls on sterling or the DM since the early 1980s. The residual French controls, removed in 1990, affected the opening of foreign bank accounts by French *individuals*. The markets were already international – and by 1989 over half the turnover in French government long bonds was accounted for by foreign investors. EC controls had the main effect of restricting retail capital movements *within* the Community.[1]

The third major factor is really a negative one. It is that, contrary to what is usually assumed and usually taken for granted by many commentators (including those from the European institutions), *a common market between the member states of the Community does not yet exist*. This apparently simple point is in reality fundamental to an understanding of economic and monetary union. If we think back to the objectives of the EC Treaty, and in particular to the logic of the Spaak Report, we will recall that the aim was to forge one market out of several, to create a large area of common economic policy where mass production could be reconciled with the absence of monopoly. This meant that, to refer to Spaak once more, economic adjustments arising from the establishment of that market should take place 'through the structure of production and costs rather than being reflected in sudden jumps in the external value of currencies' (*Rapport* 1956: 72). In other words, within one true European market economic changes would be digested *within* a national economy rather than being reflected in shifts in the external value of its currency. Economic pressures and adjustments would, one might say, be internalised rather than externalised.

Although much progress has been made towards the development of the common market, in particular through the single market programme, a situation where one true market exists between the member states, one where there is no perceptible difference between the individual national markets, does not yet prevail. The customs union of 1968 was not the same thing as the common market as it left important parts of the European economy untouched. The single market programme attempted to remedy this but is not yet complete (and was certainly not complete by 1993). Economic adjustment among the member states in the face of competitive pressures or shocks still tends to take place at the level of the national currency rather than at the level of internal production and costs. The many studies and proposals that speak of monetary union as if one European market were an accomplished fact are correct in the technical sense that most of the specific legislative programme has been adopted, but incorrect in assuming it has yet changed the behaviour of the European economies quite so radically. (Which is not the same thing as saying that it might not yet do so.)

THE DELORS REPORT

The intellectual underpinning for the moves towards monetary union which are now set out in the Maastricht Treaty can be found in the 1989 *Report on Economic and Monetary Union in the European Community* (known as the Delors Report), prepared by a committee for the study of economic and monetary union (which comprised heads of the central banks of each of the member states, plus some advisors, and which was chaired by the then President of the Commission, Jacques Delors). Although this report did not set out the timetable for moving to the final stages of Emu (and indeed argued that the setting of explicit deadlines was not advisable) it did, as requested by the European Council in 1988, set out quite clearly the concrete stages that would be needed to attain Emu if the will to do so existed.

The immediate background to the Delors Report was a decade of largely positive experience of the *European Monetary System*

(EMS), added to the impetus towards further integration created by the single market programme. The European Monetary System, founded in 1979, had three main features: a commitment to relative exchange rate stability through the Exchange Rate Mechanism (ERM) under which most participating member states agreed not to let their currencies diverge by more than a small amount (2.25 per cent) from a central pivot rate; machinery for intervention to support currencies, including significant credit arrangements between the central banks; and the creation of the basket of currencies known as the European Currency Unit (the Ecu) as the core of the system, both in terms of an account-ing unit and as the reference unit from which divergencies of currencies are calculated.

By 1989 the EMS had had a good first decade of existence. It had largely succeeded in establishing (or re-establishing) an island of comparative internal exchange rate stability in a world of currency turmoil. Exchange rate realignments became less frequent and inflationary pressures were cooled by the alignment of other member states' monetary policies on those of the Bundesbank (in itself committed by law to a policy of safeguard-ing the currency).

Yet there were imperfections. The DM (not the Ecu) had become the real core of the system. Although this brought benefits in terms of exporting German sound money policies to the rest of the EC, it also had some drawbacks. It placed undue (and unsought) weight on domestic German monetary policy decisions (such as interest rate changes) which had repercussions far outside Germany (including, it should be noted, among countries not formally members of the ERM). Yet the operating methods of the Bundesbank, drawn up on German federal lines in 1957, were never meant to apply to the whole of Europe. And, finally, there continued to be real economic divergencies among the member states, particularly in terms of budgetary policy, which were likely sooner or later to translate into pressures for exchange rate adjustments.

A combination of both these successes and these problems within the EMS, added to the fact that the single market pro-gramme was expected to increase the volume of cross-border economic transactions and thus make a single European currency more attractive, led to a majority view in the Community in around 1988 that the time was ripe for a renewed attempt at moving to Emu. (The UK dissented. For it, the time was not yet ripe even to join the Exchange Rate Mechanism of the EMS. Emu was virtually inconceivable.)

The Delors Report made a number of important points which are worth recalling. First, it contained a useful *working definition of Emu*, as follows:

Economic and monetary union in Europe would imply complete freedom of movement for persons, goods, services and capital, as well as irrevocably fixed exchange rates between national currencies and, finally, a single currency. This, in turn, would imply a common monetary policy and require a high degree of compatibility of economic policies and consistency in a number of other policy areas, particularly in the fiscal field. These policies should be geared to price stability, balanced growth, converging standards of living, high employment and external equilibrium. *Economic and monetary union would represent the final result of the process of progressive economic integration in Europe.*

(Delors Report 1989: paragraph 16; emphasis mine)

Second, the Report described clearly how the 'single most important condition' for monetary union would be to *lock exchange rates irrevocably*: only *after* which, but nonetheless 'as soon as possible', national currencies should be replaced by a single currency.

Third, the report proposed a new *European institution* to take responsibility for the common European monetary policy which would need to accompany locked exchange rates, and which would allow centralised and collective decisions on such key matters as the supply of money and credit and instruments of monetary policy like interest rates. This institution would be called the European System of Central Banks. It would be independent of instructions from national governments and it would itself have two main parts: a central body (i.e. the 'European Central Bank' proper – although that name is not in the Delors Report) and the existing national central banks.

Fourth, it suggested a series of *three stages of movement towards Emu*, of which the third stage would be the vital one of locking exchange rates. Although the Report suggested that there should be a clear indication of the timing of the first stage (and that this should be no later than 1 July 1990, when the capital liberalisation directive came into force), it added that the setting of deadlines, in particular for the move to irrevocably fixed exchange rates, was not advisable. In the light of the exchange rate crises of 1992–3 the language bears repeating: *'The conditions for moving from stage to stage cannot be defined precisely in advance; nor is it possible to foresee today when these conditions will be realised'* (ibid.: paragraph 43).

Fifth, the Report argued that although within an economic and monetary union there will still be scope for independent policy-making by national governments, there must be limits to national economic behaviour which could destabilise the monetary whole, and this applies particularly in the budgetary field, where *binding rules are required* in matters such as national budget deficits and borrowing policies.

THE MAASTRICHT TREATY AND EMU

By and large the Maastricht Treaty on European Union (signed in 1992; entry into force 1993) built on the Delors Report and wrote its main features into treaty form. Maastricht included the following noteworthy aspects. It added no fewer than twenty-one new pages to the original EC Treaty under the heading 'Economic and Monetary Policy', in which it described in the minutest detail the mechanisms to achieve Emu and the institutions and procedures involved. It also added a further forty-eight pages of detailed protocols on the status of the various monetary institutions, on national budgetary policies, on economic convergence criteria, on the transition to the third stage and on the special positions of some member states (including the UK). These sixty-nine technical pages devoted to Emu may, for interest's sake, be compared with the twenty-eight pages of the entire Single European Act. Maastricht made it clear that, as well as a single currency, monetary union would also incorporate *German sound money features*: 'The primary objective of the ESCB shall be to maintain price stability' (Maastricht Article G D (25) 105).

Notwithstanding the advice in the Delors Report, Maastricht set a clear timetable for moving to Emu. The first stage was assumed to have already begun. The second stage 'shall begin on 1 January 1994' (Article 109e). And as for the all-important third stage, a decision on setting a date for that should be taken by the end of 1997: but, if by then that date is not set, 'the third stage shall start on 1 January 1999' (Article 109j: paragraph 4). In addition a Protocol to the Treaty on the transition to the third stage drives home the point by talking about 'the will for the Community to enter swiftly into the third stage' and adds:

If by the end of 1997 the date of the beginning of the third stage has not been set, the Member States concerned, the Community institutions and other bodies involved shall expedite all preparatory work during 1998, in order to enable the Community to enter the third stage irrevocably on 1 January 1999 and to enable the ECB and the ESCB to start their full functioning from this date.

A word of comment may be useful here. Contrary to what is often assumed, *Maastricht does not, despite this apparently strong language, actually commit the Community to begin stage three by 1999 at the latest*. It would be at least theoretically possible under this formula for a decision to be taken before the end of 1997 to set a date for stage three to begin *after* 1999. Of course whether all this date-setting is in fact wise is a separate question.

Maastricht also provided more detail on the contents of the transitional (stage two) period. In particular, from 1994 a *European Monetary Institute* (EMI) was to be established to prepare the way for stage three. The EMI (now being set up in Frankfurt) is intended to promote co-ordination and consultation among national central banks on technical matters related to monetary union, including monitoring the functioning of the EMS, promoting the efficiency of cross-border payments, supervising the technical preparation of Ecu banknotes and overseeing the development of the Ecu. In addition, in stage two each member state is required 'as appropriate' to start the process leading to the *independence of its national central bank* (which France, for example, did at the beginning of 1994). During stage two member states also commit themselves in general to 'endeavour to avoid excessive government deficits' (Article 109e). However, a much more rigorous procedure is to be applied to those member states who wish to proceed to stage three. Reports have to be prepared by the Commission and the EMI on the status of each member state's national central bank and also on 'the achievement of a high degree of sustainable convergence' by each member state with reference to four specific economic criteria. No later than by the end of 1996 the European Council shall take a first (qualified majority) decision on whether a majority of

111

member states fulfil the necessary conditions for the adoption of a single currency, and will decide whether it is appropriate to begin stage three and if so set the date for it to begin. If a date for stage three is not set by the end of 1997 it will begin on 1 January 1999, in which case it will only apply to the member states which fulfil the conditions for a single currency.

The four *economic criteria* to be applied to each member state are:

1 *A high degree of price stability.* This is measured in terms of a price performance that 'is sustainable' and an average rate of inflation, observed over a period of one year before the examination, that does not exceed by more than 1.5 per cent that of, at most, the three best performing member states in terms of price stability. (All details from the Protocol on Convergence Criteria appended to the Treaty.)

2 *A sustainable government financial position.* This means a government budgetary position without an excessive deficit. This is itself to be separately determined by a (qualified majority) Council decision, on the basis of a Commission proposal, taking into account whether the ratio of planned or actual government deficit to GDP exceeds a particular reference value (3 per cent) and also whether the ratio of total government debt to GDP exceeds another reference value (60 per cent). (It should be noted here that under article 104c of the Treaty there is an elaborate procedure of assessments, opinions, private and public recommendations designed to allow an errant member state to correct its ways *before* the Council 'after an overall assessment' decides that an excessive deficit exists.)

3 *The observance of the normal fluctuation margins in the ERM for at least two years*, without devaluing its currency 'on its own initiative' against any other currency during the same period.

4 *The average nominal long-term interest rate level* should, during the period of one year before the examination, not exceed by more than 2 per cent that of, at most, the three best performing member states measured in terms of price stability. (Interest rates are measured on the basis of long-term government bonds or comparable securities).

Another comment: we should beware of observations to the effect that such and such a country 'does not at present fulfil the Maastricht criteria'. It is the position as agreed by the European Council in (at the earliest) 1996 that matters. Of these criteria, 1 and 4 are to be computed with reference to as yet unknown best performing states in (at the earliest) 1996. Point 2 looks more absolute, but there is clearly an element of judgement in the decision to declare a deficit 'excessive' (deficits can and do go up and down quite rapidly as a consequence of economic conditions affecting both public expenditure and tax intake). Point 3 is more definite: it means that if, say, the examination is made in 1996 the member state in question must have observed normal ERM disciplines at least since 1994. Following the ERM crises of 1992 and 1993 it is obviously hazardous to make predictions in this area but it should be noted that by 1994 a number of EU currencies were once again trading within the 2.25 per cent fluctuation margin – even though the margin had formally been widened to 15 per cent in the crisis of 1993.

Finally, the Maastricht Treaty has a *separate protocol on the United Kingdom*. This says that the UK is not committed to move to stage three without a separate decision to do so by its government and parliament.

CRISIS IN THE SYSTEM

In 1992 and 1993 the European Monetary System was shaken by crises so severe that to many they seemed to mark the end of the system and – *a fortiori* – the end of moves towards monetary union in Europe for the time being. In the autumn of 1992 both the pound sterling and the lira were forced to withdraw from the system and float their currencies. In the summer of 1993 speculative attacks in the financial markets on the 'core' currency relationship of the French franc against the DM put such strains on the remains of the system (and on central bank reserves) that the basic 2.25 per cent fluctuation margins had to be suspended completely and wide new fluctuation margins of 15 per cent introduced (except for the DM and the Dutch guilder, which retained the old margins). After fourteen years the EMS was not clinically dead, but it was certainly in a state of suspended animation.

What lay behind this crisis? There seem to be two main explanations. The first is linked to the Maastricht Treaty itself. Contrary to the advice in the Delors Report, Maastricht deliberately set a series of political deadlines under which the EMS would evolve into an ever tighter monetary ensemble and then into a fixed exchange rate regime. Now in some respects this may have seemed a rational approach at the time that Maastricht was negotiated (in 1991). The EMS had become increasingly stable in the 1980s, and there had been no currency realignment since 1987. In addition, the setting of political deadlines in a Treaty was of course the standard device for moving the Community and its member states forward. However, this deliberate posting of the Community's intentions in the monetary sphere meant that the EMS no longer was seen as an end in itself. It became instead a means to a different end, economic and monetary union, and as such its credibility became linked to the credibility of the latter. When in June 1992 a referendum in Denmark rejected the Maastricht Treaty, signed only the previous February, legitimate doubt was thrown over the fate of the entire Treaty, over the objective of Emu and thus over the credibility of the existing monetary arrangements (and the will of the member states to sustain them). The testing of that credibility involved mobilising the massive resources of the global financial markets.

The second explanation is linked to the way in which the DM had become the core currency in the system. While this arrangement provided benefits to the other members in terms of exporting German monetary virtues it did, of course, also have the risk that any German monetary troubles would be exported too. The massive shocks to the German economy resulting from the unification of East and West Germany in 1990 were bound to produce shocks for the European economy as a whole. Specifically, the inflationary effects of German unification led the Bundesbank to raise German interest rates higher than they would have otherwise been: simultaneously making the DM a more attractive currency to hold and forcing other European currencies linked through the EMS to raise their own interest rates to maintain the value of their own currencies. This happened at a time when, unlike in Germany, poor growth rather than inflation was the main problem. The basic (and growing) contradiction of this policy mix was the second element undermining the credibility of the EMS.

These two sets of (quite exceptional) circumstances seem to explain the general erosion of confidence by the financial markets in the official monetary policies of the member states in the period up to the crises. The crises themselves were triggered by second-order questions: the autumn 1992 crisis by unfounded fears that the French referendum on Maastricht would reject the Treaty, and the summer 1993 crisis by an unexpected decision by the Bundesbank *not* to cut a key monetary rate.

It is now, of course, difficult to say where the EMS should go after these crises. Credibility lost cannot easily be regained. The 15 per cent fluctuation margin has provided a cooling off period and (so far) member states have been reluctant (or unable) to say how long it will last and what they will do next. It might, all the same, be worth offering one or two general remarks.

First, if these explanations of the background to the crises are correct, they may be time-limited in their effect. Maastricht is now ratified; the initial shock of German unification *may* be over, or at least receding. (There is, of course, another view. This is that the system itself is fundamentally flawed and bound to fail because semi-fixed exchange rates cannot be reconciled with free capital movements and in fact exacerbate instability rather than reduce it by stopping the markets from gradually changing the value of a currency. The trouble with this view is that it is hard to reconcile with the objective fact of relative EMS stability for such a long period *before* the crises.) Second, it seems possible that the explicit visible political link between the EMS and Emu (the first a stage towards the second) may have to be broken. A series of highly visible political deadlines leading up to the locking of parities and a single currency may only produce a series of highly visible crises of confidence. Currency stability in Europe may have to be re-established as a good in its own right – and any further steps towards locking national currencies may have to be taken on an opportunistic basis as market conditions allow (rather as the Delors Report in fact implied). Third, perhaps too much confidence has been placed in the role of the DM in the system. While it is understandable that other member states might have wanted to import sound German monetary policies through membership of the EMS, there was always the risk that German monetary policy, although perfectly right for Germany, would be wrong for another member state. It seems pointless to criticise the Germans for pursuing a policy for 'selfish' or 'domestic' reasons. Those who created the Bundesbank and the way it operates never envisaged the DM becoming the reserve currency. If the other member states want to pursue sound money policies there is nothing to stop them adopting German sound money practices themselves (and, indeed, the move towards independent central banks envisaged in Maastricht may help them do this). Fourth, and finally, instead of seeing the EMS primarily as a means of importing monetary virtue it may be more productive to return to the original argument in favour of exchange rate stability in Europe – within one market it promotes a better division of labour. To illuminate this point it may (once again) be worth rehearsing the original arguments in the Spaak Report on which the common market was based:

> The progressive establishment of the rules of the common market will constitute the appropriate incentive to seek a balance in the general methods of monetary policy.
>
> Doubtless the progressive creation of the common market, and the evolution in trade which results from it, could change in unpredictable ways the equilibrium conditions of the balance of payments; subsequent adjustments in exchange rates might theoretically seem to be the useful counter-part of that evolution. *In fact, one of the reasons which justifies the very progressive character of the establishment of the common market is precisely that adjustments should be made through the structure of production and costs, instead of being reflected in sudden jumps in the external value of currencies.*
>
> *It is necessary, in particular, to guard against the risk that, despite the rules of the IMF, devaluations take place with the sole aim of obtaining a competitive advantage.*
>
> (*Rapport* 1956: 74; emphasis mine)

The Spaak Report (written under the Bretton Woods regime) did not venture very far down the technical track of monetary union, and its suggestions for combating these problems revolve around ideas for mutual support for member states in balance of payments difficulties. Nonetheless, the basic analysis remains pertinent. It is reinforced by a passage later in the Report dealing with the need for the free movement of capital:

> The most manifest difficulty is that divergencies in monetary policy or fears about currency stability produce speculative capital movements, which can take the form of sudden flights: through these unsettling movements capital ceases to move to areas where the need for funds is the most intense, interest rates the highest or the balance of payments in

deficit. *It is in the progressive development of the common market, the rules governing its functioning and the mechanisms to be set up, that there exist the most effective means to guard against such divergencies and to eliminate the speculative movements which they produce.*

(*Rapport* 1956: 93; emphasis mine)

One might observe, then, that the attempt to reintroduce Bretton Woods-style exchange rate stability within the Community was always going to be problematic to the extent that a true common market between the member states did not exist – and in fact does not yet exist. The entire process of constructing that market has taken much longer than anyone had foreseen and – in the sense that economic adjustments do not yet fully take place through the production/cost structure – it is still going on.

On the other hand, clearly economic integration in the Community *is* deepening, particularly through the progressive effects of the single market programme. The inter-penetration of the national economies of the member states, the increased mobility of economic factors, the growth in cross-border trade, the adoption of common rules in ever more areas, all serve to encourage convergence of the different economies – and also to encourage convergence of economic policies. With increased market integration the economic fundamentals which determine monetary conditions in each member state also increasingly converge.

So where does this analysis take us? It seems to suggest two things. The first is that the search for exchange rate stability in Europe cannot be divorced from the facts of real economic integration. Exchange rate stability might be used as a tool to try to *encourage* economic integration, but if too much pressure is put upon it it will snap, as the EMS snapped when it tried to do too much. Despite that experience, the objective fact of increased real economic integration in Europe does suggest that the search for exchange rate stability in that zone remains a valid one so long as it proceeds hand in hand with that integration. The second is a separate but linked point. It is that – particularly as economic integration deepens – exchange rate devaluations aimed at obtaining a competitive advantage, which are used as a deliberate tool of national economic policy, clearly can have no place. In a unified market the short-term advantages they confer on one

117

country are offset by the disadvantages in another, which means that they undermine confidence in the entire market structure and in the long run harm both. In the Europe-wide recession of 1993, for example, benefits for the whole European economy obtained by exporters in those countries whose currencies devalued in the crises of 1992 and 1993 'have been out-weighed by the negative economic impact of currency appreciation in Germany and in ERM members still linked to the D-Mark' (*Financial Times*, 15 December 1993: 13). It is one thing to have to adjust the exchange rate because economic fundamentals are out of line with the rest of the market. It is another thing entirely for member states to reserve the right to adjust their exchange rate as they see fit in line with their own economic circumstances – and for each member state to fear that each other will exercise that right.

It is perhaps here that the case for action is the strongest as the single market deepens. What may be needed is a strengthening of the original EC Article 107 requirement that changes in exchange rates be considered a matter of common concern. Perhaps the answer is linked to the general move towards independent central banks in the Community. For credibility and confidence to return to the system it may be necessary to have a kind of *double de-politicisation* of European monetary policy. In the first place this would break the essentially political link between exchange rate stability and Emu which has tended to undermine the former. In the second it would remove political calculation and uncertainty from the realm of exchange rate policy by placing monetary decisions clearly in the hands of independent central bankers who take decisions on adjusting parities on the basis of regular objective (and shared) assessments both of the overall European economy and also the place of each individual currency within it. While the aim would still be exchange rate stability, adjustments should by no means be ruled out if needed. It may be that a new economic tool should be developed to measure on a kind of matrix the degree of market integration in each member state, and thus the extent to which economic adjustment in each can be internalised or else reflected in the exchange rate.

ECONOMIC UNION

So far we have been concerned mostly with the monetary side of economic and monetary union. It has, at least, the merit of being relatively simple to describe, even if difficult to implement. But what of economic union? In what sense is economic union a necessary adjunct to monetary union? And what exactly *is* economic union? How does it differ, in particular, from the underlying concept of a unified European market?

The Delors Report addressed these points by saying that parallel advances in economic and monetary integration are indeed indispensable. As well as defining monetary union, it also says that economic union 'combines the characteristics of an unrestricted common market with a set of rules which are indispensable to its working' (Delors 1989: paragraph 25). In detail this means four things:

1 the single market within which persons, goods, services and capital can move freely;
2 competition policy and other measures aimed at strengthening market mechanisms;
3 common policies aimed at structural change and regional development; and
4 macroeconomic policy co-ordination, including binding rules for budgetary policies.

Of these, the first and second do not call for much further comment here, except to repeat the by now familiar refrain that the single market is not yet complete and that it is a major oversight to assume that it is. In paragraph 24 of the Report, for example, one can read that

> Well before the decision to fix exchange rates permanently, the full liberalisation of capital movements and financial market integration would have created a situation in which the coordination of monetary policy would have to be strengthened progressively. Once every banking institution in the Community is free to accept deposits from, and to grant loans to, any customer in the Community and in any of the national currencies, the large degree of territorial coincidence between a national central bank's area of jurisdiction, the area in which its currency is used and the area in which 'its' banking system operates will be lost.

There are, as the Report says, compelling reasons under these circumstances for co-operation on monetary policy between central banks. However, as we saw in the previous chapter, we are only at the start of creating an integrated cross-border banking market on such a scale.

But what of the third and fourth points above? It is these which are the new elements in economic union, and which go clearly beyond the single market as we have seen it so far. Common policies aimed at structural change and regional development turn out, on closer inspection, to be, essentially, existing Community expenditure policies on regional and structural programmes funded from the budget, already augmented in the context of the single market programme. For the future: 'Depending upon the speed of progress, such policies might have to be strengthened further after 1993 in the process of creating economic and monetary union' (Delors Report 1989: para. 29). But, as the Report warns, excessive reliance on financial assistance could cause tensions. And nor should the principal objective of regional policies be to subsidise incomes and simply offset inequalities in the standards of living, but rather to help equalise production conditions, for example through investment in infrastructure, communications, transport and education, 'so that large-scale movements of labour do not become the major adjustment factor' (paragraph 29). It is noteworthy also that the Report makes clear that, in an economic union, wage flexibility and labour mobility are needed to eliminate Europe-wide differences in competitiveness – a problem relevant to the argument over 'Social Europe' in Chapter 4.

It is clear then, that economic union does not of itself imply large-scale, EU-directed public expenditure; or at least that the authors of the Delors Report did not expect it to do so. In paragraph 30 the point is made clear again: 'the centrally managed Community budget is likely to remain a very small part of total public-sector spending and . . . much of this budget will not be available for cyclical adjustments.' (In other words, although the Report does not say so, it is being spent on agriculture.)

It is precisely this very limited nature of Community fiscal responsibilities that leads on to the fourth point. Macroeconomic policy co-ordination is the co-ordination of *those aspects of the economic policies of member states which would affect the stability of the monetary union as a whole*. In particular this boils down to two elements. First is a general Europe-wide 'common overall assessment of the short-term and medium-term economic developments in the Community', which would create a framework within which national economic policies could be kept consistent with the whole. The second – and principal – element is 'binding rules' on those aspects of member states' budgetary policy which would directly affect the overall policy mix in the monetary union. This means limits on the permissible budget deficit in each; the forbidding of financing national budgets by central banks; and limiting recourse to external borrowing in non-Community currencies. It does *not* mean, for example, that in this – the tightest area of co-ordination in an economic union – binding rules are needed for either the total level or the composition of public spending in any member state, as is sometimes supposed. Other areas of general economic activity, like wage negotiations and economic decisions in the fields of production, savings and investment, and the action of public authorities in the economic and social spheres would also remain either national or local decisions.

A final point should be made here about economic union as described in the Delors Report. Unlike monetary union, it does not imply new Community institutions. It implies, instead, that those existing institutions responsible for the development of the European market should act in a manner consistent with the good of the whole. In particular it addresses the public authorities in each member state and requires them to conduct national policies in a way which does not destabilise the whole. *Economic union can be defined as the European market plus some rules for the national public authorities which operate in and affect that market.*

The Maastricht Treaty in practice adds comparatively little to this basic concept of economic union, but it does enshrine the detail in Treaty form. Thus it says in Article 103 that 'Member States shall regard their economic policies as a matter of common concern and shall coordinate them within the Council'. It describes how this policy co-ordination should take place (under a method known as 'multilateral surveillance'). It incorporates the points about budget financing by forbidding, for example, overdraft facilities (or any other type of credit facility) by member states with either national central banks or the future European Central Bank itself. And, finally, it spells out the rules concerning member states' budget deficits and the economic criteria for joining the currency union which we have already seen.

EMU: AN ANALYSIS

We now need to put all these elements together and consider where economic and monetary union, as defined in the Delors Report and as set out in the sixty-nine detailed pages of the Maastricht Treaty, is likely to go next – if anywhere. There is a widespread belief that, following the EMS crises of 1992 and 1993, economic and monetary union is effectively removed from the EU agenda for the time being. Is this correct? It is worth rehearsing some of the obstacles.

First, of course, there is the paramount need to *rebuild prior confidence in the EMS (or any successor arrangement) as an instrument of relative exchange rate stability*. This is necessary not just because monetary union (locked exchange rates) is a development of semi-fixed exchange rates. It is necessary in purely formal terms because the Maastricht Treaty says that the second stage for achieving economic and monetary union 'shall begin on 1 January 1994'. A second stage – now begun – which, despite increasing economic integration, has less exchange rate stability than the first stage would indeed be a strange beast.

Second, a new set of issues has come to light in the course of *German ratification of the Maastricht Treaty* which may affect the transition to the third stage of Emu. In October 1993 the German Federal Constitutional Court approved the ratification of Maastricht, but added the following remarks:

1 The tough economic convergence criteria governing participation in stage three cannot be 'softened' beyond what is already in the Treaty;
2 the date of entry into stage three 'is to be regarded as an objective [that is, target] date rather than a legally binding deadline';
3 the Treaty does not in the final analysis rule out any member state leaving the 'community of stability' [i.e. monetary union] should it collapse.

In addition, the German authorities have promised the German Bundestag that it 'will be able to exercise its influence prior to entry into Stage Three, and it has informed the European Council, the Commission and the European Parliament accordingly.' (This and other quotations are taken from a commentary on the 12 October judgement issued shortly afterwards by the Federal German Government.)

Taken together these German reservations go a long way towards removing what appeared, at the time of Maastricht, to be the element of inevitability in the process of monetary union (or at least inevitability that Germany – the largest European economy – would take part in it). In particular, it is difficult to see how the last point, relating to the exercise of influence of the Bundestag, is materially different from the Maastricht provision that the UK government and parliament have a right to a separate decision on moving to stage three. It is of course impossible at this stage to predict the evolution of future German opinion about Emu, but this (and the problem for German opinion of replacing the DM with a single European currency) will clearly be a major factor in determining when and if stage three begins.

Third, the deep Europe-wide recession of the early 1990s (certainly exacerbated by the relayed effects of German unification through links with the DM) left member states less enthusiastic about pressing ahead with the tough Maastricht convergence criteria as their main economic targets. Growth, competitiveness and the need to combat unemployment returned as more important policy objectives. A world of German-style price stability and locked exchange rates appeared (at least temporarily) rather less attractive or necessary.[2]

These three sets of factors suggest that the 'will for the Community to enter swiftly into the third stage' (as Maastricht put it) is not quite what it was. There remains the possibility that some member states with similar monetary positions will lock currencies in advance of the others and thus form an Emu core irrespective of the Maastricht criteria, but this could not happen without Germany and German representatives have not been enthusiastic about this approach. More likely at present is that when a first decision is taken in 1997, under the Maastricht arrangements on setting a date for stage three, that date will (if set) be hedged around with German caveats which continue to make it conditional.

It has been implicit throughout this chapter, however, that if monetary union depends upon the existence of a single European market (as most commentators believe) then it follows that monetary union must inevitably be a slower process than has been generally thought (or at least than the drafters of the Maastricht Treaty thought). The problem is not fundamentally one of replacing existing national currencies with a European currency – that is a technical issue which would provide some short-term costs but also long-term advantages. (If currency transactions constitute real barriers which prevent the efficient operation of the European market then there is certainly a case for early innovative thinking to get over them: one answer would be better cross-border bank card systems). The fundamental problem with Emu is the *irrevocable locking of exchange rates which must precede the introduction of a single currency*. Unless and until member states' economies are unified in a single effective market, removing the possibility of exchange rate adjustment means that economic adjustment will take place by other means. Or as the Delors Report itself puts it:

> exchange rate adjustments would no longer be available as an instrument to correct economic imbalances within the Community. Such imbalances might arise because the process of adjustment and restructuring set in motion by the removal of physical, technical and fiscal barriers is unlikely to have an even impact on different regions or always produce satisfactory results within reasonable periods of time. Imbalances might also emanate from labour and other cost developments, external shocks with differing repercussions on individual economies, or divergent economic policies pursued at national level.
>
> (Delors 1989: paragraph 26)

To the extent that one market (including one labour market) does not exist prior to monetary union, the risk must exist that economic imbalances will not be dealt with through the structure of production and costs in any given member state (or region), but will rather be reflected in other ways: through unemployment or (to quote Delors again) 'relatively large declines in output'. These effects in turn will create pressures for increased cross-border financial transfers and these will create further problems in terms of whether such transfers promote adjustment or simply ossify outmoded practices. On the other hand, to put the problem the other way, once there *is* one European market (including one labour market, in the sense that wage levels are linked to productivity on a European basis) then the main problem of a fixed exchange rate regime falls away.

In a sense, though, this is a false dichotomy. Because, of course, such a market is being created *gradually*, without any big bang. At the same time, monetary policies of the member states are progressively overlapping as cross-border transactions increase. In some parts of the Community there will be more market integration than in others, and in some areas financial instruments may be virtually interchangeable. All this will encourage the real economic convergence that must accompany locking currencies. And so the problem is really one of how the public authorities of the member states manage (or react to) this market integration. If they move too quickly the world's financial markets (and their own electors) may punish them for hubris. If they move too slowly they risk needlessly prolonging market barriers. If they do nothing they risk being overtaken by events – by the commercial forces already set in train.

CONCLUSIONS

There is finally one other important aspect of Emu which we must consider. That is, even if it were technically and economically feasible, is it in fact *desirable*? Here the case against is put most forcefully by former British Chancellor of the Exchequer, Nigel Lawson, who in 1989 said:

Economic and Monetary Union . . . is incompatible with independent sovereign states with control over their own fiscal and monetary policies. It would be impossible, for example, to have irrevocably fixed exchange rates while individual countries retained independent monetary policies . . .. Thus Emu inevitably implies a single European currency, with monetary decisions – the setting of monetary targets and of short-term interest rates – taken not by national Governments and/or central banks, but by a European Central Bank. Nor would individual countries be able to retain responsibility for fiscal policy. With a single European monetary policy there would need to be central control over the size of budget deficits and, particularly, over their financing . . .. What organisation would really be the Government? It is clear that Economic and Monetary Union implies nothing less than a European Government – albeit a federal one – and political union: the United States of Europe. That is simply not on the agenda now, nor will it be for the foreseeable future.

(Lawson 1992: 910)

This is indeed a powerful argument from a very respectable quarter, and deserving of close analysis. What of the overall logical sequence? *Does* Emu actually mean a European government and the United States of Europe (Churchill's old phrase)? The answer to this is that it *might*. In the course of the Maastricht Treaty negotiations, for example, the French government floated the idea of a 'European economic government' as the democratic counterpart to the new European monetary authority. But again it *might not* – the French proposal did not command a consensus and the Maastricht Treaty contains no such entity. While it is certainly true that *some* of the impetus behind Emu might in some quarters come from a desire to set up a European government it would be wrong to think that that desire is necessarily widely shared. In Germany, for example, the emphasis is rather more on powers for the European Parliament than powers for the European Council, which was really what the French idea meant. The idea that A ineluctably leads to B takes no account of the aspect of *choice* in the development of the EU.

What of the detailed points in the Lawson critique? It is perfectly correct, as he says, that Emu would spell the end of independent national monetary policies: not just exchange rate adjustments but also the setting of national monetary targets and even short-term interest rates. As we have seen in this chapter, there are powerful arguments against doing this in a situation where national economies are not market integrated. But there is also the other side of the coin: what if such economies are, or become, market integrated? In those circumstances a unified monetary policy, based on common monetary targets, may make sense. And while it is true that independence of monetary policy is lost there is the compensating factor that each member state (or rather the central bank of each member state) would have a say in the setting and implementation of *joint* policy.

As for fiscal policy, it is true that individual countries *would* lose responsibility in the sense that they could not run up and finance large fiscal deficits as they pleased, and that there would have to be jointly agreed rules ('central control') about the size and manner of financing such deficits. However, this is not in itself at variance with prudent public finances and the objective of the balanced budget. The size of the budget, how it is broken down into expenditure programmes and how taxes are raised to finance it would all remain up to the individual member state (subject, it is true, to some constraints like European agreements on minimum levels of VAT, which exist for a different reason). The Delors Report put it this way:

Many developments in macroeconomic conditions would continue to be determined by factors and decisions operating at the national or local level. This would include not only wage negotiations and other economic decisions in the fields of production, savings and investment, but also the action of public authorities in the economic and social spheres. Apart from the system of binding rules governing the size and the financing of national budget deficits, decisions on the main components of public policy in such areas as internal and external security, justice, social security, education, and hence on the level and composition of government spending, as well as many revenue measures, would remain the preserve of Member States even at the final stage of economic and monetary union.

(Delors 1989: paragraph 30)

Assuming this analysis is correct (and it is the basis on which the EU has been proceeding) then any new European government would enjoy far fewer powers than any government which has existed so far. It would not have the power to raise taxes or direct expenditure; nor would it have much influence in the monetary sphere, since the European System of Central Banks is of course supposed to be independent (the role of the Council under Maastricht is restricted to a say in determining the *external* value of the Ecu against a third currency). It could set broad guidelines for European macroeconomic policy and oversee national deficits, but important matters like defence policy, internal security, social policy and education policy would pass it by completely. It would in fact largely be a government in name only (which begs the question whether it deserves that name).

This analysis of the Lawson critique does not deny its force. Under certain circumstances, and if pressed in some quarters, Emu *could* be used as a lever to concentrate more economic and political power at a European level than is wise or necessary (and more than is suggested in the Delors Report). There *could* be pressure for vastly increased cross-border financial transfers, particularly if fixed exchange rates create regional economic declines in output (or, in other words, if market integration had not succeeded). But these are not inevitable consequences, and matters could turn out otherwise.

One solution to the problem of uncertainty of outcome would be to adopt the method for introducing political reforms recommended by Popper in *The Open Society and Its Enemies*. As he points out:

> Social life is so complicated that few men, or none at all, could judge a blueprint for social engineering on the grand scale; whether it be practicable; whether it would result in a real improvement; what kind of suffering it may involve; and what may be the means for its realisation.
>
> (Popper 1971: 159)

Faced with this difficulty he recommends not trying to change everything at once, but rather conducting discrete social experiments which allow theoretical ideas to be tempered by the process of trial and error elimination since, as he puts it 'the whole secret of scientific method is a readiness to learn from mistakes' (ibid.: 163).

For Emu, then, perhaps the only answer would be to try a regime of locked exchange rates on a limited basis first – among member states whose economies are most market integrated. If it works without undue strain over a period of time lessons can be learnt and the system applied more widely to those other member states who wish to participate.

7

AGRICULTURE

INTRODUCTION

It may not be at first sight obvious why separate consideration should be given to agriculture within the European political economy. Agricultural support was one of the last things on the minds of those concerned with the post-war unification of Europe (see Chapter 1). And agriculture at present contributes only about 2.5 per cent to total EU GDP, and employs less than 7 per cent of the total EU workforce.

Nonetheless, it is impossible to have an understanding of how the EU functions without an understanding of its agricultural policy. For many years agricultural support took up about two-thirds of expenditure from the EC budget (and it still takes about half – far more than any other expenditure block). The Common Agricultural Policy was widely considered for a long time to be the most developed area of Community policy, and thus in some sense a model of how the Community might develop. Given its central role within the EC system, agriculture has played a dominant part in external trade negotiations (most notably in the Gatt Uruguay Round). So, although there is a strong tendency to treat agriculture as a separate 'technical' subject, in a different compartment from matters of high policy like the single market or monetary union, it cannot be ignored or left solely to the farm experts (although the organisation of business in the EU in fact tends to encourage this).

For a policy which has come to dominate everyday EU life, agriculture had rather quiet beginnings. In the momentous first decade after the war it was not seen as a leading candidate to help the unification of Europe. Monnet himself had little to do with or say about agriculture within the European economy. His collaborator Richard Mayne recounts an anecdote which shows how Monnet once dealt with rural economics. Having moved into a house in the country outside Paris, where most of his neighbours were farmers, Monnet was confronted with the same problem that the previous owner of the same house had faced:

> One of [the farmers] owned a field adjacent to the Jean Monnet property, which gave it an odd shape. The predecessor of Jean Monnet had tried to buy the field, but the owner had refused to sell. 'As long as I have this bit of land I can tell everyone to go to hell,' he used to say. Faced with the same refusal, Jean Monnet bought an area of land of better quality elsewhere in the village, and offered it in exchange. The deal was struck on the spot. Each had found his equal.
>
> (*Témoignages* 1989: 358)

THE LINK WITH THE COMMON MARKET

It was, as in other areas, the Spaak Report of 1956 which set the scene for the introduction of agriculture into the Treaty of Rome. And an important point should be noted here. From the outset the wider objective was the creation of the common market, within which agriculture was but one economic sector:

> It is not possible to conceive of establishing a general common market in Europe without including agriculture in it. It is one of the sectors where the progress in productivity resulting from a common market, that is the progressive specialisation of production and the widening of outlets, could have the greatest effect on the standard of living of producers as well as consumers. In addition, including agriculture in the common market is a condition for balancing trade between the different economies of the member states.
>
> (*Rapport* 1956: 44)

Rather as for any other economic sector, the authors of the Spaak Report believed that creating one European market for agriculture would be a good thing in itself. The problem was that there already existed a large array of internal national regulations in the farm sectors of the member states, which covered all matters such as the fixing of prices for farm products, volumes of production, timetables for sales, purchases, market intervention and the liquidation of surpluses by stockpiling, destruction or subsidised export. 'The de facto situation is therefore more complex in agriculture than in other economic sectors, with the exception perhaps of services' (*Rapport* 1956: 45).

As in the case of services, the Spaak Report did not spell out in detail how the common market was to be extended to agriculture. But it did set out the broad guidelines which, during the transitional period leading up to the establishment of the common market, would enable the Commission and the member states to create an agricultural policy. The basic idea was that at the same time as reducing and then eliminating national obstacles to trade within the common market, and disparities in regulation established behind such obstacles, there should take place the establishment of a common policy 'and even, for certain products, a common organisation instead' (ibid.: 48). (The underlying idea that in a highly regulated sector common rules should replace national rules figures elsewhere in the Report, and can be found also in the section on the services sector.) The Report also suggested that, as well as encouraging product specialisation, the general objectives for an agricultural policy should be the stabilisation of markets, security of supply, the maintenance of a sufficient level of income for 'normally productive farm enterprises' and the gradual necessary adjustment of agricultural structures and farms.

In the *transitional period* the Report suggested that customs duties on agricultural products should be reduced in line with other duties, quotas on farm trade eliminated, and national organisations of trade turned into a common organisation. For external tariffs, it suggested,

> the general method of establishing a common tariff will apply to agriculture; at the outset the maintenance of certain internal quotas in the Community will permit quotas established by the member states towards third countries; but the easing of the former will lead progressively to the harmonisation of the latter, up to the establishment of the common commercial policy.
>
> (*Rapport* 1956: 49)

Finally, the problem of member states' regulation of the farm sector ('the most important to resolve') would require that such regulations were examined in the process of creating a common regime and put to the proof that they are not more restrictive than necessary to achieve the basic objectives.

Beyond the valid objectives to which they are a response, it cannot be disguised that in many cases they have allowed the continuation of abusive protection, un-exportable surpluses or old-fashioned methods of development.

(ibid.: 50)

A word about external tariffs. As the above indicates, the development of a common tariff for agriculture seems to have been expected to be no different from other sectors. And, as the Spaak Report makes clear elsewhere, the common market was to be based on a customs union established under Gatt rules, one of which was that the general level of common tariff should not be higher than that of the separate tariffs which it replaced:

The rules for establishing this external tariff will be such that they satisfy this condition. In this way, the common market will avoid the risk of constituting a zone of high external protection, tending to isolate itself from the rest of the world or distorting trade flows. *A high level of protection is excluded a priori.*

(*Rapport* 1956: 22; emphasis mine)

Under the *final agricultural regime* (that is, after the transitional period had led to the establishment of the common market), the Spaak Report envisaged that different solutions would apply to different farm products. For a 'limited number' of products their particular problems and their significance for farm income would justify an organisation of the market on a European level. To do this a forward programme would be established of resources and sales affecting consumption patterns, measures to be taken with regard to surpluses and the degrees of protection necessary. The market organisation would involve establishing stabilising mechanisms, based in particular on import monopolies selling on to the internal market at a fixed price. In addition, if these indirect means were inadequate, they could be accompanied by stockpiling or price guarantees. In an exceptional case, where a national economy was both too small and insufficiently diversified to absorb 'fundamental and persistent' problems affecting the farm sector, 'special solutions' could be applied if necessary, in addition to the stabilising mechanisms.

132

For other farm products, the intention should be to let a free market function within the Community and to limit external protection to customs duties, including defensive anti-dumping measures, preferably through quotas. And such quotas, insofar as they are compatible with international obligations should themselves, as far as possible, not be permanent but seasonal.

The Spaak Report also considers some problems concerning competition with third countries. One is that some markets are distorted by large producers who liquidate their surpluses at prices which are lower because they keep prices on their domestic market higher (and thus increase production).

It would not be giving Community countries unusual preference to buy their products when their prices are reasonable by comparison with the internal prices in third countries, without trying to align them on the prices at which third countries are forced to liquidate their stocks.

(*Rapport* 1956: 51)

Nor, on the other hand, should it be underestimated how far world prices could rise if some European production was reduced following the setting of prices incompatible with production costs. A long-term view is particularly important, taking into account a renunciation 'by certain partners of the Community' of the short-term advantages obtained from the pricing practices of some third countries. The general warning of the Spaak Report in this area is in fact clear (and remarkably prophetic):

No doubt it is necessary to guard against the risk that organisation measures for the whole of the market, in replacing national regulations, tend to create a large area protected against the exterior and aligning its prices on marginal internal production.

(Rapport 1956: 51; emphasis mine)

In the *EC Treaty* itself (1957) agriculture within the common market is covered in much the same way as the other economic sectors mentioned by Spaak. The *objectives* of the common agricultural policy, to be established at the same time as the common market for agricultural products, are set out in Article 39:

1 To increase agricultural productivity;
2 thus to ensure a fair standard of living for the agricultural community (in particular by increasing the individual earnings of persons engaged in agriculture);

133

3 to stabilise markets;
4 to assure the availability of supplies;
5 to ensure that supplies reach consumers at reasonable prices.

The *mechanisms* for achieving the above objectives involve a 'common organisation of agricultural markets' (Article 40), through one of three forms, depending on the product concerned: common rules on competition; a compulsory co-ordination of the various national market organisations; or a European market organisation. The common organisation of the market (which 'shall be limited to pursuit of the objectives set out in Article 39') may include all measures required to attain these objectives, in particular the regulation of prices, aids for the production and marketing of the various products, storage and carry-over arrangements and common machinery for stabilising imports or exports. Any common price policy shall be based on common criteria and uniform methods of calculation.

Under the EC Treaty specific proposals for working out and implementing the common agricultural policy are to be made by the Commission after a conference of member states has allowed a comparison of their national agricultural policies, including an assessment of their resources and needs.

It may be worth pausing a moment here to recapitulate. Agriculture has not figured as a subject in the later Treaty amendments (the Single European Act and the Maastricht Treaty). This means that the Treaty base is solely the original EC Treaty, drawn up in 1957 on the basis of the Spaak Report. What general observations can we make about the situation as it appeared at that time?

First, it is important to recall the relatively backward nature of the farm sector among most of the member states in the 1950s. Farms were small, productivity was low, farming methods were largely unmodernised and labour intensive (over 10 million people worked in the farm sector among the Six), food shortages rather than surpluses were commonplace and the Europe of the future common market was far from self-sufficient in most farm products. Agriculture everywhere (and not just among the Six) was propped up by national support systems intended to smooth out seasonal price variations and to mediate between the farmer and the consumer. The UK was no exception. Its system of deficiency payments meant that farmers were compensated financially when market prices fell below a certain level.

Second, the fundamental policy problem which the EC Treaty had to address was how to integrate this backward, inefficient, highly protected and nationally sensitive sector into the one European market which was to be created. On the one hand, the very creation of the new market was likely to stimulate farm trade and thus help to modernise and develop the sector; on the other hand, the existing barrage of national support measures which fragmented the market meant that European rules for market organisation would have to replace national rules.

Third, it is noteworthy how, by and large, the European rules which were to replace national rules were drawn up in neutral terms. The objectives set out at Article 39 are framed in terms of balance and equilibrium: to ensure a 'fair standing of living', to 'stabilise markets', to 'assure the availability of supplies', to ensure 'reasonable' consumer prices. It is true that there is also the open-ended aim of increasing agricultural productivity, but Article 39 makes clear that this should be through promoting technical progress and modernising farm methods – and it is by this method that a fair standard of living and increased individual earnings are to be obtained. The Treaty is open about the mechanisms for achieving its objectives. It says they may include price regulation (but does not specify at what level – although Spaak implies linking some internal Community prices to internal third country prices); it says they may include aids for the production and marketing of various products, storage and carry-over arrangements (but does not specify what these might be); and it says that there may be common machinery for 'stabilising' imports and exports (but not on the other hand for stimulating or restricting either). What it does make clear is that it is *only* in pursuit of the Article 39 objectives that there may be a common organisation of the market (and not, for example, in pursuit of different objectives such as promoting Community exports, winning market shares or stimulating consumption).

THE DEVELOPMENT OF THE COMMON AGRICULTURAL POLICY (CAP)

The development of the CAP from these arguably slightly contradictory but nonetheless relatively balanced beginnings is a gradual and salutary tale of how a policy, over many years, can become distorted through losing touch with its original objectives, and develop a life of its own with little regard to the economic reality shaping the rest of the Community. The CAP today is a bloated and isolated policy relic within the EU, consuming vast resources, prey to fraud and criminality, subject to seemingly perennial reform and increasingly getting in the way of other important Community objectives. What has gone wrong? It is not necessary here to give the history of everything that has happened since the signature of the EC Treaty. Four major factors contributed to this policy disorientation. We shall now examine them.

First, the *farm support mechanisms* developed after the EC Treaty was signed, essentially over the period from the Stresa Conference of Agriculture Ministers in 1958 to 1968 (i.e. in the run up to the creation of the customs union), contained inherent distortions. The simplest thing is to quote from the 1992 Commission publication explaining the early days of the CAP (*Our Farming Future*):

> In order to create a single market for agricultural products, *prices were unified*. To prevent farmers in any one country from having to accept cuts, the price set for each product was generally the *price of the country where the product was most expensive*. The gap between world market prices and EC prices, which were already higher for most products, widened.
>
> So as to respect the principle of Community preference, EC products had to remain cheaper than imports on the European market. *Imports were therefore subject to import duties or levies* which ensured that they were more expensive than competing home products. By the same token, a system of *export subsidies was put in place* to enable EC products to be competitive on world markets.
>
> Financial solidarity was guaranteed by making the *EC budget the main financial instrument for operating and managing the CAP*. Member States no longer paid their own farmers directly; they made a contribution to overall costs via the budget.
>
> (p. 7; emphasis mine throughout)

It will be clear from this that the *price mechanism* became the heart of the farm support system, and it is also clear that the initial prices to be set were deliberately high – generally on the basis of the price that was the highest in the Community – and that these internal prices were increasingly divorced from world market prices.

How does this mechanism work in practice? There are, in fact, many different types of intervention, depending on the farm product in question (the main expenditure programmes are for support for cereals production, dairy products, olive oil, beef and veal, and sugar). The following is a (rather simplified) description of the classic price support mechanism as it was developed for cereals:

1 Every year a *target price* is set, which is the internal wholesale price for cereals thought to be obtainable in the highest cost, least agricultural region of the Community (in fact in the middle of the industrial Ruhr area in Germany).

2 From this is calculated the *threshold price*, which is below the target price, and represents the price at which imports are thought to be able to enter the Community without undercutting the target price (taking into account the handling charges and transport costs in moving such imports from the port to the Ruhr area).

3 Somewhere below these two prices is the *intervention price*, which is the minimum price within the Community below which cereals cannot fall, and at which the Community guarantees as buyer of last resort to purchase and take off the market all stocks presented to it, provided they meet certain specified criteria.

4 But somewhere below all of these is the fluctuating *world price* (which is the price which cereals are actually fetching on the market outside the Community). To ensure that such cereals only enter the Community at the above threshold price they are subject to import levies (or duties) based on the difference between the world price and the threshold price. And, in counterpart, because internal Community prices are higher than world prices, Community cereals can only be sold on the world market with the aid of subsidies (known as export restitutions) which make up the difference between the Community price and the world price.

There are therefore *three* specific types of potential market distortion inherent in this system. First, the effective internal EC price is high: it is derived from the highest obtainable internal market price. Second, imports into the Community are taxed (and thus restricted). Third, exports from the Community have to be subsidised from the Community budget.

In the early days of low productivity and low food self-sufficiency, such a farm support system may well have been appropriate. But clearly much must depend on the relationship between such an open-ended price support mechanism and the changing pattern of the Community economy. And this brings us on to the second main factor affecting the development of the CAP: the *rigidity of the system* – and in particular its inability to modulate the price mechanism in line with supply and demand.

The point is illustrated by the figures in Box 11. These show the degree of self-sufficiency in the Community for the main agricultural products since 1968 (in other words since the main mechanisms of the CAP came into effect). The structural economic change is fairly clear. During this period, across the spectrum of its farm output, *the Community shifted from being in a general position of under-supply to being in a general position of over-supply.* In other words, the Article 39 objective of increasing agricultural productivity was being met in spades.

The consequence of this is illustrated in Box 12, which shows the rising level of food stocks in the Community arising from the

Box 11 Agricultural self-sufficiency in the EC (%)							
	Total cereals	Wheat	Sugar	Fresh fruit	Butter	Cheese	Beef	Sheep and goat meat
1968/9 (EUR 9)	86	94	82	80	92	99	95	56
1973/4 (EUR 10)	91	104	100	82	98	103	96	66
1984/5	118	129	101	83	134	107	108	76
1985/6 (EUR 12)	119	120	126	88	130	106	106	80
1986/7	111	119	127	85	105	106	108	80

Source: *A Common Agricultural Policy for the 1990s* (1989)

Box 12 Level of public stocks in the Community (1000 t at end of year)				
	1979 EUR 9	1983 EUR 10	1986 EUR 10	1987 EUR 12	1988 EUR 12
Cereals	2,677	9,542	14,717	8,147	8,312
Olive oil	53	121	283	299	346
Skimmed milk powder	215	957	847	600	11
Butter	293	686	1,297	860	120
Beef (carcasses equivalent)	310	410	576	776	425
Alcohol (1,000 hl)	[–]	[–]	4,026	9,000	10,556

Source: *A Common Agricultural Policy for the 1990s* (1989)

guaranteed intervention mechanisms of the CAP in various types of farm product.

What appears to have happened is that, at some time during the mid-1970s, with some variation from product to product, the CAP began to get fundamentally out of balance, with a diminishing link between farm support prices and what the Community market actually needed or could consume in terms of farm products. This growing imbalance had a number of consequences, such as the mounting costs of intervention, to which we will turn in a moment.

The general point about the rigidity of the system leads, however, on to a third policy problem: *the way in which the detailed price mechanism was flawed in its execution.* As I have mentioned briefly, each year the Community sets prices for its main farm products (in the annual negotiation known, appropriately enough, as the 'price fixing'). These prices are crucial in that they determine the minimum price at which the Community guarantees to buy in products. However, until the most recent reforms, which we will come to, such prices bore little or no relation to the supply and demand situation within the Community. They were instead fixed by Agriculture Ministers in the Council in relation to the previous year's prices and as a function of a negotiation among member states over a global package of farm products, each seeking special treatment in the sectors of greatest national concern. In other words, the crucial price support levels within the Community were determined each year not by supply and demand, or even by objective economic criteria (for example, a Commission assessment of market needs), but by *political decision* – and by politicians under much more pressure from national producer interests to maintain high prices than from consumer interests to keep food prices low.

Why the pressure to keep prices high? The reason is fairly simple. Within the Community there is a wide variation in farm structures. Average national farm sizes vary from 65 hectares in the UK down to 4 hectares in Greece. The Community average size is only 9 hectares. The three top agricultural producers – France, Italy and Germany (in that order) – have average farm sizes of 27, 6 and 16 hectares respectively.[1] In simple numerical terms, small (relatively inefficient) farms greatly outnumber large (relatively efficient) farms across the Community. But in terms of farm output the position is reversed. About 80 per cent of all farm production is concentrated in the hands of only 20 per cent of farmers – the high-performance farm businesses. Prices – which are uniform across the Community – tend to be set at levels insufficient to keep small farms satisfied but nonetheless high enough to encourage big farms to overproduce. And because of this the political pressure is nearly always for prices to ratchet upwards, irrespective of the effects on larger, more efficient producers. It is rare for the Agriculture Council, for example, to agree on any farm prices that are *below* what the Commission have recommended.

Box 13 illustrates the trend of market support prices in the Community in the period 1980 to 1988, expressed in terms of annual percentage changes, in Ecus. In this period (as we have already seen) the Community was already more than self-sufficient in most products covered by the CAP (or in other words, demand was already saturated). And yet average Ecu support prices rose by as much as 28.8 per cent in the first four years of the decade, before being more or less frozen thereafter. In other words, even in a situation of structural surplus, prices rose and then remained pegged at a relatively high level, providing a continuing incentive to efficient producers to overproduce (although, as we shall see, not in fact providing enough for the average small farmer to make ends meet). (Against this it should of course be added that annual inflation would erode the effects of frozen farm prices: but then it should also be taken into account

Box 13 Support price changes (Ecu)	
1980	4.9%
1981	9.3%
1982	10.3%
1983	4.3%
1984	−0.4%
1985	0.1%
1986	−0.3%
1987	−0.2%
1988	−0.1%

Source: A Common Agricultural Policy for the 1990s (1989)

that regular annual increases in farm productivity – at an average rate of about 2 per cent a year – offset this).

The fourth factor contributing to a loss of policy direction was the *ending of the semi-fixed exchange rate regime within the Community* (see Chapter 6). As we have already seen, the fundamental principle of the CAP, as developed in the 1960s, was that there should be common prices for farm goods within the Community. But this can only work in a situation of exchange rate stability, otherwise a price expressed in common terms in one country will come to mean something different in another if the exchange rate between the two countries shifts. The ending of the Bretton Woods system in 1971 and the beginning of an era of floating currencies has made the objective of common farm prices much more difficult to put into practice.

The answer to this problem has been the development of an extraordinarily complicated and arcane system of shadow currencies, applied solely to agricultural goods in the Community, known as the *green currency system*. The origins of the green currency system in fact go back to 1969, when the French franc was devalued against the DM for the first time after the establishment of the main CAP support mechanisms. If the common support prices had continued as before, the result of this exchange rate realignment would have been increasing farm prices in France and decreasing prices in Germany. Neither country wished this to happen. France wanted to avoid it because higher farm prices would have meant higher food prices, at a time when domestic inflation was a problem: and Germany because lower farm prices would have meant a reduction in support for German farmers.

Thus it was agreed that farm support prices would continue to be expressed in the old exchange rates and these became known as the 'green' exchange rates. This idea became the basis of the green currency system: it is essentially *the deferral or lagging of effects of previous exchange rate realignments on farm support prices.*

Introducing green currencies for agricultural goods brought in its own problems, however. In the first place, in the real world, trade in farm goods continues to take place in market currencies (which will have just been realigned against each other). This means that a tonne of cereals produced at the intervention price in France (in this case) will, if shipped to Germany and converted into DM, be below the intervention price in Germany. This is what happened in 1969: cereals moved from France to be sold for DM in Germany, filling intervention stores in Germany and leading to undersupply in the French market. To get round this problem a system of Monetary Compensatory Amounts (MCAs) was developed, calculated to reflect the difference between green and market rates of exchange. These MCAs act as taxes on exports from the devaluing country to the revaluing country (in this case on exports from France to Germany) and also as sub-sidies on imports (in this case into France). They are levied at the border and administered by national agricultural authorities. In other words, the end result of the creation of this green currency system was the strengthening of the network of national border controls for farm products: precisely the opposite of the original intention of developing a common market in agriculture. The MCA system of border taxes and subsidies, with its array of taxes and subsidies varying from product to product, was done away with under the single market programme. But the green currency system remains.

Nor does the story end there. The very possibility of managed shadow 'green' currencies, which differ from real market curren-cies, throws up new policy problems. How long should green rates be allowed to diverge from market rates? To what products should green rates apply? In the UK in 1991, for example, there were four different green rates in force, depending on the farm product. Who decides, under what criteria, whether to realign on market rates? What to do in the case where one country (Germany) has a currency which is usually rising compared to the others, but where there is extreme reluctance to see real support price cuts to farmers? And so on.

Perhaps not surprisingly, what has happened in practice is that management and adjustment of the green rate system has become one more factor (and a very important one) in the political negotiations among agriculture ministers leading to the setting of farm support prices. Adjustment of the green currency to offset some of the effects of changes in common support prices has become a classic way of reaching agreement. Box 14 shows the effects of the same changes in support prices in the period 1980 to 1988 as in Box 13, but in this case taking into account green currency adjustments. The two columns of figures show how in nominal terms the end result of the common price changes in Box 13, expressed in national, market currencies, becomes a continuing stream of price rises. In real terms, that is after allowing for inflation in each member state, support prices in national currencies fell: but again, constant rises in farm productivity – particularly in intensive farming – offset this.[2]

Box 14 Support price changes (after green rate adjustments)		
	Nominal	*Real*
1980	4.5%	−3.9%
1981	13.3%	0.9%
1982	10.5%	0.6%
1983	6.6%	−2.5%
1984	3.3%	−3.5%
1985	1.8%	−4.5%
1986	2.2%	−0.7%
1987	3.3%	−1.1%
1988	0.6%	−3.2%

Source: A Common Agricultural Policy for the 1990s (1989)

One further refinement of the green currency system is that, to get round the problem that a country with a strong currency (Germany) will tend to see its support prices reduced as its currency rises, it was agreed in 1984 that a special co-efficient should be introduced which also revalues upward the central rate from which national green rates are calculated (the so-called 'green Ecu') and which thus drags all national support prices upward. In 1990 the Court of Auditors put the total additional cost of the green currency system to the EC budget at 1.8 billion Ecu (or about 7 per cent of farm support expenditure), of which the lion's share was due to this strong currency system.

My main point here, however, is that the green currency system, added to all the other distortions we have seen, is simply one more way of jamming the signals of the normal market price mechanism in European agriculture.

THE RESULTS

Reform of the CAP has become a way of life in the Community, from the introduction of quotas on milk production in 1984 to the MacSharry reforms of 1992 (currently under implementation). Before looking at what is being done it is worth considering the consequences of the developments we have just reviewed.

On the positive side, there can be no doubt that the CAP has achieved many of the original Article 39 objectives. Productivity has increased, food is abundant, markets have been stabilised (in the sense that prices do not fluctuate wildly), supplies reach consumers at 'reasonable' prices in Community terms (albeit higher than world prices) and, thanks to the effects of increased trade within the common market, the variety of foodstuffs actually on sale in Europe is probably greater than ever before. Nor can it be denied that other countries outside the EU also protect their agricultural systems, sometimes with even higher price support systems for some goods. In that sense the CAP is merely one manifestation of a global pattern of farm support systems, practised in a number of developed countries. And, when compared with the poverty of agricultural exploitation in eastern Europe, it can easily be demonstrated that too much food is better than too little. And yet enormous problems have built up.

One is the *budgetary cost* of maintaining a system of open-ended, demand-led support. It has meant that agriculture has from the outset dominated the Community budget, and still in 1993 represented about half of budget expenditure (while, at the same time, agriculture contributed only about 2.5 per cent to total EU GDP). Over the ten years to 1989 CAP expenditure almost quadrupled. From 1975 to 1989, in terms of *constant prices*, it expanded at a rate of about 7.5 per cent a year (three-and-a-half times the rate of increase in total EC GDP). In 1987 the CAP budget of almost Ecu 27 billion was rather larger than the

144

national budgets of Greece or Ireland. By 1992 the figure had risen to Ecu 36 billion, with a projection that without reforms it would rise to Ecu 42 billion by 1997 (and, even *with* the MacSharry reforms, would rise to Ecu 39 billion).[3]

Where does the money go? It goes, by and large, on storing and disposing of agricultural surpluses, the production of which has been encouraged by the price support mechanism. When Commissioner MacSharry presented his package of reform measures in 1991 he observed the following:

We have 20 million tonnes of cereals in intervention and that is predicted to rise to 30 million tonnes. We have almost one million tonnes of dairy products in stock. We have, also, 750,000 tonnes of beef in intervention which is rising at the rate of 15,000 to 20,000 tonnes a week. As no markets can be found for these products, they are being stored at taxpayers' expense; and we have run short of storage space.

(Preface to the *Development and Future of the Common Agricultural Policy*, contained in Bulletin of the European Communities, Supplement 5/91)

Thus it is that the bizarre situation has arisen that by far the largest part of CAP expenditure (and thus a dominant part of total EU budget expenditure) is devoted to purchasing, storing and disposing of surplus agricultural products which by definition cannot be sold on the saturated European market. In 1987, for example, about 55 per cent of total CAP expenditure went on either storing or disposing of surpluses (through export refunds or subsidies to bring the cost of products down to world price levels).[4] This means that over one-third of the entire EC budget in that year was spent simply on getting rid of unwanted foodstuffs.

Yet for all this expenditure the CAP has not helped farm incomes. As MacSharry pointed out: 'even with a 30 per cent increase in the farm budget, from 1990 to 1991, farmers' incomes in all Member States are set for further decline' (*The Development and Future of the Common Agricultural Policy* 1991). In fact, the problem is even worse if viewed over the long term. According to Commission figures, until 1978 average farm incomes in the Community remained approximately in step with those in other sectors of the economy, albeit with much greater year-to-year

145

variations. But from that time on they began to deteriorate and in 1988 the average real income of European farmers was actually below the level of the mid-1970s.[5] Why should this be? Mainly because, as we have seen, from about this time the Community started to move into a position of excess production, and the pressure of this surplus production had the effect of depressing both world and European markets.

But, it may be objected, did not agriculture ministers, as we have just seen, keep support prices at artificially high levels during this entire period? To which the answer is yes: but the common prices – although adequate to stimulate overproduction – were not high enough to satisfy the majority of farmers whose incomes make up the average. In fact, as MacSharry pointed out in 1991, 80 per cent of support goes to 20 per cent of farmers – the same 20 per cent who are responsible for 80 per cent of farm production.[6] Why is this? Because the price support system is linked to volume. The greater the production in volume terms, the greater the support. The principle of open-ended intervention simply means that, the more that is produced, the more subsidy is received (and, thanks to economies of scale and ever more intensive farm methods, the cheaper it is to produce also). But the majority of farms – the small, relatively inefficient farms which still constitute the EU norm – cannot enjoy such economies of scale, cannot produce in large enough volume to obtain sufficiently large subsidies to live off, yet nonetheless still suffer from relatively depressed markets caused by the surpluses of the over-producer. Once the EU moves into structural surplus for a farm product it is the majority who suffer, and they are forced under the price support system to take ever lower incomes or else move out of farming completely – as in fact a large proportion of the farm population have done.[7] This may of course over time lead to better farm structures through the survival of the fittest, but it is a Darwinian form of restructuring never intended by those who sought to modernise farming in Europe.

REFORMS

The unwinding of this situation is now being attempted through the major package of reforms known as the MacSharry Plan. Agreed by the Council in 1992, this is the most radical attempt ever to return the CAP to a situation of balance. The reforms are being put into place over the marketing years 1993–4, 1994–5 and 1995–6 and will affect most areas of the CAP. The main elements of the reform package are as follows:

- A substantial (29 per cent) cut in the support price for cereals over the three-year period (at the end of which cereals prices are expected to be close to current world market prices).
- At the same time cereals farmers will be eligible for direct financial compensation for the loss of earnings arising from price cuts. But to receive this they must also take part in a scheme to take a proportion of land out of production (set-aside) – for which they will also receive compensation. (NB: small farmers will receive more favourable treatment.)
- Beef prices will be cut by 15 per cent over the three years (with farmers compensated by payments per head of beef cattle, themselves linked to less intensive forms of animal rearing).
- There is a range of accompanying measures aimed at developing more environmentally friendly types of farming (less pesticides and fertilisers), afforestation and other types of land management. There will also be EU finance for an early retirement scheme for farmers.

The heart of this plan is the attempt to de-link financial support from the price mechanism: and thus both to target assistance to where it is needed and at the same time reduce the incentive to overproduce. Such a reform package is certainly not cheap (and, in the short term, may be even more expensive than the unreformed CAP). Nor is it easy to administer. Nor is it at first sight easy to defend a payments system linked to doing nothing with land (set-aside). But, taken as a whole, it is hoped that the package will, over the long term at least, be better and cheaper than the status quo and that it will end by returning European agriculture to some kind of balance. The high cost of doing so is essentially the price of accumulated policy failures of the past.

Irrespective of the details of the MacSharry Plan (which, like everything in agriculture, are being permanently modified and re-negotiated), some useful points of principle seem at least to have now been established. One is to have agreed a pluri-annual scheme with an element of predictability in it, which allows all concerned in the farming sector to make better long-term plans. Hitherto, everything depended upon an annual negotiation in the price fixing, the outcome of which was always unclear. Another point is that support prices for the main crop (cereals) are finally to be determined by reference to some objective criterion rather than by political negotiation among the member states. A third, obviously, is the introduction of the idea that farm support can come from something other than the price mechanism. A fourth is the reference, albeit tenuous, to the idea that internal prices might bear some relationship to world price levels. Were this actually to happen, the savings from the high cost of subsidising exports (export restitutions), traditionally taking up some 40 per cent of CAP expenditure, could be switched to better internal use. Running down CAP surpluses which overhang the market and bringing EU prices nearer to world prices would probably also help stagnant world prices rally.

It was in fact this prospect which helped unlock the negotiations concerning world trade in agriculture in the Uruguay Round of the Gatt, begun in 1986 and concluded in 1993. There was no formal linkage between the MacSharry reforms, which were always justified by the Commission as being needed purely on internal grounds, and the external negotiations in the Gatt which, for the first time ever, brought world trade in farm products within international rules. But the latter could not have happened without the former. The Gatt agreement, in so far as agriculture is concerned, is intended to reduce general levels of farm subsidy in all developed countries over a six year period, and in particular to reduce levels of subsidised farm exports on the world market and also to cut restrictions on imports of farm goods. Subsidised exports are to be cut by 36 per cent in value and 21 per cent in volume; and all import barriers are to be converted into tariffs (as for industrial goods in the Gatt) and cut by 36 per cent. The importance of reducing internal farm prices within the EU might now be clearer: the nearer they are to world prices the less the subsidy (export refund) needed to sell them on the world market, and also the lower the scale of duties on imports into the EU.

CONCLUSION

This battery of reforms, on both the internal and the external sides, may with luck return the CAP to some form of balance. But it is too early to say. Many other incremental reforms which have been tried since the 1980s have proved to have unforeseen drawbacks. A powerful case could be made that in such a complex area as agriculture, with so many variables of crop, climate and geography, and with such a wide disparity of structure and development among the farm holdings employing 9 million or so individuals, it is literally impossible to be certain of the implications of any large-scale plan. Set-aside schemes, for example, are always difficult to implement and, as has been found in the US, are by no means as effective as they seem in reducing output (since farmers tend to compensate by concentrating production on other land). Equally, direct income support involves a complicated network of payments, which may well develop its own problems (not to mention the potential for fraud). Moreover, there are plenty of new problems on the horizon: one such is the incorporation of the new agricultural area of East Germany, which was collectivised under communism and is now broken up into small family farms, into the new reformed CAP. Another will be the incorporation of Nordic and Alpine farm support systems, if and when Sweden, Finland, Norway and Austria join the EU.

Looking further ahead, the liberalisation of eastern Europe from communism will have its own impact on the CAP. Land reform there, and the ending of collective farms, will almost certainly lead to increased output, putting further pressure on the CAP. Indeed former Agriculture Commissioner Sicco Mansholt, who was directly involved in the early formation of the CAP, has suggested that the implications of changes in eastern Europe will be even greater for the CAP than the Gatt negotiations. In Mansholt's view, the MacSharry reforms will prove too complicated to work, and the debate on the future of the CAP, rather than ending, has only just begun. As a contribution to the debate he proposes shifting the basis of all future aid away from income support linked to set-aside and price cuts and towards a simpler per hectare partial compensation for the fixed costs of production.[8]

The main point on which I would like to conclude is to recall that the *objectives* of the CAP, and the way in which they are set out in the Treaty, have never really been the problem. One might of course argue that there should not have been an agricultural support policy in the first place, but, given the fact of pre-existing agricultural support mechanisms in the member states and their widespread use throughout the world, it is difficult to press this argument very far. Nor were the *principles* on which the CAP was later developed (a single agricultural market, Community preference and financial solidarity) necessarily outlandish (although it is much better to define 'Community preference' in terms of a global system of rules, as is now the case in the Gatt).

The real problems began when, gradually, the price support mechanism for farm products – the main determinant of supply – drifted away from any relationship with underlying demand, and prices became largely determined by the outcome of political negotiation among member states, themselves subject to differing pressures and requirements. Overlaying this basic distortion, the subtleties of the green currency system and the countless administrative changes introduced on an ad hoc basis (often in the name of reform) served only to increase the complexity.

This kind of administered farm economy, with ballooning costs and diminishing success in maintaining farm incomes, was a peculiar growth on the European body politic, owing little to the vision of those who drew up the Treaties. One might even argue that it was partly the absence of development of other parts of the EC Treaty (and in particular the inability to complete the common market) which contributed to this lop-sided growth. In 1989 agriculture was responsible for 7 per cent of employment in the Community, while industry accounted for 32 per cent and services 62 per cent.[9] But even in 1958 agriculture was only responsible for 19 per cent of employment, while industry accounted for 42 per cent and services 39 per cent. It is hard to avoid the conclusion that, had more attention been paid to services and industry and less attention to agriculture, the overall European economy would have been in a better shape, and quite possibly so would the farm sector.

In the period ahead – which no doubt will present new challenges, including the need to address post-communist eastern Europe, as we shall see in Chapter 9 – it will be important to distinguish carefully between the essential attributes of the CAP and what were in fact distortions which developed piecemeal and which should certainly not be allowed to stand in the way of future progress.

8

EXTERNAL RELATIONS

INTRODUCTION

The way in which the EU conducts its affairs with the rest of the world is distinctive and unusual – but perhaps no more distinctive and unusual than the way in which it conducts its internal affairs. It is no coincidence. There is a close link between the manner in which European integration has developed and the manner in which various types of collective relations are maintained with external bodies. In one sense, the EU is clearly a big player on the world stage. It is the world's largest trader; and now the European Economic Area accounts for some two-fifths of world trade. In global economic matters the EU, the US and Japan are predominant. By 1991 some 150 third countries had established accredited diplomatic missions to the Community in Brussels. Yet the EU has no seat at the UN Security Council, no unified diplomatic service, no military command, no armed forces and no weapons.

There are two legally distinct means by which the EU maintains external relations. The first is in the economic sphere and arises from the fact that certain economic powers, in particular in trade matters, have been transferred under the treaties from member states to European institutions. In such areas the Community (with the Commission as spokesperson) has real and distinct authority to represent the interests of the member states with third parties. The second is in the political sphere, and here the member states themselves (with the Presidency as spokesperson) combine to pool their national foreign policy objectives and instruments, with the aim of maximising their collective influence on the world outside. The second type of activity has been refined in the Maastricht Treaty into a 'common foreign and security policy' and it is put into a separate category from the first. (It will be recalled that there are three 'pillars' to the Maastricht Treaty: the first comprising the Community and its policies, including external trade matters; the second the common foreign and security policy; and the third co-operation in the fields of justice and home affairs.) Although in legal and procedural terms the economic and political spheres are distinct, the Maastricht Treaty does commit both European and national institutions to act in a consistent manner: 'The Union shall in particular ensure *the* consistency of its external activities as a whole in the context of its external relations, security, economic and development policies' (Article C). And it is in the European Council where the varying policies are, in the final analysis, intended to be reconciled under general policy guidance.

In this chapter I propose to look first at Community external relations proper and then at matters of common foreign and security policy. I shall then attempt some general conclusions about the role of the EU in the world.

EXTERNAL ECONOMIC RELATIONS

Even before the creation of the European Economic Area in 1994 (see below), the Community of the Twelve was the largest single trading unit in the world. In terms of overall trade with the rest of the world in 1989 the Community, with 16.2 per cent of world imports and 15 per cent of world exports, was slightly ahead of the United States (15.6 per cent and 12 per cent respectively) and much further ahead of the third major world trader, Japan (7 per cent and 9.1 per cent respectively). (It should be noted that this is only in terms of external trade – trade *between* Community countries is additional.) The main trading partners of the Community, in order of priority, were, in volume terms (again, before the creation of the EEA), the EFTA area, the United States and Japan. It is rarely appreciated just how big a market the EFTA area is for the Community: but it accounted for 23 per cent of Community imports and 26 per cent of Community exports in 1989 – considerably more than twice the share of trade with Japan.

The fact of being such a large trader itself (and having a comparatively large part of its total GDP arising from external trade) means that the Community has traditionally had a strong interest in an open world trading system. The preamble to the EC

Treaty talks of the desire 'to contribute, by means of a common commercial policy, to the progressive abolition of restrictions on international trade', and Article 110 sets out the aims of commercial policy as follows:

> By establishing a customs union between themselves Member States aim to contribute, in the common interest, to the harmonious development of world trade, the progressive abolition of restrictions on international trade and the lowering of customs barriers.

Despite the difficulties of reaching a final settlement on agricultural trade in the latest Uruguay Round (see Chapter 7) the Community is, in the words of the Commission, 'an enthusiastic supporter'[1] of the multilateral trading principles of the Gatt, which entered into force in 1948 and on which the world trade order has since been built. Successive rounds of tariff cutting plus the adoption of international trade rules within the Gatt have stimulated a strong steady growth in world trade over the post-war period (at an average growth rate of 8 per cent a year in the period 1950 to 1970), from which the Community has been a major beneficiary. Studies on the economic benefits of the Uruguay Round suggest that the EU once more is a strong beneficiary, with the bulk of its benefits coming from the reforms in agricultural trade.[2]

External trade policy for the EU is a direct consequence of the establishment of the customs union in 1968 as the basis of the (still developing) common market. The customs union, having abolished internal tariffs on trade, led to a common commercial tariff on goods from third countries (which, once they are within the customs union, circulate freely). By 1989 the Community's weighted average tariff level for industrial goods had, as a consequence of successive Gatt rounds, fallen below 5 per cent and the effective level, having taken into account various tariff preference agreements, was nearer 1 per cent.[3] (This excludes trade in the major agricultural goods covered by the CAP, subject to variable but high import duties, as explained in the previous chapter.)

Under Article 113 of the EC Treaty the common commercial policy is to be based on 'uniform principles, particularly in regard to changes in tariff rates, the conclusion of tariff and trade agreements, the achievement of uniformity in measures of liberalisation, export policy and measures to protect trade such as those to be taken in case of dumping or subsidies'. It is the Commission which has the responsibility of conducting negotiations on trade matters with third parties, in consultation with the Council. The Commission submits proposals to the Council and the Council, by qualified majority vote, approves both them and also the final agreement.

The Community has evolved a complex web of bilateral relations, codified in various types of agreements, with many of the world's industrialised and developing countries. We shall look at some of these in more detail. In addition, because of its competence in external commercial matters, the Community is represented in its own right in a number of multilateral spheres, including within the Gatt, in the OECD, in the Economic Summits of the G7, in various UN bodies and also as signatory to an increasing number of international agreements which touch on Community activity. The precise division of authority between the Community and the member states on some complex international issues is not always clear, and is sometimes in dispute. In the Gatt, for example, the member states are the contracting parties, since the Gatt predated the Community, but the Community has de facto sole negotiating authority. The relevant phrase from Article 116 of the Treaty is that 'Member States shall, in respect of all matters of particular interest to the common market, proceed within the framework of international organisations of an economic character only by common action' – which is clearly open to some differences of interpretation.

RELATIONS WITH THE UNITED STATES

It has often seemed in recent years that the relationship of the Community with the United States has been an uneasy one, characterised by trade tensions, threats of retaliatory action on the most esoteric goods and major disagreements within the Gatt.

Yet to imagine that the Community was from the outset conceived as an economic or political irritant to the United States could not be further from the truth. It is worth once more referring back briefly to the early days of European integration, after the Second World War.

Monnet, who contributed more than anyone to the creation of the Community, had the closest possible relationship with the

Americans both during and after the war. During the war he worked in Washington, first on negotiations on behalf of the French government for the purchase of military aircraft and then, after the fall of France in 1940, as a member of the British Supply Council. There, as an advisor to Roosevelt, he played a major role in the development of the crucial American military production plan, 'The Victory Program', which supplied weapons to the Allies, and in particular to the UK. After the war, Monnet maintained particularly close links with key American figures. He integrated the post-war French Modernisation Plan (for which he was responsible) into the US Marshall Plan for Europe. He made sure that Secretary of State Dean Acheson was briefed about the Schuman Plan for coal and steel from the outset. He even allowed American anti-cartel expert Robert Bowie to draft key anti-trust articles of the Treaty for the European Coal and Steel Community (see Chapter 1).

It was never Monnet's intention to unify Europe in opposition to the United States. His aim was precisely the opposite: it was to unify Europe so that it could work in co-operation with the United States in addressing the wider problems of the world. Monnet wrote:

> The United States and Europe share the same civilisation based on individual liberty and conduct their public life according to common democratic principles. The essential is there.
>
> (Monnet 1976: 689)

For Monnet the high point of transatlantic co-operation in the post-war period came with the brief Kennedy administration of 1961–3, when Monnet believed that there existed in Washington an echo of the spirit of the Roosevelt era. Kennedy's proposal in a speech in 1962 of a *partnership* between the United States and a united Europe, working on the basis of equality in dealing with global issues of common concern, was exactly in line with Monnet's own thinking. Monnet foresaw that economic and commercial differences between the two could only be kept in a proper context within the framework of a wider political whole:

> The countries united in the Community belong to the same western civilisation whose principles also rule American society: between these two great entities, very close but

155

distinct, a deep and constant dialogue is possible, in the ways established which are those of democracy.

(Monnet 1976: 710)

Monnet hoped that Kennedy's partnership idea would be put on a solid footing, to give body to this 'deep and constant dialogue'. To this end, in 1964 he proposed that there should be instituted a working committee comprising the United States and Europe. This would prepare common positions on current problems and thus help American and European institutions to arrive at decisions affecting both their economic relations and also their respective negotiations with the rest of the world.

What happened to this idea? It never bore fruit in Monnet's lifetime, to his disappointment. On the American side the assassination of Kennedy, the Vietnam war, and the tensions of the cold war all combined to reduce the urgency of the idea of a partnership with western Europe. On the European side, the anti-Americanism of de Gaulle in particular ensured that little progress could be made in his lifetime. De Gaulle's double veto of UK entry into the Community was linked to his fear that the UK was the American Trojan horse. Both Monnet and Kennedy, however, had hoped on the contrary that UK entry into the Community would help the policy of a partnership of equals to work. It was not until a full twenty-eight years after Kennedy's partnership speech that EC and US relations were put on to something like a formal footing with the joint 'Transatlantic Declaration' of 1990. In the intervening period a deep and constant series of trade disputes had replaced any idea of a deep and constant dialogue.

Monnet had originally envisaged a formal treaty between the United States and the Community, and the Transatlantic Declaration is something less than that (indeed in 1993 the Commission suggested that it would be 'premature' to institutionalise relations further).[4] Nonetheless, the Transatlantic Declaration does formalise a regular series of meetings and contacts between the two sides, including between the US President and the EU Presidents of the Commission and the Council, and between EU foreign ministers and the US Secretary of State. In addition, individual Commissioners with responsibility for policy areas overlapping with American concerns have established better contacts with their American counterparts.

What are the two sides talking about? For the most part about the very wide range of commercial problems thrown up by transactions between the two large trading economies. The foremost problem area has long been the Uruguay Round of trade liberalisation negotiations in the Gatt. From 1986 to 1993, when agreement was finally reached, this subject (and in particular the handling of trade in agricultural goods) dominated the agenda. The bilateral Blair House Agreement of 1992 set the basic terms under which subsidised farm exports would be reduced and (with some modifications) this was carried over into the final Gatt agreement in 1993 (see Chapter 7). Other recent items of EU–US discussion have included each other's public sector procurement policies, problems caused by world steel overcapacity, US taxation policy, public sector support to the aircraft industry and the reconciliation of differing industrial standards.

The successful conclusion of the Uruguay Round, despite the fact that, at least in agriculture, the two sides started out with positions far apart, might suggest that the EU–US relationship could well be further developed in the period ahead. There are many strong reasons for mutual understanding and agreement on the widest range of policy problems. The two regional economies depend on each other. The bilateral trading relationship is the most important in the world. In 1992 the EC took almost a quarter (23 per cent) of US exports and the US almost a fifth (17 per cent) of EC exports. In 1991 EC firms had accumulated a stock of investment in the US amounting to $232 billion (57 per cent of total foreign direct investment stock in the US) and US firms had accumulated a stock of investments in the EC worth $190 billion.[5] The creation of the North Atlantic Free Trade Area (NAFTA) in 1994 and the simultaneous development of the European Economic Area has widened the scope for transatlantic consultations. Completely new areas might yet arise where mutual agreements could be beneficial. One such could be global monetary policy and another could be the development of post-communist eastern Europe (on which see Chapter 9).

RELATIONS WITH JAPAN

When the Community was formed comparatively little thought was given to relations with the then under-developed Japan, although there is some evidence that Monnet hoped from the beginning that, in addition to the United States, the Community would also work with either Japan or China in a new organised world order.[6]

It was the more recent rise of Japan as a world trading power that brought EC–Japan relations more clearly to the foreground. More specifically, it has been the relative imbalance of the mutual trading relationship which has tended to dominate thinking. (As the Commission puts it: 'Trade tensions and trade disputes form a more constant feature of EC-Japan bilateral relations than between the Community and the USA.')[7] It is not so much the *volume* of trade between the Community and Japan which is the problem (the absolute levels have been much less than with either EFTA countries or the US) as what trade there is tends to be much more in the form of exports from Japan to the Community than the other way round. In 1991 the Japanese trade surplus with the EC amounted to $27 billion, which was itself a 48 per cent increase on the year before. While Japanese firms had by 1991 invested some $60 billion in EC firms, EC firms held only $3.5 billion worth of investments in Japan.[8] The contrast with the more or less balanced EC-US investment patterns mentioned above is striking.

In 1991 an EC–Japan Joint Declaration was signed. This was the first attempt to put the relationship on a more formal footing. The Declaration covers economic relations and includes a clause calling on both sides to allow equitable access to their respective markets and to remove obstacles in the way of expanding trade. The Declaration also aims at expanding political links and, for example, has established the practice of holding annual EU–Japan summits to discuss matters of joint interest.

However, on the Japanese side there has long been the concern that the relationship focuses too much on the economic problems caused by Japan's export surplus and not enough on other major global economic and political issues. The EU trade problem with Japan can be broken down into two parts: the difficulty which European firms have in obtaining access to the Japanese market; and the fears in the European market of being swamped by Japanese imports. The first problem is connected to the internal workings of the Japanese economy and is not just of concern to the EU; it has also been the source of much recent US–Japanese friction, including threats of US trade sanctions. It seems the more likely, therefore, that it can only be resolved on a wider basis than one of purely EU–Japan bilateralism. The strengthening of the rule-based trading system of the Gatt in the Uruguay Round might be of help here (and see below for more on this point). The second part of the problem, the purely domestic EU effects of large-scale Japanese exports and investment, turns out on closer inspection to be partly a problem and partly a solution – or at least a contribution to stimulating better EU economic performance. Inward investment as such, from whatever source, is invariably welcomed by the host country (and, by 1991, it was estimated that Japanese investment in the EC had created an additional 182,000 jobs).[9] The *dumping* of exports on the EU market at artificial prices is (if it can be upheld) a more serious matter – but here the EU has trade defence mechanisms and the strengthened anti-dumping rules in the Gatt Round will help clarify what is or is not dumping. In one sector deemed particularly sensitive – that of cars – the EC resorted to a somewhat dubious trade agreement in 1991 under which Japanese car manufacturers agreed not to exceed 16 per cent of the European market by the year 2000 (after which trade in principle will be liberalised). Although dubious on grounds of intent and likely effect, however, one should be fair and add that this kind of managed trade deal has to be seen against the background of increased market liberalisation in Europe through the single market programme – which benefits third country firms too – and an absence of matching liberalisation of the Japanese market.

I will add a little more in the conclusion about general EU–Japanese relations, but will leave the last word on this particular subject to US economist (and subsequently Labour Secretary) Robert Reich, who argued in *The Work of Nations* (1991) that, rather than attempting to restrict Japanese or other imports or investment, the US authorities should actually encourage them in areas where they increased the value added of American workers:

Government policy makers should be less interested in helping American-owned companies earn hefty profits from new technologies than in helping *Americans* become technologically sophisticated. It makes perfect sense, then, to encourage Sony, Philips, Thompson, NEC or any other global company to train Americans to design and make advanced semiconductors, high-definition televisions,

159

complex parts for jet aircraft, and other exotica of the future. Invite them in; we need the training.

(Reich 1991: 163; emphasis in original)

FROM EUROPEAN FREE TRADE AREA TO EUROPEAN ECONOMIC AREA

I have already mentioned that the European Free Trade Area, comprising Austria, Finland, Iceland, Liechtenstein, Norway, Sweden and Switzerland, was the single largest trading zone for the Community, responsible for around a quarter of total external trade. In 1994 there entered into force an agreement between the EU and all the EFTA countries (except for Switzerland) instituting the European Economic Area (EEA), creating what has been described by the Commission as the world's biggest integrated market, responsible in itself for more than two-fifths of all world trade. Total EEA GDP is put at $7,501 billion. This can be compared to the total GDP of $6,770 billion for the US, Canada and Mexico which at the same time in 1994 joined together in the North American Free Trade Agreement (NAFTA).

What is the European Economic Area, and how does it differ both from the existing European Free Trade Area and also from the process of straightforward enlargement of the EU to include the candidate countries of Austria, Finland, Norway and Sweden (a process still incomplete at the time of writing)? It may be helpful here to recall the original distinction between a common market and a free trade area, which was first covered in Chapter 1. The Spaak Report, when setting out the basis for the original EC Treaty, considered that, although both types of arrangements included the abolition of customs duties between member countries, there were two essential differences between them. First, a simple free trade area, by permitting the existence of separate national tariffs and, as a consequence, separate tariff negotiations with third countries, would in practice run into almost insurmountable practical difficulties among countries sharing common borders, as among the Six. Differing tariff regimes with third countries would mean that distortions of trade could only be avoided by somehow differentiating between member states' products and external products, and this would mean maintaining frontier controls between the member states.

160

The second objection was of an economic order. A free trade area would allow differing commercial and tariff policies towards third countries and thus the maintenance of differing exchange rates towards third countries. This would affect the equilibrium conditions and the nature of trade within the common market, and be an obstacle to the establishment of conditions guaranteeing stability and prosperity within the internal market.

For these two technical reasons the Spaak Report argued that a customs union, with a common external tariff, should be the basis of the common market. And, going beyond this, the whole thrust of the Spaak Report is that the creation of a common market implies the creation of an array of common economic machinery replacing national controls and regulations, if one market is really to replace individual national markets. That degree of economic integration is a step beyond free trade between separate national markets. Monnet, for his part, put the difference this way:

> There is a fundamental difference . . . between the Community, which is a method to unite peoples, and the Free Trade Area, which is a commercial arrangement. Our institutions take an overall view and establish a common policy; the Free Trade Area seeks to settle particular difficulties without placing them in the perspective of common action.
>
> (Monnet 1976: 668)

However, notwithstanding this difference of approach, the Spaak Report by no means ruled out the grafting of a free trade area on to the future common market of the six:

> [I]f there are decisive economic and technical reasons for the countries of the continent to opt for the formula of a customs union, they do not exclude the possibility of adding on to it a free trade area with another country where distance, transport and handling costs allow the maintenance of a separate tariff with regard to third countries without the risk of trade distortion.
>
> (*Rapport* 1956: 22)

What did happen was that after the signature of the Treaties of Rome in 1957 the UK, plus Austria, Denmark, Norway, Portugal,

Sweden and Switzerland, created between them the European Free Trade Area (EFTA). When the UK and Denmark joined the Community in 1973 individual free trade agreements were then negotiated between the Community and each of the remaining EFTA countries over the period 1972–3, which abolished all customs duties and quantitative restrictions on industrial goods between the signatories. These formed the basis of EC–EFTA relations until the entry into force of the EEA agreement in 1994 (although it had already been agreed ten years earlier that efforts should be made to intensify co-operation).

What does the EEA agreement add to these existing free trade arrangements? In the first place it takes into account the deepening of economic integration within the Community itself since 1972–3. As we saw in earlier chapters, the single market programme extended the common market beyond industrial goods, and the Single European Act of 1986 enshrined the principles of the free movement of goods, services, people and capital. The EEA agreement accordingly extends these principles to the entire eighteen nation bloc (albeit with some limitations). The liberalisation of public procurement markets and the free movement of services and capital within the entire area are likely to be particularly important innovations. Financial services, for example, will be subject to the same single passport procedure that has been introduced for Community firms, as we saw in Chapter 5. In the area of technical standards, mutual recognition (Chapter 3) will be the rule.

In the second place the EEA agreement creates a new institutional system to enforce common rules in this wider market. The EFTA countries have set up a body which in some respects mirrors the Commission, known as the Surveillance Authority, which has the responsibility of ensuring that contracting parties fulfil their EEA obligations. An EFTA Court has also been set up to arbitrate on differences within the EFTA area. Under the EEA agreement both competition policy and state aid rules fall to the Surveillance Authority to administer.

In the third place the EEA agreement extends a number of co-operation-type arrangements which have been developed within the Community to the EFTA nations. Examples are co-operation in the areas of research and development, social policy, the environment and education.

At the same time, however, the EEA agreement falls short of

extending to the EFTA countries the entire degree of economic and political integration which had taken place within the Community even before the Maastricht Treaty came into effect. A number of points are noteworthy here.

First, the EEA is not a formal customs union. There is no common commercial policy. Relations with third parties will, as the EFTA Secretariat has put it, 'inevitably have to be co-ordinated to some extent', but this is to be on a case by case basis. There is, in particular, no transfer of member states' authority to a single body responsible for maintaining EEA external trade policy.

Second, some areas of economic integration are still excluded from the agreement. One such is the Common Agricultural Policy (and the counterpart to this is that trade in agricultural goods is still restricted within the EEA). Another is harmonisation of fiscal policy. A third is monetary integration, either in the shape of the EMS or through economic and monetary union.

Third, the political aspects of integration, notably the creation of a common foreign and security policy under the Maastricht Treaty, are also excluded. There is no formal citizenship of the EEA.

Finally, the constitutional/legal relationship between individual EFTA country and the EEA is not that of the member state to the EU. As the EFTA Secretariat has put it: 'Unlike in the Community there will be no transfer of legislative power from the contracting parties to the EEA institutions'.[10] Although this might look at first sight like the holy grail of integration without tears, things are not that straightforward. Instead, through the act of signing the EEA agreement, the individual EFTA countries have committed themselves to incorporating within their national legislations a backlog of some thirty years of Community legislation, most of it concerning the common market and none of which they had direct control in drawing up. In addition, the degree of influence of EFTA countries over *future* EU legislation affecting the EEA will be limited. There will be an EEA Joint Committee, comprising the Council of the EU and the Standing Committee of EFTA, which will endeavour to reach a consensus between them on decisions affecting the overall EEA, but in which the institutions of the EU retain decision-making authority.

It is difficult to be categorical about the content of and prospects for the EEA. On the one hand it is clearly something more than a free trade area. It creates a wider rule-based system, and through that it extends the four freedoms of the single European market (at least in principle) to most of western Europe ('from the Arctic to the Mediterranean', as the Commission puts it (*European Economic Area* 1992: 1)). On the other hand it is something less than an extended EU – and even less than an extended common market, as developed since the 1950s. The fact that it is less than the EU, and that EFTA countries have less of a say than EU member states in common decision-taking, have been factors behind the decisions of Austria, Finland, Norway and Sweden to apply for full membership of the EU more or less at the same time as negotiating the EEA agreement. In 1994 these candidate countries agreed basic membership terms with the EU and (following referenda in each) Austria, Finland and Sweden were set to join the EU in 1995, but with Norway once again voting not to participate.

So what will remain of the EEA? In a national referendum in 1993 Switzerland voted not to join it. Once the three candidate countries do actually join the EU the EEA will then in effect be shrunk to a trading area between an enlarged EU, Norway, Iceland and Liechtenstein. This seems little to show for one of the most complicated pieces of international legislation in modern times. On the other hand, the process of incorporating EU legislation by the EFTA countries will have been started (which will have made the formal accession negotiations easier). If any of the four applicants vote not to join the EU the EEA will remain as a safe haven. The innovations in institutional terms which the EEA introduced might yet have some future bearing elsewhere – for example in relations with post-communist eastern Europe.

RELATIONS WITH DEVELOPING COUNTRIES

The Community and the member states, if added together within the EU, would constitute the largest donor of aid to developing countries in the world. They were responsible for some $22.8 billion of assistance in 1989 – three times that of the United States. In practice, however, this assistance is split in various ways according to both donor and recipient, and so the net effect is rather more one of dispersal of effort than concentration of resources to achieve certain specific goals. Differing member states have differing types of aid programmes and differing regional and

164

political priorities: nor do these necessarily coincide with EU priorities as such. There are in particular differing views about how far aid should be linked to economic and political reform.

Within the strictly Community sphere of operations the principal instrument of assistance is the *Lomé Convention* between the Community and sixty-nine *African, Caribbean and Pacific* (ACP) countries. Updated regularly (the most recent Convention runs from the period 1990 to 2000), the Lomé Convention provides both a package of financial aid and also preferential trade access for exports from the ACP states to the Community market. The total amount of aid most recently made available comes to Ecu 12 billion, paid for by the member states into a fund separate from (and additional to) the normal EU budget. All aid is now non-repayable, with the exception of risk capital and European Investment Bank loans. Virtually all (99 per cent) of ACP products are allowed into the Community market duty free.

In addition, there are a number of co-operation agreements with the developing countries of *Asia and Latin America*, who receive some project aid from the budget and who are also (as are the ACP) eligible to receive food aid, if necessary. Trade access is not as generous as for the ACP, but manufactured and semi-manufactured goods are offered duty free access under the Community's Generalised System of Preferences (which is of UN origin).

Finally, in rather a separate category are the various co-operation or association agreements which the Community has signed with the *countries of the Mediterranean*. Although these differ in their political content and form (the agreements with Turkey, Cyprus and Malta, for example are each intended to lead to the establishment of a customs union; and the agreement with Turkey envisages full membership of the Community), they do contain some common features. In particular they allow for unlimited duty free access for industrial goods into the Community market, plus some concessions on Mediterranean agricultural goods like fruit and vegetables, wines and olive oil. (Following the accession of Spain and Portugal in 1986 the Community committed itself to try to maintain traditional trade flows for agricultural goods from the Mediterranean). In addition each agreement contains a financial protocol setting out the terms of loan and grant finance made available by the Community.

FROM POLITICAL CO-OPERATION TO COMMON FOREIGN AND SECURITY POLICY

So far virtually everything we have looked at in this chapter could be considered to be part of the first 'pillar' of the Maastricht Treaty, which means that it touches on the legal competence of the Community proper. But there is next the question of the foreign and security policy of the EU itself, which falls into a different legal category, one where the member states meeting within the Council retain their own authority.

The basic ideas behind the creation of a European foreign policy are not new, and can be broken down into two essential parts: first that there should be the maximum consultation *between* the member states on all matters of international relations, so that there is the greatest possible mutual understanding of each other's positions; and second that as far as possible the member states should present a common front towards third parties, to the extent of taking *joint action* where necessary.

This kind of political co-operation between the foreign policy authorities of the member states, based on the idea of maximising their influence on the world outside, has been taking place for some time, and long before there was any formal Treaty basis. Since 1970 a machinery of consultations has been developed involving regular meetings of EC foreign ministers, the creation of a network of official-level contacts and committees, and a direct telegram communications system between foreign ministries (which by-passes local embassies). In this way a 'reflex of co-ordination' has been established among the member states which, at the very least, has reduced the scope for misunderstandings about each other's intentions when external crises occur. This may seem a routine matter, but one has only to think back to the traditional methods of conducting foreign policy among the European powers, and how rapidly differences of view about external events can become part of internal conflicts. Here I would simply quote from a speech which Churchill made in the House of Commons in 1934, when he wished to show how quickly war can break out:

> Let me remind the House of the sort of thing that happened in 1914. There was absolutely no quarrel between Germany and France. One July afternoon the German Ambassador drove down to the Quai d'Orsay and said to M. Viviani, the

French Prime Minister, 'We have been forced to mobilise against Russia, and war will be declared. What is to be the position of France?' The French Prime Minister made the answer, which his Cabinet had agreed upon, that France would act in accordance with what she considered to be her own interests. The Ambassador said, 'You have an alliance with Russia, have you not?' 'Quite so,' said the French Prime Minister.

(Cannadine 1989: 109)

As well as developing the habit of co-ordination, real joint action *has* often been undertaken by the member states. Examples include economic sanctions against Argentina after the invasion of the Falklands and various measures against South Africa aimed at combating apartheid. It is the Presidency of the day which usually takes charge of decision-taking.

The 1986 Single European Act largely codified existing practice within what were called 'Treaty Provisions on European Co-operation in the Sphere of Foreign Policy'. Under this part of the Treaty the member states (known as 'High Contracting Parties' to differentiate them from Community institutions) agreed to 'endeavour jointly to formulate and implement a European foreign policy' and to ensure that 'their combined influence is exercised as effectively as possible'. It was also agreed that 'The external policies of the European Community and the policies agreed in European Political Co-operation must be consistent' (SEA: Article 30). On the institutional side there was created a small Secretariat, based in Brussels, to assist the Presidency in preparing and implementing the activities of political co-operation, and also to deal with administrative matters (communications, meetings and so forth).

So it was that the drafters of the Maastricht Treaty of 1992 had two decades of experience to draw on when they set out in Title V the 'Provisions on a Common Foreign and Security Policy'. In substantive terms the basic ideas have changed little. In Article J.2 the member states agree to inform and consult one another on matters of foreign and security policy (that is similar to the internal function mentioned above). In Article J.3 a procedure is elaborated for taking joint action (in other words the external function mentioned above). So what is new?

In the first place there is an attempt, for the first time, to put into

Treaty form what the objectives of a common foreign and security policy might be. These are set out in Article J.1 but cannot be said to be inspired in their drafting. They include 'to safeguard the common values, fundamental interests and independence of the Union', 'to preserve peace and strengthen international security' and 'to promote international cooperation'. There is though a potentially useful reference 'to develop and consolidate democracy and the rule of law, and respect for human rights and fundamental freedoms'.

In the second place the former High Contracting Parties have become the member states. And this connects to the institutional architecture of the Maastricht Treaty itself – the member states meet within the Council, and the Council has a dual purpose. On the one hand it is the decision-taking body of the Community – a Community institution, in other words – and on the other hand it is the place of assembly of the member states – a forum for intergovernmental co-ordination and co-operation. It is the same representatives of the member states, however, who meet and act in these two legally distinct ways: in the former sense as legislators (whose laws are subject to review in the Court of Justice) and in the latter sense as foreign ministers, who may engage the political responsibility of their governments but whose decisions do not have the force of law. This dual function has existed within the Community from the outset, and there have been numerous cases of member states' representatives switching from legislative to political mode while hardly being aware of doing so. What Maastricht does is to build on the dual function of the Council by putting into Treaty form the concept of the European Union, which includes both the Community and also types of intergovernmental co-operation. The 'common' in common foreign and security policy is (perhaps deliberately) misleading. It is common in the sense that it takes place within the Council but there is no implied transfer of legal authority as in other Treaty areas where a common policy comes into effect: and (as Article L of Maastricht says) the powers of the Court of Justice do not apply to this area of the Treaty.

Third, an elaborate procedure is invented whereby in certain areas 'joint action' may be undertaken, not on the basis of consensus or unanimity, but by qualified majority vote. There is a catch, though. First the Council must decide the area for joint action, then only within that those matters on which decisions are to be taken by a vote. Since such prior decisions are to be unanimous the practical scope for voting is much circumscribed. Moreover, issues having defence implications (see below) are excluded entirely.

Fourth and finally, this element of *defence* is brought into play for the first time. In the Single European Act the High Contracting Parties considered that 'closer co-operation on questions of European security would contribute in an essential way to the development of a European identity in external policy matters' (SEA: Article 30). This is strengthened in Maastricht: hence 'common foreign *and security* policy'. Maastricht makes clear in Article J.4 that 'The common foreign and security policy shall include all questions related to the security of the Union.' And, it continues, 'including the eventual framing of a common defence policy, which might in time lead to a common defence'.

There is a long history to the idea of a common European defence. It was the failure to get agreement on the European Defence Community Treaty in 1954 (which took the institutional arrangements for the Coal and Steel Community and applied them to setting up a European Army) which caused the crisis among the Six out of which the Treaties of Rome were born. The basic argument over the years has been the extent to which any European defence identity is linked to or separate from the existing defence arrangement for western Europe within Nato, which in turn depends upon the American guarantee for its credibility. (This is not the place for a discussion of military doctrine, but it is interesting to note in passing that the European Defence Community itself *would* have been linked to Nato, and that there was close American involvement in its creation since it was designed essentially as a means to rearm Germany without alarming France. In addition one should remember that Nato itself is no stranger to the debate about the credibility of the American guarantee to Europe: indeed much Nato strategic thinking has revolved around this very subject.)

The Maastricht Treaty deals with this issue by saying in Article J.4.4 that the policy of the EU 'shall respect the obligations of certain Member States under the North Atlantic Treaty and be compatible with the common security and defence policy established within that framework'. It proposes, not that the Community or its institutions should take on defence responsibilities, but rather that a wholly separate body entitled (somewhat confusingly) the Western European Union (WEU) should be charged with elaborating and implementing 'decisions and actions of the Union which have defence implications'. And – illustrating the way in which the concept of the European Union is something rather elastic – it says also that the Western European Union 'is an integral part of the development of the Union'.

What is the Western European Union? And how can it be considered an integral part of the development of a European Union established by the Maastricht Treaty itself? The WEU was the successor arrangement to the failed European Defence Community. It arose in the 1950s from the continuing American pressure to find another vehicle for the rearming of Germany as a contribution to European defence against the Soviet Union. In 1954 Germany and Italy signed a modified treaty from 1948 which covered defence relations between the UK, France and the Benelux countries, and this then became the stepping stone to full German membership of Nato in 1955. This 1954 treaty established the WEU, but the WEU itself was never much more than a shell because between 1948 and 1954 the Atlantic Alliance had come into being, with the additional American commitment to European defence. Nonetheless, the WEU does continue to exist, with a current membership of nine of the EU member states (all except Ireland, Denmark and Greece), and it provides a distinctive point of co-ordination of European views on defence matters.

Under the Maastricht Treaty this somewhat ancient institution, which predates the Treaty of Rome, is intended to become part of the development of the European Union itself. However, the Treaty is not crystal clear as to precisely how. In a Declaration on the WEU annexed to it, it suggests that this will be a gradual process involving successive phases: 'WEU will form an integral part of the process of the development of the European Union'. A first phase will be the development of a close working relationship between the WEU institutions and those of the EU, helped by the transfer of the former to Brussels. A progress report will be made by the WEU on developments in 1996, and this will form the basis of a report to the European Council (which presumably will take account of such suggestions in the revision of the Maastricht Treaty in 1996).

Behind these institutional complexities the underlying idea is that the WEU should become the 'defence component' of the European Union, 'as a means to strengthen the European pillar of the Atlantic Alliance' (Declaration on WEU annexed to Maastricht: Articles 3 and 4). To help this all EU member states are invited to become members or observers of the WEU.

Since this development of a defence component of the EU is self-evidently a gradual business, it is difficult to say anything conclusive about it at this stage. It is certainly a radical step for the EU to develop a defence dimension. But, on the other hand, it is made very clear in the Treaty that this will be in close collaboration with Nato: 'Close cooperation will be established between the Secretariats-General of WEU and Nato' (Declaration on WEU: Article 4). Equally, it has long been common currency on both sides of the Atlantic that more should be done to strengthen European defence, if only to continue to encourage the American commitment to the continent. In certain respects the WEU appears to be seen by the drafters of the Maastricht Treaty as a kind of *bridge* between the European Union and the Atlantic Alliance, which may prove to have its uses.

However, there is room for some doubt over the overall approach adopted. It is hard to avoid the general impression that the Maastricht Treaty was driven by questions of internal procedure without any clear connection to events in the world outside. In the past, developments in European defence have usually been linked to fairly clear objective problems (the post-war threat from the Soviet Union, the problem of rearming Germany). Here the impulsion was from within – the desire to round off the foreign and security policy of the EU with a defence component. There is no apparent reference or connection to the two momentous events which have completely changed the strategic landscape in Europe: the unification of Germany in 1990 (and the integration of former East Germany into both the EU and Nato) and the winding up of the Warsaw Pact itself. This changed strategic landscape suggests that the most urgent task facing the WEU is not so much working out a defence organigram as defining a new defence philosophy. This is certainly not to deny the usefulness of a European defence identity; it is merely to suggest that unless it is related to external developments – and in this case the effects of the collapse of communism in eastern Europe – it risks remaining a paper exercise. At present the more immediate threat to general European security seems to arise not so much from an organised military attack from the east as from organised crime benefiting from economic dislocation.

It is equally a little early to say anything definitive about the wider concept of a common foreign and security policy. The Maastricht Treaty only entered into force in late 1993, and at the time of writing it would be difficult to point to the EU doing anything (other than internal re-organisation) which was not already done under political co-operation. The European Council at the end of 1993, for example, adopted various declarations of a foreign policy nature, concerning the holding of a conference on a Stability Pact for Europe, on former Yugoslavia, on the Middle East and on relations with Israel, none of which differ materially from what might have been agreed prior to Maastricht.

The problems of the former Yugoslavia are often held to be the test case of the usefulness or otherwise of a common foreign and security policy. But here again it is hard to be conclusive. On the one hand it is clearly highly desirable for the EU to speak with one voice about such a sensitive and volatile conflict taking place right on its borders. On the other hand, it would be a mistake to assume that even a common European policy will of itself solve all such complicated external problems, particularly those where the logic of reason and legality which underpins the EU is suspended. The fact that, in relation to Bosnia, it required the threat of military action by Nato to make progress – and subsequently the political engagement of both the United States and Russia – merely shows that after conflicts have degenerated beyond a certain point they require greater force to resolve. That does not detract from the usefulness of a united European view – indeed the historical dangers of disunited European views about events in the Balkans have often been pointed out. And nor should one extrapolate from events in the former Yugoslavia to assume that the EU is hopelessly ill-equipped to deal with the rest of eastern Europe. On the contrary, as I shall suggest in the next chapter, the EU is in fact rather well-equipped and well-positioned to put in place a wider policy towards eastern Europe – one designed to ensure that such a breakdown in the structure of society does not repeat itself.

CONCLUSIONS

So far much attention has been paid, particularly within the EU member states and institutions, to the developing nature of the EU in the world: how it should organise its decision-making; how it should aim at a common voice; how it should 'safeguard the common values, fundamental interests and independence of the Union', as the Maastricht Treaty puts it. But perhaps not enough attention has been paid to the nature of the world which the EU is actually coming to inhabit. It is on this point that I would like to conclude.

The ending of communism may be thought of as the ending of the last systematic attempt by national political authorities to direct and control economic activity. The world that has emerged at the end of the long communist experiment is not the same as it was at the beginning. In the intervening period a global economy has been developing, with economic factors and information technology rapidly eroding the meaning of old political boundaries. There seems every reason to assume that this process will continue, and perhaps accelerate, in the future. That process no doubt contributed to the collapse of communism, just as it makes the retention of any system involving the restriction of information less viable.

It is in this emerging global market that the EU must make its way. The growth of international factors of production, and the mobility of many of today's most advanced industries, have already led to existential worries about the EU losing competitiveness, or being overtaken by other fast-growing regions of the world. Such concerns may or may not be valid. There is at least an element of cyclical pessimism about them. But there is another side to the story, which is relevant to this chapter. That is that the global market is not just affecting the EU. It is affecting all the major economies of the world. The US and Japan, as much as the EU, are seeing their power (or 'sovereignty') eroded by this global revolution. The attempt to control the economy swept away the former Soviet Union; and the same forces are now weakening public controls everywhere. In Japan the conclusion of the Uruguay Round will mean a change in the relationship between government and the private sector (initially in agriculture, but also in wider terms). And in the US Robert Reich – a prominent member of the Clinton administration – has written an entire book on the implications of his thesis that the massive US economy has become but a region of the world economy (Reich 1991).

This general global trend has, I believe, important implications for the development of the EU. On the negative side it suggests that to see the EU as only becoming something like one large nation state, on the traditional model, is to miss an important point. In the global economy nation states – even large ones – are simply being overtaken by events. To recreate on a bigger scale a model of society which has proved to be inadequate, first on a European and now on a global level, would be to replace one error with another. That is the intellectual weakness of all models which take what has simply been the norm at the level of the nation state and transpose it onto the European level. It is quite true to say that in many areas the EU would be better for stronger powers, or for concentrating its existing powers better. But that is quite different from saying that *all* powers should be unified, or that only by a unification of powers can the EU have any real influence on the world outside. On the contrary: a pluralistic system, with a separation of powers, may well be better adapted to the world that is emerging.

Indeed one might go further. The fact that European integration has allowed a rule based political economy to develop among the member states of the EU may actually have prepared them all the better, individually and collectively, for the emerging global economy. Having become used to operating in an environment which encourages the settlement of individual differences in favour of the common good – no matter how difficult that may prove to be – may actually prove an advantage in a world where Europe is but one region among several. In particular, the setting up of the World Trade Organisation as a consequence of the agreement on the Uruguay Round in the Gatt, which will help extend international rules throughout the world trading economy, may do something similar in terms of minimising unilateral state interference with world trading matters to what the Treaties have done within Europe.

If the extension of a rule-based international trading system can be seen as a natural counterpart to the economic aspects of EU external relations, what of the second of the two spheres with which I began this chapter? What about the *political* dimension of external relations in this unifying world economy?

Here I would make a specific suggestion. This is that the EU cannot proceed unilaterally. It needs political allies. Not allies so much in the old balance of power sense of projecting influence over the rest of the globe. In a global economy 'power' as traditionally understood, except in the narrow meaning of military power, simply escapes the control of those who would attempt to use it. What the EU needs instead are allies who share similar political and economic values, and in particular the commitment to *share power* through the development of a wider pluralistic international society.

The original Monnet idea of the Community and the United States working together could certainly form part of this approach. In the post-cold war (and post-Uruguay Round) world there may be at last the opportunity to develop the idea of *partnership* which has been elusive for so long. But we could perhaps do better. There could be added to the relationship a new third partner – that of Japan. The EU, North America and Japan jointly account for more than 70 per cent of total world GNP. Their mutual trading relations dominate the world economy. A trilateral system of political co-ordination – a trilateral 'deep and constant dialogue', possibly enshrined in a new trilateral treaty – would not of course solve all the problems of the world. But it might be the best place to start when addressing many of them. Such an approach could have benefits for each partner. For the EU it might be the basis from which post-communist Europe is brought further into the world economy (for more on which see Chapter 9). For Japan it would be an opportunity to develop wider political responsibilities to match its economic strength. And for the United States it might be the venue to draw up the rules of the 'positive economic nationalism' which Reich has called for, one 'in which each nation's citizens take primary responsibility for enhancing the capacities of their countrymen for full and productive lives, but who also work with other nations to ensure that these improvements do not come at others' expense' (Reich 1991: 311).

For all three partners – who between them exercise predominant influence in the American, European and Asian regions – trilateral co-ordination could be the starting place for building on the success of the Uruguay Round in extending the rules of the world trading sector. It could be the starting place for creating a wider rule-based international order, governing all aspects of political and economic life in a world economy where the division of labour is becoming ever greater.

9

THE COLLAPSE OF
COMMUNISM

INTRODUCTION

It was the refusal by the Soviet Union and its satellites to participate in the formulation of the United States-led Marshall Plan in
1947 – on the grounds that it would infringe national sovereignty
– that confirmed the rupture in the political economy of Europe
and the reality of the iron curtain. In the west, post-war reconstruction under the Marshall Plan led to the rebuilding of market
economies, first on a national and then on an international scale.
To the east, state-controlled and centrally planned economies
developed on completely different lines, linked by a framework
of co-operation with the Soviet Union (enforced if need be by
military strength).

At about the same time as the logic of a unified western
European market was being explored in the Spaak Report (see
Chapter 1), an ostensibly parallel process was under way in eastern Europe. Only two years after the Treaties of Rome were
signed, the Council for Mutual Economic Assistance was
launched in 1959 between Albania, Bulgaria, Czechoslovakia, the
German Democratic Republic, Hungary, Poland, Romania and
the USSR. It is illuminating now to recall the original purposes
and principles of the CMEA (or Comecon, as it was widely
known). According to its 1959 Charter, they were as follows:

1 The purpose of the Council for Mutual Economic Assistance is
to promote, by uniting and co-ordinating the efforts of the
member countries of the Council, the *further deepening and
perfecting of co-operation and the development of socialist economic
integration*, the planned development of the national
economies and the acceleration of the economic and technical

progress of those countries, the raising of the level of industrialisation of the countries with a less-developed industry, a continual growth in productivity, the gradual approximation and equalisation of the levels of economic development, together with a steady increase in the well-being of the peoples of the member countries of the Council.

2 The Council for Mutual Economic Assistance is based on the principle of the *sovereign equality of all the member countries of the Council.*

Economic and scientific-technical co-operation between the member countries of the Council shall take place in accordance with the principles of *socialist internationalism*, on the basis of *respect for state sovereignty, independence and national interest, non-interference in the internal affairs of countries*, complete equality of rights, mutual advantage and friendly mutual aid.

(International Organization and Integration 1983, Vol. II. C. 2a: 1; emphasis mine).

It is interesting how, with all its emphasis on sovereignty, independence and the national interest, the CMEA had in fact very little to do with economic integration as we have seen it so far. In the jargon of the EU it could be described in fact as a huge exercise in inter-governmentalism – it concerned a network of government to government, state sector to state sector and bureaucracy to bureaucracy relations. It was precisely the opposite of what Monnet had once said the Community should be:[1] it was not a union of peoples but instead a coalition of states – and, moreover, states exercising dominant control within each nation (and, of course, themselves dominated by the largest state of all).

The economic principles underlying the Community and the CMEA could not have been more different. Whereas the common market was based upon the principle of the division of labour and the objective of merging separate national markets into one, the CMEA was based upon the idea of managed trade – managed, that is, by official economic planners in each country who shifted resources around in line with Communist Party thinking (in itself, of course, reflecting priorities set by Moscow). In the Community strong rules of competition (as we have seen from Chapter 4) allowed the price mechanism to operate in allocating resources and kept national authorities in check: in the CMEA global annual plans for cross-border volume flows were drawn up and each individual member state had a firm role in implementing them by allocating import and export quotas to (state-owned) companies, as well as fixing border prices.

Increasingly seen in its latter years as a hindrance rather than a stimulus to trade (which had in fact been stagnating since the mid-1980s), the CMEA was wound up by its members when they shifted to market-based systems following the collapse of communism in eastern Europe. It was formally dissolved in 1991 (the same year that in western Europe the Maastricht Treaty was being drawn up). But dismantling the CMEA did not bring in a sudden increase in trade flows between former members. On the contrary, the immediate effect was that (partly because the old CMEA settlement system disappeared, but also because of general economic dislocation) there was a sudden and dramatic drop in volumes of regional trade (by around one-half in 1991 alone). Trade to and from the former Soviet Union was particularly badly affected. Trade between what was the GDR and the other CMEA countries virtually came to a standstill following German reunification in 1990.

RE-INVENTING THE STATE

The collapse in trade in central and eastern Europe was only one of the effects of the collapse of communism. Although it is difficult to measure what has happened precisely, it seems clear that there have been large drops in economic output more or less everywhere. Real GDP appears to have been falling since 1990 and is estimated to have dropped in aggregate terms in central and eastern Europe as a whole by 11 per cent in 1991 and 4 per cent in 1992: and in the former Soviet Union by 11 per cent and 19 per cent respectively.[2] Thus, at a time when western Europe has been worried by growth levels which have at least been positive, eastern Europe has experienced severe economic contraction (and, of course, from a much lower starting point). Monetary conditions have been chaotic. Although in some central European countries inflationary pressures seem to be cooling, hyper-inflation has ravaged much of the former Soviet Union. There has, partly as a consequence, been massive capital flight from the Russian Federation in particular. Unemployment is either rising or set to rise throughout the region as state-run enterprises are run down. In particular, the conversion to anything remotely productive of the massive military–industrial complex of the former Soviet Union (taking up at least 15 per cent of Soviet GDP, and probably much more) dwarfs any comparable western difficulty in adjusting to a post-cold war world.

There are all kinds of difficulties in making comparisons between countries in the two halves of Europe. But the reunification of Germany in 1990 gives some indicators of the gap that has opened up since 1947. The GDR was generally reckoned to be the economic success story of the communist world, yet it was discovered at the time of unification that the average age of its capital stock was over twice that of the Federal Republic, while average productivity was only about one-third. When it came to trying to privatise state-dominated industries in the former GDR, the specialist agency, the Treuhand, found that, by western standards, most GDR firms were actually insolvent. The net value of the companies on the opening balance sheet of the Treuhand was a minus figure. Around 30 per cent of the total portfolio was considered beyond redemption and was liquidated at the outset: the remainder has only been privatised at the cost of massive subsidies from the Federal budget (subsumed in the huge net transfer figures for 1991, 1992 and 1993, amounting to DM 357 billion (£143 billion) for these three years alone).[3]

Such a comparison of a relatively strong communist economy with a western European analogue suggests that the economic picture at the outset of transition elsewhere in post-communist Europe will have been much more bleak. And this is not the only problem. At the same time as coping with the economic shock of adjusting to the market order – and the macroeconomic crises mentioned above – each state in post-communist Europe also has the difficulty of constructing (or in limited cases reconstructing) national democratic political institutions after several generations of totalitarianism. This in turn is linked to the problem of boundaries and lines of demarcation *between* states, and the proliferation of new states after the end of the Soviet-dominated system. Of the states which were party to the CMEA in 1959, one (the GDR) has disappeared, one (Czechoslovakia) has split in two and the largest (the USSR) has fragmented into fifteen separate parts. To this, of course, should be added the fragmentation of former Yugoslavia into half a dozen separate parts, some at war with each other. In this volatile post-communist world ethnic and border conflicts are always a possibility since there is little correlation

179

between political boundaries and ethnic groups. The absence of mature political systems and parties has in some cases allowed racist or fascist groups to assume power (as in former Yugoslavia). The risk of political instability remains great almost everywhere.

The problem in post-communist Europe could be described as twofold. It is partly one of introducing the market economy into an area where it did not exist before. But it is also a political problem of rebuilding civil society as the foundation of stability. Laws, institutions, parties, the press, the armed forces, even constitutions themselves have to be rethought in non-communist terms. This is easier for some countries than others. They either have previous political traditions to draw on (such as Poland) or they can define themselves in opposition to Soviet rule (such as Czechoslovakia at the moment of the transition to democracy – but this did not stop the split of that country into two). For the former Soviet Union, however, it is not freedom from foreign domination that is at stake but rather freedom from domestic domination, and the mistakes of the past. Yet we should never under-estimate the desire of ordinary people for the ordinary decencies. The Russian expert Hélène Carrère d'Encausse quotes an opinion poll in Russia in 1990 in which 60 per cent of those asked 'What is the best thing for a people?' gave the answer 'Good laws' (Carrère d'Encausse 1992: 190).

There seems to be no way of by-passing the reconstruction of political and economic life in post-communist Europe through the rebuilding of nation states. No other framework has yet been developed which allows the organisation of political pluralism by providing the means of introducing laws, of ensuring civil security, of guaranteeing freedom of expression and restraining abuses of power. The host of economic reforms needed in post-communist Europe – from putting into effect laws on private property to introducing fiscal stability and market mechanisms in state-dominated industries – require effective political structures and also the acceptance by the people that they are involved in political terms with such reforms. The nation state is the building-block in this process. Only the GDR – by adopting overnight the Federal German constitution, laws and institutions – has side-stepped the problem.

Yet there are obvious dangers. One is that a proliferation of nation states could lead to a proliferation of antagonisms. Border and ethnic disputes, fuelled by widespread economic and political dislocation, can easily translate into political or military tension. This in turn becomes a disincentive to investment and thus a brake on further economic development – as parts of former Yugoslavia show only too clearly. There is always the risk that the nation state will define itself in terms of opposition to certain groups: or that within any state an ethnic majority will seek to exclude from power a minority group which it fears has links with a neighbouring state.

Thus there are clear political risks in rebuilding a mosaic pattern of autonomous nation states. But there are economic risks too. Few post-communist countries (one possible exception may be Poland) are large enough to be able to develop significant domestic markets as the basis of economic activity. Economic autarky would be equivalent to further stagnation. This means that, like it or not, the countries of post-communist Europe have to take part in the international division of labour to make their way. And this means, as night follows day, that they need to recreate market-based trading relationships amongst themselves: but also, and above all, they need to build up trading relationships with the largest trading bloc on the planet, which they happen to share the continent with.

THE MOTOR OF GROWTH

The ending of the CMEA in 1991 did not mean that former communist countries ceased trading completely with the outside world. Instead there was a strong shift in the direction of trade, away from the collapsing economies of central and eastern Europe and towards the developed markets and hard currencies of the west. After being stable in the 1980s, levels of exports to OECD countries from Czechoslovakia, Hungary and Poland increased by 41 per cent, 22 per cent and 15 per cent respectively in 1991 alone.[4] The trend continued in 1992, with these and other central European countries showing a continuing strong growth in exports to the OECD (but this excluded the former Soviet Union, whose exports to the OECD area actually fell in 1992). In addition, of course, the former GDR switched its trading relationship around completely in this period from the CMEA to the Federal Republic of Germany (and thus to the EU too).

Within the OECD area the EU has become far and away the major market of post-communist Europe. Figures for the first nine months of 1992 show that, for example, for Czechoslovakia, Hungary and Poland, the EU market was responsible for respectively 78 per cent, 71 per cent and 81 per cent of all exports to OECD countries. (If EFTA markets are included the total becomes respectively 94 per cent, 92 per cent and 94 per cent.) Exports by these same countries to the other major markets of the OECD (the US and Japan) remained at trivial levels: around 3–4 per cent to the US and none measurable at all to Japan. Even for the former Soviet Union the same figures show that the EU took 70 per cent of OECD exports, EFTA 12 per cent and Japan 8 per cent.[5]

These figures underline one inescapable fact. *The EU has become by far the dominant market-economy trading partner for post-communist Europe.* This fact has important implications. There are broadly three main ways of reconstructing post-communist Europe. The first – the mobilisation of internal resources – is (even assuming a basic commitment to reform in each country) hampered by weak domestic demand, rudimentary or chaotic markets, financial institutions and cross-border payments systems. The second – financial transfers from the outside – can only be of limited help given the limited resources available at subsidised rates, the need not to increase already heavy debt burdens and the need for private capital to find bankable projects. This means that the third way – increasing trade with the rest of the world – is of crucial importance to restarting growth, raising living standards, creating employment and earning foreign exchange. So it is that, although public opinion in western Europe still tends to see the collapse of communism in terms of former superpower military relations, and perhaps assumes because of that that responsibility for reconstructing eastern Europe lies elsewhere, *it is western Europe in general and the EU in particular which will in fact have the main external role* (in addition to the efforts of the countries themselves) in encouraging the transition of central and eastern Europe from communism to the market economy.

This policy conclusion – inescapable though it seems to be, and profoundly important though it clearly is – has not so far been explicitly drawn. Instead, although credit must go to the EU for many aid initiatives which have been helpful to eastern Europe, and some more recent trade concessions, since 1989 the policy stance of the EU towards post-communist Europe has been ambiguous. It is as if the countries of central and eastern Europe are seen as distant third parties – or at worst potential competitors – rather than a divided part of the same continent for which the EU has unique responsibility. (A straw in the wind: the 1993 Commission White Paper on *Growth, Competitiveness and Employment* has remarkably little to say about post-communist Europe. It mentions improved transport links to eastern Europe at p. 32, but in the same breath as improved links to north Africa!)

In the absence of a clear sense of overall direction, EU policy towards eastern Europe, in particular in the trade field, has been driven by incrementalism. The EU has, for example, been negotiating separate individual trade and political agreements ('Europe Agreements') with a number of former communist countries. Agreements with Czechoslovakia, Hungary and Poland were signed in 1991, and with Bulgaria and Romania in 1992. Different 'Partnership and Co-operation Agreements', also covering trade access, are being negotiated with countries of the former Soviet Union, and yet other 'Trade and Cooperation Agreements' with the Baltic States, Albania and Slovenia. At the top of the hierarchy though are the Europe Agreements, and these then subdivide into two: a trade element (an Interim Agreement) which, because it lies within Community competence, does not have to be ratified by EU member states; and a non-trade element (including, for example, a framework for political dialogue) which does require such ratification.

There have been endless complications in the negotiation and implementation of virtually all these types of agreement. The break-up of Czechoslovakia in 1993, for example, meant that EU import quotas then had to be divided between the two new countries. The Interim Agreement with Bulgaria (supposed to have come into force in 1993 at the same time as that with Romania) has been held up in the EU Council on purely internal procedural grounds. EU member states' ratification of the Europe Agreements with Romania, Hungary and Poland have all been delayed for one reason or another. Partnership and Cooperation Agreements with Russia and the Ukraine were only signed in 1994. By early 1994 – over four years after the collapse of the Berlin Wall – the EU had only formally ratified two of its flagship Europe Agreements (with Poland and Hungary).

The practice of negotiating separate agreements with each former communist country has also meant that the trade regimes

183

vary. For example, the Interim (i.e. trade) Agreements with Romania and Bulgaria differ in certain respects from those with Hungary, Poland and the former CSFR, which in itself discourages the *reintegration* of trade between these former members of the CMEA. Then there is the additional problem of trade with the EFTA countries (linked to the EU from the beginning of 1994 through the EEA). Free Trade Agreements have also been signed between EFTA and individual former communist countries (and also between individual EFTA members and the Baltic states of Latvia, Lithuania and Estonia). However, the EFTA agreements, although similar to the EU agreements, are not identical and thus the same problem of discouraging trade *between* former communist states arises.

Apart from these basic problems of methodology, the *contents* of the Europe Agreements have been widely criticised. They offer a free trade area between the EU and partner country over a ten-year period, with the general principle that import restrictions on the EU side will be lifted faster than by the partner country. However, a range of restrictions – actual or potential – remains in place for 'sensitive' products (like agricultural products; and basic industrial products like coal, iron and steel and textiles) which themselves account for a very large part (up to a half) of what the former communist countries *can* actually export, given the unmodernised nature of their economies. The EU has resorted to restrictions on a number of occasions already. Virtually all farm products from eastern Europe were banned completely for three weeks in 1993 following an outbreak of foot and mouth disease in former Yugoslavia. Penal anti-dumping duties were imposed on various iron and steel products from Hungary, Poland and Croatia in 1993. Voluntary Export Restraints on steel products were negotiated with the Czech and Slovak Republics in 1993 which set quota limits on what these countries can export to the EU up to 1995. And so on. (It is interesting that there is a close correlation between 'sensitive' sectors and areas of high subsidy within the EU – including by means of dubious (and possibly illegal) state aids (see Chapter 4).)

To set against this it should certainly be added that the EU has gradually *improved* its trade access offers to eastern Europe. Thus, at the Copenhagen European Council in 1993, it was agreed that some timetables for reducing duties on imports from eastern Europe should be accelerated, that some quotas and ceilings on volumes of sensitive goods should be increased faster, and that a Commission proposal to cumulate some rules of origin for trade purposes (which would ease inter-regional trade) should be 'studied'.

While it is true that each individual step and each individual concession in this general area of trade with post-communist Europe has its merit, and is better than nothing, it is hard to avoid the overall impression that in this field the EU has been making it up as it goes along rather than having a clear overall policy objective. As a result, a web of complicated (and shifting) bilateral managed trade arrangements has been constructed, adjusted here and there on an ad hoc product by product or country by country basis, subject to the vagaries of negotiation and comprehensible only to a handful of experts in trade ministries around Europe. And for what? While EU spokespeople are quite correct to say that the EU is taking the lion's share of exports from central and eastern Europe (compared with, say, the US or Japan), the volumes in question, expressed as a proportion of total EU imports, are microscopic – about 3 per cent (less than from Norway). And, of course, trade is a two-way process, not a unilateral concession. It is not simply a matter of the EU taking imports from eastern Europe. The EU sends its exports there too, and its trade deficit with these countries had in fact turned into a trade surplus by 1992.[6]

This entire subject cries out for a major policy review by the EU. The benefits to the fragile east European economies of an *early* boost to trade are overwhelmingly greater than any conceivable disadvantages to the much stronger EU economy. The incorporation of the EFTA countries into the trading bloc of the European Economic Area from 1994 (which thus accounts for some 90 per cent of eastern European exports to OECD countries) only reinforces the need for a global review.

THE RULE OF LAW

On the one hand the collapse of communism has led to the multiplication of individual nation states in eastern Europe, nearly all attempting in one way or another to move towards a market economy. On the other hand the need to trade with the rest of Europe means that each state must remain in touch with the wider market. On the one hand new political borders cut across ethnic groups and create tensions among minority groups. On the other hand economic requirements dictate that such borders become meaningless if growth is to resume. This problem – the squaring the circle of allowing nations to co-exist and develop without mutually destructive tension – might be described as the *European problem*. The unsurpassed degree of ethnic, linguistic, political, cultural and even religious differences across the continent of Europe means that it can never be avoided. Some means or other has always to be found to allow diversity to flourish in peace.

It has been the theme of much of this book that, by and large, the development of the Community since the Second World War has allowed western Europe to solve or at least contain the worst aspects of this problem. Economic integration through the development of an ever deeper market, based on common institutions, common decision-taking and common rules, has removed at least some of the stresses and strains of European life. (Of course solving some old problems only means that new problems take their place. But that really is an inescapable fact of political life.)

Are there aspects of European integration since the war which might be relevant to the situation of post-communist Europe today? Possibly there are. First, the need seems to exist once more to build a market which will allow the division of labour to function and (in the words of the Spaak Report) 'reconcile mass production and the absence of monopoly' (*Rapport* 1956: 13). The vacuum caused by the collapse of the CMEA-managed trade regime in eastern Europe, the move of each post-communist state towards the market economy and the need to stimulate trade as the motor for growth all point to the need for a new – international – economic framework encompassing both the EU and post-communist Europe. Whether that should involve the creation of a new free trade zone with separate national tariff arrangements or a common market-type arrangement with a customs union remains open for consideration.

Second, there are parallels to be drawn between the withdrawal of the state as the dominant force in the economy in eastern Europe and the restraints on state activity which economic integration has entailed in western Europe. Monopoly practices, state subsidies to national industries, state-sponsored discrimination against foreign goods, services and individuals, have all been circumscribed (if not banned outright) in the west.

As we have seen in some earlier chapters, one of the main difficulties in achieving the aims of the EC Treaty has been, not so much that the private sector in each member state has resisted change, as that the *national apparatus* in each member state – the complicated infrastructure of administrative, fiscal and social arrangements which each has developed piecemeal (particularly since the war) – is not always compatible with that in other member states. In the services sector it was only when the Community gave up administrative harmonisation in despair and turned to mutual recognition that progress was possible. There are surely lessons here for the future development of state/economy relations in eastern Europe.

Third, the EU has developed, on the basis of the Treaties but also on the basis of the findings of the Court of Justice, a corpus of economic law which has direct effect in each member state, which takes precedence over national law and which underpins the functioning of the wider European market. Here is something of great potential value – perhaps a jewel beyond price. Each former communist state is developing, separately, its own regime of economic law governing such matters as the ownership of property, the position of monopolies, the status of companies, the role of competition, the rules of financial institutions, the avoidance of cartels, the safeguarding of investment, and so on. Each is starting from a different position, which is whatever happens to have been left over after the ravages of generations of totalitarian rule. Sooner or later, however, the problem will arise in each country of making its market economy compatible with that of its neighbour – and compatible with that in the rest of Europe. Having a ready-made corpus of economic law to hand may then be of enormous advantage. This does not mean that everything on the EU statute books is necessary or suitable for eastern Europe. Community law itself has evolved over the years. But some sort of *codification* should be possible. What benefits might not arise if, say, foreign investors in eastern Europe were sure of a common body of transparent, directly applicable, market economic law that applied from one country to the next and which in cases of doubt *took precedence over national law*? Of course eastern European countries would have to agree they wanted this and some new judicial body may be needed. But these are not insoluble problems.

All these points – added to the need to overhaul its own trade policy – suggest that the EU could if it wishes do much more for post-communist Europe. There are many other quite obvious ideas, such as improving communications and transport links ('Trans European Networks'), helping rebuild cross-border payments systems, providing aid and assistance for the training of officials, lawyers, market regulators, economists, teachers, politicians – the list is endless. The problem is not finding good and useful things to do (and I would not wish to downplay the many things the EU *has* done in these areas). The problem for the future is rather more one of finding an overall strategy to replace the outmoded cold war strategy of containment. And this brings us to our next topic.

THE PROBLEM OF METHOD

The 1993 Copenhagen European Council offered the possibility of EU membership to associated countries of central and eastern Europe upon fulfilment of a number of general economic and political conditions, including the 'capacity to cope with competitive pressure and market forces within the Union' (Presidency Conclusions: Copenhagen, 21–2 June 1993). But no target date for membership was set and, after Copenhagen, EU energies were largely devoted to the enlargement negotiations with the EFTA countries of Austria, Finland, Norway and Sweden. In 1994 both Hungary and Poland formally applied for EU membership.

The general approach in the EU so far could be described, perhaps unkindly, as one of getting the EFTAns in first, making whatever internal institutional changes are necessary at the 1996 inter-governmental conference and then turning a rather leisurely collective attention to post-communist Europe, the countries of which might become members sometime later this century, or perhaps early in the next, as and when they reach specific standards of economic and political probity (and as and when the EU can resolve its own institutional differences). And in the meantime fire-fighting in the former Yugoslavia is to continue. But this must be the wrong strategy. We have already seen how the former GDR was found to be in a much worse economic position than the Federal Republic at the time of unification. Nobody is making any predictions now, but with luck the former GDR – after receiving vast amounts of public subsidy and with all the benefit of the introduction of the Federal constitution, laws and institutions – might be on the road to economic recovery towards the end of the century. It was estimated in 1992 that investments of the order of DM 120 to 150 billion (£48 to £60 billion) per year *over a period of around fifteen years* would be needed to bring former GDR capital and infrastructure up to west German levels.[7] To expect the countries of the rest of eastern Europe to engineer their own recovery and then – as if they were the same as the incomparably wealthier EFTA countries – to come up to the competitive pressures and market forces of the EU *before* anything further is done is to ask too much. The unprecedented economic and political instability of post-communist Europe demands action now – not early next century. Once the situation deteriorates beyond a certain point – as in former Yugoslavia – the difficulties of recreating stability mount exponentially. The lesson to be drawn from the tragedy of Yugoslavia is not so much that the EU is powerless in the face of determined and unprincipled combatants as that it should make it a matter of clear priority to see that no such breakdown in the social order takes place again. It is a mistake to assume that because not everything can be done nothing can be done. It is quite true that immediate EU enlargement *would* pose insuperable difficulties, not just to the candidate countries but to the EU itself. A classic enlargement negotiation – as for Spain and Portugal and as for the EFTAns – might well entail complete paralysis.

The answer is not to become overwhelmed by problems of procedure but rather first to define the problem and then work backwards, adapting the procedure to the solution. It is absolutely clear that the Community institutions were not designed with the collapse of communism in mind. It does not then follow, though, that Community *principles* – of which the institutions are merely a reflection – cannot still apply.

We cannot know now what those who founded the Community after the Second World War would have made of the end of communism. They left no blueprint. Nonetheless, as I have suggested in Chapter 1, some basic ideas can be derived from the thinking of Monnet in particular – based upon his observations and experience of European events in the first half of this century – which are perhaps of universal, not just local, application. What are those ideas? A key one is that it is preferable to create a system of rules of conduct between nations rather than to allow differences between them to be resolved by the use of force (as has usually been the case in Europe). Another is that we should resist attempts to establish positions of crushing domination which, although they might provide short-term gains (such as a quiet life), only store up resentment and the desire for revenge. The corollary of this is that as far as possible interlocutors should be treated as equals. A third is that it is more fruitful to pursue a common objective in the common interest than for each party in a transaction to seek to achieve purely individual, reciprocally negotiated advantages.

Refreshed, as it were, by drawing on such ideas, are there comments we can now make about relations with eastern Europe? First, the temptation to achieve or maintain a position of domination must be avoided. It is precisely when countries are in a relatively weak position (as they are now in eastern Europe) that the temptation to dominate is strongest – and most dangerous. Those who have come off worst from the cold war need not punishment but rapid rehabilitation. Churchill's motto for his history *The Second World War* should be recalled: 'In War: Resolution. In Defeat: Defiance. In Victory: Magnanimity. In Peace: Goodwill' (1965: vii). Now, doubtless the EU will deny vehemently that it has any intention of seeking a position of domination. Against that one should note that some eastern European leaders (President Walesa of Poland, President Havel of the Czech Republic) clearly seem to think that it does. The latter, for example, complained about the 'protectionist egoism' of western Europe in a speech in late 1993.[8]

Second, a means should be found to discuss common interests on a basis of equality, excluding no interested interlocutor. This may require institutional lateral thinking, but so be it. The collapse of communism happens only once.

Third, and perhaps most importantly, a common approach must be developed and as far as possible common solutions sought for common problems. This is a complete reversal of the policy of reciprocally negotiated advantages which has been the main approach so far and which has tended to freeze positions. It is only when both sides feel that they have important greater objectives that comparatively minor problems can be by-passed.

What might such common solutions to common problems be? Nobody knows. The important thing first is to have a shared analysis of each other's objectives as the basis on which a common approach can be built. As a matter of fact there are any number of issues where a clear community of interests can be identified. I have already made some specific suggestions. It is obviously in the interests of both sides that economic and political stability is maintained across the continent. It is in the interests of both sides that growth resumes as soon as possible in the east. It is in the interests of both sides that there are better communications, better markets and clear economic laws. There are vast natural energy resources in the former Soviet Union which can be exploited for the benefit of everyone. It is in the interest of no one for anti-competitive practices to prevail any-where which falsify markets and distort prices. And so on. Perhaps the first step should be to draw up a 'balance sheet': a shared assessment by experts from both sides of the real economic strengths and weaknesses throughout the continent, which would clear minds and form the basis for any further action.

The point is to arrive at shared objectives which allow both sides to make progress, which if they do not solve problems directly then contain within them the seeds of future solutions. This can only be done on a basis of equality of treatment – which means a say for everyone in what happens next. None of this need mean the same as EU membership in the classical sense. Again, both sides could probably agree that this could be harm-ful in the short term, given what we know of the real economic discrepancies between eastern and western Europe, and the problems it would pose for the EU in institutional terms. Some entirely new, hybrid, arrangement might be needed, which applies or adapts some EU practices and makes up others com-pletely. It remains to be invented. The search for it – if conducted by both sides – will be part of the solution.

There is no other option than to innovate in this entire field. Existing rules and institutions were not designed for this situa-tion and are not flexible enough to cope. This does not mean that the *principles* should be jettisoned. On the contrary, the sooner we arrive at a wider Europe, based on a system of commonly accepted binding rules, the better it will be for everyone.

CONCLUSIONS

It is hard to think of a more important task facing the EU today than to help establish stability and economic growth elsewhere on the same continent now that communism has been over-turned. The price of failure is so great – including the possible break-up of everything that has been achieved in the west so far – and the potential for success so enormous, that by comparison virtually anything else that the EU does in the next few years will be of secondary consequence. This does not mean that the EU should stop developing, but unless it does so within the frame-work of a clear policy towards post-communist Europe any development risks being rendered futile.

Nobody else can really take on this task. The United States can certainly help provide military stability, and perhaps financial assistance, but by themselves those are not enough. Nor are the international financial organisations able to do much more than provide emergency relief. That is not enough either. In the end it is the clear responsibility of the wealthy market democracies on the same continent, unified by force of law into one increasingly powerful economic ensemble, to take the initiative. The Marshall Plan in 1947 was conceived originally as American support in favour of a common programme which the Europeans were to draw up themselves. (Its co-ordination mechanism later became the OECD.) Times have changed. Needs are different. Post-communist Europe suffers not so much from a capital stock destroyed through war as a capital stock which exists but which is unsuitable. Nonetheless, the same principles of organisation could perhaps apply. If post-communist Europe could put together a common recovery programme (which may not rest upon financial transfers as much as a co-ordinated approach to modernisation) it should be the responsibility of the west of Europe – the beneficiary of Marshall aid so long ago – to help implement it and to help mobilise the assistance of both the United States and Japan in doing so.

Throughout this chapter I have deliberately avoided trying to distinguish between one former communist country and the next. In practice, as is well known, some are in a better state than others. Some are more clearly on the path to a market economy than others. Yet in very few cases can it be stated with certainty that the worst is over. It is my thesis that it is the most difficult cases of transition which require the most urgent attention rather than, as at present, offering the greatest inducements to those which have made the most progress – essentially Poland, Hungary and the Czech Republic.

This leads, inescapably, to the problem of the former Soviet Union, and in particular the problem of relations with the Russian Federation. Should Russia be part of any common European grouping? Can it, with its vast size, enormous problems of transition and uncertain political future, take part in the same sense as other countries? There can be no clear answer as yet. On the one hand Russia may still wish to cling to its old superpower status. In effect this would mean projecting influence by means of force, and this is obviously unacceptable. On the other hand, many Russian leaders have spoken about rejoining the 'community of civilised states', which implies a new approach to relations with the west of Europe.

Part of the problem is purely conceptual. If we were talking about Russian membership of the EU then I would agree that this is not a practical proposition in the foreseeable future (and it is the foreseeable future which is the problem). But if, as I have suggested, it is better to talk about creating a general system of commonly accepted binding rules, then I would argue that anyone who accepts the rules should be able to take part. It is in the interest of *everyone* for the zone of stability to be as wide as possible. In practice there is a close correlation between acceptance of a rule-based system and political pluralism. In practice the problem usually resolves itself. So while it is difficult to be categoric about Russia, I would certainly say it should be offered the *possibility* of participating in any common endeavour, on the same basis of equality as others. There should at least be a seat at the table.

10

WHAT IS EUROPEAN INTEGRATION?

INTRODUCTION

When, in 1992, the 1958 French constitution was amended as part of the process of ratification of the Maastricht Treaty the following explanatory clause was added:

> The Republic participates in the European Communities and the European Union *comprising states which have freely chosen, in accordance with the constituent treaties, to exercise certain of their powers in common.*
>
> (New Article 88-1 A; emphasis mine)

In 1993 the German Constitutional Court was required to comment on the compatibility of Maastricht with the German constitution. It observed the following:

> The democratic principle does not exclude the Federal Republic of Germany from membership of a (*supranationally organised) international community . . .. If a union of democratic states performs sovereign tasks through the exercise of sovereign authority* it is first and foremost the citizens of the Member States who must legitimise such action through a democratic process via their national parliaments.
>
> (Judgement of 12 October 1993; emphasis mine)

Finally, as we saw in Chapter 1, Monnet defined the basic objective of the European Community as follows:

> To create progressively between the people of Europe the greatest common interest *managed by common democratic institutions to which is delegated the necessary sovereignty.*
>
> (Monnet 1976: 786; emphasis mine)

Although there are differences between these three definitions, they share one important characteristic. They see the Community (or the Union) as involving a deliberate decision to share a common exercise of national powers, authorities or 'sovereignty'. That decision rests upon the idea of transfer: transfer of these national attributes to a European level. It also involves, however, a mechanism (institutions) to manage those attributes once transferred. The institutions themselves (or the form of that organisation) may remain open, and the powers exercised in common may remain open. In addition both the French and German constitutional readings assume that the state remains the essential building-block in this process. As a statement of fact this seems incontestable – otherwise why did German unification involve the merging of the two Germanies into one entity, rather than each within a federal system taking part in a United States of Europe, as Churchill had suggested in 1946 (Cannadine 1989: 313)?[1]

The important point here is that this process of transferring and organising actual power is the kernel of what is usually meant by European integration. It is different in character from simple co-operation between individual nation states, either on a multilateral or bilateral basis, because it implies some new body or new institution which has real delegated authority, legal personality and independence of its creators. It is in fact an innovation in the means of organising relations between nations.

Two out of the three definitions quoted above invoke the idea of 'sovereignty'. In fact, the classical definition of the Community process is usually one of a 'transfer of sovereignty'. Monnet himself spoke in those terms. In his work *L'Ordre juridique communautaire*, J.V. Louis develops the (slightly different) idea of 'dividing sovereignty' as being at the heart of the integration mechanism:

> This is certainly not a quantitative conception which would bring together sovereignty in the area where the parties have given it up. It is more a question of determining as a function of the attribution of competencies to the Community and the exercise of them made by it which, between the State and the Community, has the control on such and such question, without excluding, according to the case, either joint actions or the carrying out of subordinate tasks by the State.
>
> (Quoted in Mattera 1990: 645)

The continuing use of the idea of 'sovereignty' in this context, however, even 'divided sovereignty', may provoke needless confusion. The ambiguities surrounding the word 'sovereignty' are the cause of the problem. Using the very concept seems to imply creating a 'sovereign' institution – perhaps even some kind of a superstate with greater powers than any existing state. It seems to invoke a loss of something vital to the nation, almost as if it were some mortal wound to the national body politic. As it is both controversial and such a key part of European integration it clearly deserves further examination.

THE PROBLEM OF SOVEREIGNTY

What is sovereignty? Where does it reside? In practice sovereignty proves to be a remarkably difficult idea to pin down. Its manifestation varies from place to place. In the UK sovereignty is usually thought to reside in Parliament (or more specifically in the House of Commons: 'The ultimate authority in the English Constitution is a newly-elected House of Commons' (Bagehot 1983: 219)). But this is the outcome of a historical battle of power between the Monarchy, the Commons and the Lords, each of which still retains a role. In the United States, the Declaration of Independence places sovereignty in the people, whereas the constitution divides effective power between the individual states and the federal government. Within the federal institutions it is further subdivided between the President, Congress and the Senate. In France the current constitution states at Article 3 that 'national sovereignty belongs to the people who exercise it through their representatives and by means of the referendum'. In Germany the 1949 Basic Law avoids the issue and says simply at Article 20 that 'All state authority shall emanate from the people'. (Although it does add at Article 24 that 'The Federation may by legislation transfer sovereign powers to intergovernmental institutions'.)

As the above examples illustrate, 'sovereignty' has meant – and still means – different things to different people. Often it shades into a kind of shorthand for 'ultimate authority'. If we look at the problem from the other end – where exactly in the Community institutions would transferred sovereignty (if it is transferred) reside? In the Commission, as the main management organ? In the Council of Ministers, as the main legislative body?

In the European Parliament, as the directly elected body? Or perhaps even in the Court of Justice as the final arbiter of EC law? In all of these? Or in none of them?

The problem of the search for sovereignty in the modern world is a little like Descartes' problem of searching for the seat of consciousness in the human body. Even supposing sovereignty were found and everyone agreed where it lay, at both national and European levels, where would that leave us in the global market place, with instantaneous capital movements and virtually free dissemination of information? How could Europe exercise its own sovereignty in this fluid and interdependent world?

In his monumental work *The Open Society and Its Enemies* (1971, 1990), the philosopher Karl Popper already expressed serious misgivings about the relevance of theories of sovereignty to open democratic societies, on the grounds that all such theories are paradoxical. They assume an absolute authority somehow agreeing to limit its authority in the name of democracy. In fact, he argued that it was possible to develop a theory of democratic control which was free of the paradox of sovereignty by making as its policy objective the creation, development and protection of political institutions for the avoidance of tyranny (Popper 1971: 125).

Likewise, in *Justice and World Order* (1992), Janna Thompson observes the distinction between closed societies and open societies, and how the two inter-relate in the world:

> The fluidity of nations poses a problem for a system of states, whatever form this system takes. For states, if they are to exercise sovereignty over a territory, must have fixed borders; they must divide up the world's territory and population into mutually exclusive entities.
>
> (Thompson 1992: 181)

Philosopher and theologian Jacques Maritain, writing in 1954, looked at the problem in some detail. Maritain found, in fact, that the modern idea of sovereignty was linked to the development of absolute monarchy in Europe and could be traced to the attempt to compare the relationship between the king and his subjects to that between God and man. He found that in the writings of Jean Bodin in the sixteenth century, the king (or prince) was held to exercise an absolute and transcendent authority (or sovereignty), answerable only to God and shared with no one. He was,

197

literally, cut off from the people and transcended the political whole in the same way that God transcends the cosmos. Hobbes, with his idea of the Mortal God (or Leviathan), had suggested something similar when he placed all political power and strength in the Sovereign, in whom 'consisteth the essence of the Common-Wealth' (quoted in Maritain 1954: 35).

Maritain suggested that, by a curious and mistaken intellectual shift, the idea of sovereignty (royal, absolute, God-like) was carried over from the person of the monarch to the abstract entity of the state when Rousseau, after the French revolution, placed the Popular Will where the monarch had been and subsequent theorists (notably Hegel) followed him in ascribing to the state virtually divine powers:

> Rousseau, who was not a democrat, injected into nascent modern democracies a notion of Sovereignty which was destructive of democracy, and pointed towards the totalitarian State; because, instead of getting rid of the separate and transcendent power of the absolute kings, he carried, on the contrary, that spurious power of the absolute kings to the point of an unheard-of absolutism, in order to make a gift of it to the people.
>
> (Maritain 1954: 40)

Maritain thus argued (following a similar logic to Popper) that, as a tool of political theory, the concept of sovereignty was impossible to divorce from its original absolutism and that, when considering democratic societies, we were better off without it: 'The two concepts of Sovereignty and Absolutism have been formed together on the same anvil. They must be scrapped together' (Maritain 1954: 48). Maritain's point was not simply linguistic. He was not arguing that any other word (like 'autonomy' or 'independence') would do in place of sovereignty, or that we should change the meaning of sovereignty so that it became something different. He was arguing that the very *idea* of sovereignty, because of its origins, belonged to the sphere of the absolute; and that because of this it is out of place in democratic, non-absolutist societies. Here is Maritain on attempts to explain away or redefine the problem:

> Now it is not enough to say that modern bodies politic have ceased in actual fact to be 'sovereign' in that improper sense

which means full autonomy. It is also not enough to seek from sovereign States limitations and partial surrenders of their sovereignty, as if it were only a matter of limiting in its extension a privilege naturally and really inherent in the State, and as if, moreover, sovereignty could be limited in its own sphere.

That is not enough. We must go down to the root, that is, we must get rid of the Hegelian or pseudo-Hegelian concept of the State as a person, a supra-human person, and understand that the State is only a *part* (at the summit, to be sure, but still a part) and an *instrumental agency* in the body politic – thus bringing the State back to its true, normal and necessary functions as well as to its natural dignity. And we must realise that the State is not and never has been sovereign.

(Maritain 1954: 178; emphasis in original)

Neither Maritain nor Popper address the specific problem of European integration. Both were concerned with finding a non-absolutist framework for the development of democratic civil society. However, all the countries which take part in European integration are (and must be) democratic civil societies. What then if we adopt the radical approach and, if only for argument's sake, we remove completely the concept of sovereignty from the notion of transfer which lies at the heart of European integration?

The first point to make is that 'something' is still transferred. This is not some linguistic device to try to define away the problem. A real operation of transfer still takes place. If it is not sovereignty it must be something else. Perhaps a better word would be 'power'. That seems a more accurate description of what is at stake, one more suited to the dynamic process that is taking place and one more suited to the realities of democratic politics. 'Authority' might be another possibility, but it is rather static. Concepts like 'independence' or 'autonomy' seem meaningless in this context. Although I tentatively suggest 'power', I am not wedded to the word. The important point is that we should choose some concept which reflects the limited, democratically-authorised, finite attributes of the modern state rather than one which is *only* proper to the realm of the absolute.

The second point is that if we remove what is absolutist from this operation of transfer we can arrive at a better understanding of what European integration actually is. It is *not* the building up of one more absolutist authority drawing all existing absolute authority to it. Nor is it the creation of a superstate exercising sovereign authority on the world stage in the same way that individual nation states once believed they exercised sovereignty in Europe. Nor is it even necessarily a simple answer to the old political question 'Who should rule?' Because, as Popper pointed out, the question 'Who shall rule?' in itself presumes absolute political power, or rather unchecked sovereignty. In an open democratic society the proper question is rather the following:

> How can we so organise political institutions that bad or incompetent rulers can be prevented from doing too much damage?
>
> (Popper 1971: 121)

Now on the European stage this question takes on a whole new meaning. Bad or incompetent rulers have indeed inflicted an extraordinary amount of damage on their own countries and on the rest of Europe during the twentieth century. The damage done in central and eastern Europe is still with us, but it is only the last in a series of totalitarian failures. Yet European integration, as developed through the European Community, presumes that those taking part are open market economies, governed according to democratic principles. As a contrast we have seen in the previous chapter that a parallel non-market, non-democratic attempt at forced integration of communist countries in the shape of the Council for Mutual Economic Assistance (CMEA) failed miserably. It was dissolved by its members in 1991 as soon as they had the chance. European integration can be thought of as a means of *stopping* bad or incompetent rulers from dominating the continent, rather than adding to the list.

It may be worth borrowing a further concept from Popper here, that of historicism. *The Open Society and Its Enemies* is a sustained attack upon the belief in historical necessity, of the existence of laws of history which enable prophets to foresee the future and which thus absolve the present generation from personal responsibility for anything. Popper argued that Marx was the latest such prophet, but that similar thinking can be traced further back to Hegel and indeed to Plato. Now it may well be that, as in other walks of life, there are traces of historicist thinking among some adherents of European integration. Behind some of the rhetoric in favour of European unity, a kind of sub-Marxist, sub-Hegelian belief in the ineluctable working out of historical laws can occasionally be glimpsed: for example, the process of the Commission–Council dialectic and the widespread idea that progress can only come out of crisis; or the argument that the Commission as guardian of the Treaties can do no wrong; or the belief that, somewhere in the future, there lies a perfect European political constitution of which present day reality is but an imperfect shadow.[2] Some of the draft treaties or constitutions for a future Europe have this utopian flavour, as do some of the intellectual models which are used, which frequently seek to project onto a European scale what was once national practice. (In the nineteenth century Saint-Simon argued in favour of a European monarch, government and parliament. Today the prevalent model is usually some kind of European federal republic.)

If we agree with Popper and put historicist thinking behind us (as the collapse of communism in eastern Europe surely encourages us to do), does that invalidate European integration itself? Surely not: it merely invalidates one particular approach to the problem, one based on inevitability, on historical rules, on domination, on the vestigial belief that the starting point of politics is 'Who shall rule?' One, in other words, based upon the idea of the closed society. If, on the contrary, we start from the premise that the European Community is a set of institutions put in place by open societies to help resolve some previously insoluble problems we are in a better position to appreciate its true worth. Because, as Popper argued, institutions are essential to democracy:

> Democracy . . . provides the institutional framework for the reform of political institutions. It makes possible the reform of institutions without using violence, and thereby the use of reason in the designing of new institutions and the adjusting of old ones.
>
> (Popper 1971: 126)

So an important point seems to arise here. The institutions of the Community are not perfect (indeed they could *not* be perfect) but – like anything else in democracy – they are reformable and can be improved, *as they themselves represent an improvement upon what existed before*. They do not necessarily replace existing democratic institutions – they are additional to them. The Community (or Union) as a whole – that is, the sum of the member states and the Community institutions – is a highly complex political entity devoted to problem-solving on many levels. As such it is a completely original political experiment, bearing little resemblance to anything that has gone before or anything that exists anywhere else.

A final point could be made here. If the absolutist concept of sovereignty is put to one side in the Community context, the relationship between the individual nation and the Community loses much of its tension. Transferring power to an independent body which exercises that power to achieve common objectives which could not otherwise be attained is a much more rational footing for debate than transferring (absolute) sovereignty to an external entity, which accumulates such sovereignty and grows by feeding on that which it destroys. Such an approach does not pre-judge *which* powers should be exercised in common; it merely allows the policy debate to be shifted onto a clearer plane of likely costs and benefits. It also clears the way to a better relationship between national institutions and Community institutions, since neither is inevitably at war with the other. Both are necessary, and rather than seeing themselves as locked in some kind of conflict they each can learn from the other.

Whether one follows the logic of this argument over sovereignty is perhaps a matter of personal taste and conviction. It may seem to some that sovereignty is such an important political symbol that to do without it is to undo the fabric of the nation, and thus ultimately to lead to a Hobbesian form of anarchy. Against this it can only be remarked that democratic models *can* exist free of the problem of sovereignty; and that, ironically, camping on sovereignty locks the debate into the absolutist one of 'Who shall rule?', conceding the agenda to the proponents of the closed society at the outset.

THE MOTOR OF INTEGRATION

The member states of the EU (still the most important elements in the ensemble) are all market economy democracies. There are, of course, some differences in their individual economic arrangements, just as there are differences in their precise constitutional arrangements, but all the same the similarities override the differences. The candidate countries for the next round of enlargement (Sweden, Norway, Finland, Austria) are all market economy democracies. And now, after the fall of Soviet-led communism, most of the states of central and eastern Europe are also aspirant market economy democracies.

The essential motor of integration in the Community (and the Union) has so far been the deepening and the widening of one European market. It is this process, even more than treaties, declarations of intent or common expenditure programmes, which has acted like a magnet in drawing the individual economies of the member states ever closer together and which has constituted the prime rationale for building and maintaining common institutions. At the heart of the original Coal and Steel Community was one market in coal and steel. The objective of the common market was the fusion into one of six national markets for all goods and services. The single market programme was an updating (or deepening) of this. The project for monetary union is a further deepening. Widening has taken place through the progressive enlargement of the Community from six to twelve member states (and it will continue as other countries to the north and east of Europe join in).

The Community (and Union) institutions are at their strongest precisely where they are concerned with the operation of this market. The High Authority had to be strong *because* the existing national markets for coal and steel were fragmented, cartellised and intimately linked to the old war economies. The European Commission was given its strongest powers (in relation to competition policy, for example, or in relation to the abuse of state aid to industry) in areas where distortions of the market would be most significant. The Court of Justice has forced member states time and again to remove market-distorting measures. The primary objective of the European System of Central Banks, if monetary union ever moves into the final stage, will be to maintain price stability and in doing so to 'act in accordance with the principle of an open market economy with free competition, favouring an efficient allocation of resources' (Maastricht Treaty: Article 105). Even in the area of policy where the law of supply and demand has most notably been defied – agriculture – the *aim* was to allow one market in agricultural goods to function, not to regulate for the sake of it.

The question can be thought of in this way: if the member states are individual market economies, is it better to create one large market between them or instead to stay with a looser array of several smaller markets? In a free trade area, for example, there can be open commerce between individual market economies, each of which can maintain their characteristics and each their separate tariff regimes. But that is a rather different proposition from the actual merging of each individual market into one, with a common external tariff, no internal barriers to the economic factors of production and common market institutions. On grounds of economic efficiency and because of the previous history of division leading to warfare, it has been the second route that the signatories to the various treaties have chosen.

It may be objected here that the Community (and even more so the Union, as it emerges from Maastricht) is not just a market. And, of course, this is true. But those aspects of it which are most integrationist in character *are* market-related. Article G.3 of the Maastricht Treaty (see Box 15) lists the activities of the Community. From this list it can be seen that activities (a) to (h) are unambiguously market-related measures; that (i) to (n) and (s) are measures which in one way or another are meant to improve certain aspects of the functioning of the market (concerning the merits of which there may of course be differing views within the Union); and that only (o) to (r) and (t) seem clearly unconnected to the market. These latter areas (contributing to a high level of health protection, better education, measures in the spheres of energy, civil protection and tourism, development policy and so on) are vague, clearly of mixed competence between member states and the Community or so undeveloped that they have had little integrating effect. Finally, of course, Maastricht adds new policies and forms of co-operation as well, but these (a common foreign and security policy and co-operation in the fields of justice and home affairs) are more inter-governmental than integrationist in character (and remain outside the jurisdiction of the Court). The very idea of *citizenship* of the Union (which Maastricht introduces) builds on the economic freedoms implied by one market.

If the motor of integration is the market, this must affect the kind of economic policy which each member state adopts. As factors of production become ever more mobile within that market, the option of running an economic policy at variance with that market becomes less feasible. But that is the price that is paid for access to the market. And this notion of paying a price for something leads us to the next topic.

Box 15 Activities of the Community

(a) The elimination of customs duties and restrictions on trade between the member states;

(b) a common commercial policy;

(c) an internal market characterised by the abolition of obstacles to the free movement of goods, persons, services and capital;

(d) measures concerning the entry and movement of persons in the internal market;

(e) a common policy in the sphere of agriculture and fisheries;

(f) a common policy in the sphere of transport;

(g) a system ensuring that competition in the internal market is not distorted;

(h) the approximation of national laws required by the functioning of the common market;

(i) a policy in the social sphere comprising a European Social Fund;

(j) the strengthening of economic and social cohesion;

(k) a policy in the sphere of the environment;

(l) the strengthening of the competitiveness of Community industry;

(m) the promotion of research and technological development;

(n) encouragement for trans-European networks;

(o) a contribution to the attainment of a high level of health protection;

(p) a contribution to education and training and 'flowering of the cultures of the Member States';

(q) a policy in the sphere of development co-operation;

(r) the association of overseas countries and territories;

(s) a contribution to the strengthening of consumer protection;

(t) measures in the spheres of energy, civil protection and tourism.

Source: Maastricht Treaty: Article G.3

THE MULTIPLIER EFFECT

Even if 'sovereignty' is not quite the right word for what is pooled at a European level, nonetheless, something real is pooled. I have suggested that a better term might be 'power'. There is, however, a question which still cannot be avoided. Why should any free individual – or any free member state – actually *want* to pool power?

The answer can only be that it has a reasonable expectation that it will gain something in return. And this calculation –

conscious or otherwise – is the basis of membership of the Community. It is the general expectation of each member state that, although it might lose specific, real power in certain areas, that loss is offset by real gains which are greater and which could not otherwise be obtained. It would be pleasant to think that altruism guided member states, but in fact the more usual motive is a kind of enlightened but calculating self-interest.('We are not choirboys' Monnet used to observe (*Témoignages* 1989: 359).) It is a similar kind of self-interest to that which leads individuals or companies to take part in commercial transactions with others from which they have an expectation of gain. Indeed, it would not be incongruous to conceive of the EU institutions as providing a kind of political market place for the exchange of interests and the doing of deals, equipped with machinery for the enforcement of the contract or bargain. In this sense it channels and uses national self-interest in the way a market channels the search for profit.

We have already seen that the most significant aspect of the Community (and the Union) is economic. Broadly speaking, the main calculation which member states make is that, although they may lose individual economic autonomy, they gain in terms of general economic welfare through being part of a larger market. Another general calculation is that, although they may lose the political independence to do just as they please, they make real gains in terms of enhanced security of their environment and the stability of their neighbours.

But are these kinds of political calculations legitimate? Are they even democratic? Is it *permissible* to hand over a portion of national power to an independent institution and thus remove it from the national debate? The answer is surely yes, provided the consent is freely given (or 'freely chosen' as the French constitution puts it), provided what is at stake is fully appreciated and provided that a system of checks and balances prevents abuses of power. Although the EU institutions have a different function from national institutions they are not alien to them. They occupy what one might term the same political space.

A further point arises here which often clouds the argument. While it is often quite easy in any one member state to perceive the inconveniences or disadvantages of any particular line of EU action, it is sometimes more difficult to perceive the advantages. That is because the advantages are usually on a European scale (in which the member state is but one beneficiary among others) while the resistance to change is usually localised. This is a problem which is linked to the *multiplier effect* of EU decision-taking. In other words, while it is (apparently) quite easy to measure what is taking place within one's own member state, it is much more difficult to measure what is happening in all the others. Thus it is easy to fall into the habit of thinking that the burden of adjustment, of reform, of modernisation or what-ever is falling disproportionately in one country. Whereas, in fact, for any given item of European legislation there are two types of effects: those which, viewed from the standpoint of the member state, are felt domestically and those which are felt in every other member state too. It is arithmetically the latter which are likely to be the more important. As in business, a negotiating strategy can be either negative or positive; it can be a concentration on the defence of certain interests or instead a more active use of the multiplier effect to try to improve (from one's own point of view) the wider environment in the other member states. It can be (and is) argued that it is the role of the Commission to consider the whole problem since only it can take a European, as opposed to a national, view. This is certainly true up to a point but there would seem also to be a case for improving knowledge *within each member state* of the overall impact of Community business.

THE DEMOCRATIC SURPLUS

The member states are both market economies and democracies. Whereas it is fairly straightforward, at least in theory, to conceive of one European market, it is much more difficult – even in theory – to conceive of one European democracy. Does this mean a European government? And if so, elected under which rules? Would there be a head of state? Which constitution would apply? Which language would be used? What would happen to all existing national governments, heads of state and national con-stitutions? Would such an arrangement be accepted everywhere? Could any part of the whole secede? And so on and so forth.

Even to ask these sorts of questions illustrates the conceptual difficulties involved. And this probably explains why, unlike economic union, European political union has made compara-tively little progress. There is no one agreed definition of what it might amount to (unlike, say, the admirably clear description of a common market in the Spaak Report). But perhaps this is not at all surprising. If, as has been suggested, the Community (or Union) is a highly complex entity which has no model either in the past or anywhere else in the world, it clearly *will* be a challenge to standing political theory. If we start from the ancient premise 'Who shall rule?', we shall soon become bogged down in impossible calculations of who dominates whom and thus who wins and who loses. If, however, we start from the premise that the EU comprises democracies – open societies – which have already developed some institutions for the peaceful organisation of domestic life and which have also developed between them some common institutions for the organisation of their common interests it may then become conceptually easier to make progress.

It can now perhaps be seen why removing the problem of sovereignty from the equation can help matters. The EU institutions, in this approach, can be thought of as *an extension of national democratic institutions*. Rather than being seen as locked into opposition, either in a battle of sovereignty or a Hegelian conflict of thesis and anti-thesis, the two levels of institutions in fact form part of the same political whole, each with its different area of operations.

It has sometimes been said that the Community suffers from a democratic deficit, in that the chief decision-taking body, the Council, is not responsible to the directly elected body (the Parliament). However, a closer examination of the complex whole which is the EU might lead one to the conclusion that, on the contrary, it enjoys a *democratic surplus*. European institutions plus national institutions, (plus, one might add, regional or local institutions) combine to form several layers of effective democracy which overlap, intermingle and sometimes compete with one another. It may be that this is an untidy and complicated arrangement, but, given the differing national constitutions of the member states, that is only to be expected. Integration *needs* open (and thus democratic) societies. It depends upon observance of the rule of law and, sometimes, acceptance of the majority opinion – or vote – by states in a minority.

An appreciation of the point that Community institutions start, as it were, where national institutions stop but that, nonetheless, they are all serving similar democratic ends, might make it easier to establish a better working relationship between them. National parliaments, for example, generally embody the democratic opinion of a particular nation, while the European Parliament aims to embody democratic opinion on a European scale. Better co-operation between the two levels (and indeed also between individual national parliaments) might provide benefits to both and re-invigorate both. Since Community law takes precedence over national law, national legislatures might want to do everything possible to be informed about and if possible to influence the shape of European law – including for example by keeping in touch with the Commission and specialised committees of the European Parliament.

There are many possible ways of building bridges and conduits between the different types of institution in Europe, and it seems likely that this problem will be considered the next time institutional issues are discussed in depth (at the inter-governmental conference in 1996). Some have already suggested a European Congress or Senate of national parliamentarians. This idea featured among French proposals when Maastricht was under discussion. The Maastricht Treaty contains a declaration inviting the European Parliament and national parliaments to meet when necessary as a Conference of Parliaments, which Commissioner Sir Leon Brittan has proposed building on to develop a functioning Committee of Parliaments (Brittan 1994: 226). In addition, at a national level, there has been widespread renewed interest in improving parliamentary treatment of European questions. Examples range from the constitutional amendments made in France in 1992, which give a much greater scrutiny role over Community legislation to the French Parliament, to the German Constitutional Court requirement in 1993 that the German Bundestag must retain substantial tasks and powers in the European Union, and to the suggestion in the UK that a reformed House of Lords could be given a larger role in the debate and scrutiny of European issues.[3]

Much more useful research could in fact be done on what might be termed the *interface* between the differing national and European institutions in Europe before the 1996 discussions. These are difficult but not insoluble problems; indeed they are exactly the kind of reasoned, non-violent improvement of institutions which Popper might commend. The scope for rational reforms and thus for an improvement in effective democracy on a European scale seems quite large. Maastricht introduced the idea of *citizenship* of the Union. It may be a concept ripe for further development (for example by increasing cross-border political rights in line with the increase in cross-border economic rights, and exploring ways by which citizens can participate in various forms of political activity). As the then President of the Commission, Jacques Delors, put it in an article in 1993: 'The debate on the political form of Europe is open, it is before us.'[4]

THE ORGANISATION OF EUROPE

Monnet did not think the Community was an end in itself. He believed instead that it was rather a *process of transformation*, following in a direct line from the process which led to national patterns of existence. The concluding words of his memoirs were the following:

> The Community itself is only a step towards the forms of organisation of the world of tomorrow.

(Monnet 1976: 788)

Yet it is doubtful that by this Monnet meant simply that the Community could be enlarged indefinitely to end up by forming some kind of world government. Although he believed in the importance of institutions, Monnet also preferred human, small-scale solutions to large powerful bureaucracies. There is an anecdote by his collaborator Richard Mayne about a visit in 1973 of the 85-year-old Monnet to the labyrinthine Berlaymont building in Brussels, which houses the European Commission. Viewing the rows of offices and the officials rushing about, Mayne remarked to Monnet '"Isn't it strange to think that all this was only a piece of paper in your office?" Monnet raised his eyebrows. "Yes, it's extraordinary." Then, with a smile: "It's frightening"' (*Témoignages* 1989: 360).

It is more likely that Monnet thought that the *principles* which underlie the Community are generally valid and exportable to the world at large. The *mechanisms* (the institutions) which put those principles into effect may well change from place to place depending upon circumstance (and, indeed, as we have seen in the course of this book, may also change over time too, as has happened in the Community).

What are those principles? As I have suggested in Chapter 1, three essential ones can be derived from Monnet's thinking. First, that it is better to construct rules of conduct between nations than to rely on force as the arbiter. Second, that it is better to aim at establishing equality of treatment than positions of crushing domination (even though these may give temporary advantage). Third, that it is better to pursue common objectives in the common interest than to aim for individual reciprocal advantages.

It follows from the foregoing that some *means* is required to put these principles into effect (and hence the Community) and it also follows that the participating nations should be prepared to abide by the rules (which means that they cannot be governed in an arbitrary or autarkic manner). It does *not* follow that the European institutions are necessarily perfect and unreformable. Like all other political institutions they are open to abuse and to bureaucratic vices. It is up to the members to improve them.

Although it was felt most necessary to establish institutions embodying such principles in post-war Europe, the rapid transformation of the world as a whole into one global economic entity suggests that they do have general applicability. When the idea of the common market was developed in the Spaak Report, it seemed already that the individual European nation was too small to be able to exercise effective influence and thus that a bigger European market was necessary. Today, even the largest economies in the world are dwarfed by the growing global economy and the mobility of factors of production and information. The post-war superpowers have been no exception. The Soviet Union and its system proved completely inadequate to resist the encroachment of the global economy. Even the United States economy is, in the words of Robert Reich, 'but a region of the global economy – albeit still a relatively wealthy region' (Reich 1991: 243). It may be, therefore, that the days of a global application of Monnet's principles still lie ahead, and in that sense an organised world order remains to be constructed.

The immediate concern, however, and the scope of this book, is the European stage. It is here where the *mechanism* of organisation has been most developed. And it is here where we must conclude our remarks.

It will be evident now that when talking about the organisation of Europe I do not mean a bureaucracy, or even necessarily a grand design. Market democracies contain a life of their own which evade too much planning. What I do mean is the development of a rule-based society on a European scale which operates *in the margin* between nation and nation, that is in precisely the area where conflict has arisen so often in the past. Rules of society have developed *within* nations. This is usually what we mean by civilisation. What is at stake now in Europe is the development of rules *between* nations. Immanuel Kant once observed that 'Right (or justice) is the sum total of the conditions which are necessary for everybody's free choice to co-exist with that of everybody else, in accordance with a general law of liberty.'[5] This idea – that conditions are necessary for the widest possible freedom of choice – may be said to be the organising principle of the Community. It may also help understand why it is difficult to define the end point of European integration. A system which in effect creates increasing choices is by definition non-deterministic.

This process remains a man-made and quite possibly fragile political experiment. It contains no guarantee of success. A return to the old order based on attempted domination and the rule of force is always possible. However, the collapse of communism and the end of the cold war in Europe provides an extraordinary opportunity to consolidate it. In the previous chapter we reviewed some of the economic and political issues which arise from the integration of the two halves of the continent. Here I would like to make a more general point. The collapse of communism signals not so much the end of history but rather the end of historicism – a phase of European society marked by attempts to align the world on supposedly inevitable, hidden laws of history and economics, and which led ultimately to the totalitarian society. The discrediting of that approach to politics – at least for the moment – forces a re-evaluation of other forms of society, and it forces a re-evaluation of their purpose. It requires western Europe, in particular, for the first time to consider collectively what it is *for* rather more than what it is *against*. This assumption of a new and not necessarily welcome responsibility may not be easy, but it will be necessary if post-communist Europe is to be helped out of the morass.

It is perhaps time for a reconsideration of democratic values. The idea of the open society is old, much older than the Community (and also much older than its member states). Popper identified its spirit in the magnificent funeral oration of Pericles of Athens over 2,400 years ago:

Our political system does not compete with institutions which are elsewhere in force. We do not copy our neighbours, but try to be an example. Our administration favours the many instead of the few: that is why it is called a democracy. The laws afford equal justice to all alike in their private disputes, but do not ignore the claims of excellence . . .. An Athenian citizen does not neglect public affairs when attending to his own private business . . .. We consider a man who takes no interest in the state not as harmless, but as useless; and although only a few may originate a policy, we are all able to judge it. We do not look upon discussion as a stumbling-block in the way of political action, but as an indispensable preliminary to acting wisely.

Democritus too was caught by the same spirit: 'The poverty of a democracy is better than the prosperity which allegedly goes with aristocracy or monarchy, just as liberty is better than slavery . . .. The wise man belongs to all countries, for the home of a great soul is the whole world.' [6] Such words have lost nothing of their resonance today. Perhaps the most moving reaffirmation of the principles of the open society in recent years is to be found in the New Year's Address of January 1990 of President Václav Havel to the newly liberated Czechoslovakia. He marked the ending of forty years of totalitarian rule by concluding with the words 'People, your Government has returned to you!'[7]

With the end of totalitarianism in Europe what is at stake now is the general development of democratic principles. At one stage in European history they were only possible at the level of a fortunate city state. Much later they became feasible at the level of some lucky individual nations. The question now is how to expand such principles by multiplying freedoms on a continental scale – or in other words by organising the open society on the level of Europe itself.

NOTES

PREFACE

1 By Éric Roussel (Fayard) 1994. The quotations are from an article by Roussel entitled 'Monnet et les Américains', published in the 1993 *Revue des débats Européens*, by the Groupe des Belles Feuilles, Paris.
2 Ibid.
3 Ibid.
4 This anecdote is reported by Jean-Louis Mandereau in his contribution to *Témoignages à la mémoire de Jean Monnet* (1989: 342).

1 INVENTING THE EUROPEAN COMMUNITY

1 Keynes made this remark to his French colleague Emmanuel Monick, who mentioned it in his account *Pour Mémoire* (p. 67), subsequently quoted in Monnet (1976: 255).
2 Derek Urwin points out in his guide to post-war European integration *The Community of Europe* (1991: 44) that the idea of pooling coal and steel was in the air in this period, and had already been suggested by reports produced by the Council of Europe and the UN Economic Commission for Europe. It is possible to trace the paternity of the idea even further back. The French Ambassador to London at the time (René Massigli) records in his own memoirs that in 1948 he first heard from *American* officials responsible for Germany the idea of internationalising German industrial production on a non-punitive basis (Massigli 1978: 192).

It is fascinating also to note that, even though no direct link seems to exist, Karl Popper had had a similar idea when in 1943 he wrote *The Open Society and Its Enemies*. He explores a method of treating individual citizens fairly while breaking up the power-organisation of an aggressor state:

> The fringe of the aggressor country, including its sea-coast and its main (not all) sources of water power, coal and steel, could be severed from the state, and administered as an international territory, never to be returned . . . .. The danger that the

214

internationalisation of these facilities might be misused for the purpose of exploiting or of humiliating the population of the defeated country can be counter-acted by international legal measures that provide for courts of appeal, etc.

(Popper 1971: Chapter 9, note 7)

It is of course one thing to have ideas. It is another to persuade others to put them into practice.

3 According to Spaak the report bearing his name 'is largely the fruit of [Uri's] efforts. Uri was one of the principal architects of the Treaty of Rome' (Spaak 1971: 231). Uri was recommended to Spaak by Monnet, and had also worked closely on the economic aspects of the Coal and Steel Community.

4 The figures in this paragraph come from an amalgam of sources: Donaldson's *Guide to the British Economy* (1973: 222), Mattera (1990: 4), and Goodman (1990: 44).

2 THE SHAPE OF THE UNION

1 If Austria, Sweden, Finland and Norway join as planned in 1995 the first two will each receive 4 votes, the latter two 3 votes. The total will be increased to 90 and the number of votes needed to adopt a proposal raised to 64.

2 French Constitutional Council Decision No. 92–308 DC of 9 April 1992, p. 11.

3 German transfer figures from the 1993 OECD *Economic Survey of Germany*, p. 78.

3 THE PRINCIPLES OF THE SINGLE EUROPEAN MARKET

1 Mentioned in an article by Christian Lequesne in the *Revue du Groupe des Belles-Feuilles* (1991).

2 Ibid.

3 Ibid., article by 'Tiresias' (pseudonym of a senior French civil servant).

4 THE SINGLE MARKET IN PRACTICE

1 Both quotations are from a Commission press release on the single market, 10 November 1993.

2 Figures given by Jacques Fournier, President of the European Centre for Public Enterprises, at a conference on the role of the state held in Paris in 1991 (proceedings published by Le-Monde Éditions in 1992 under the title *Où va l'État?*).

3 Suggested by Fournier (at the conference mentioned at 3) and also by MEP Gérard Fuchs (in an article in the *Revue des Débats Européens* by the Groupe des Belles Feuilles (Paris 1993)).

4 The examples are culled from the 1990 publication *Labour Relations in 18 Countries* by Christian Bratt of the Swedish Employers' Confederation.
5 All material from a *Financial Times* survey, 'Business Locations in Europe', October, 1993.

5 FINANCIAL EUROPE

1 'Transparency and Performance of Remote Cross-Border Payments: a Survey by the Commission of the European Communities', summarised in the November 1993 edition of the Commission monthly newsletter *Frontier-Free Europe*.

6 ECONOMIC AND MONETARY UNION

1 French statistics from the French Ministry of Finance. From 1987 to mid-1989 foreign investors purchased almost FF 80 billion worth of French government securities, and were positively encouraged to do so by the French authorities. This liberalisation coincided with the beginning of a long period of franc/DM stability.
2 Although, as Sir Leon Brittan points out (1994: 59), even in the European recession of 1994 ten member states either meet the inflation criterion or are very close to doing so and ten member states also meet the long-term interest criterion. In addition, a majority either meet or are not too far from meeting the two fiscal ratios.

7 AGRICULTURE

1 Figures from Commission publication *A Common Agricultural Policy for the 1990s* (1989: 7).
2 According to the Commission publication *Our Farming Future* (1993: 7), over the twenty years 1970 to 1990 cereal yields almost doubled in France and the Netherlands, and milk yields in France and the Netherlands, sugar yields in Italy and rape yields in Germany increased by almost 50 per cent. Potato yield per hectare doubled in France and Italy between 1960 and 1985.
3 Figures from *Our Farming Future* (p. 25).
4 *A Common Agricultural Policy for the 1990s* (p. 54).
5 Ibid.
6 In the paper *The Development and Future of the Common Agricultural Policy*, published as Bulletin of the European Communities Supplement 5/91, it is stated that 6 per cent of cereals farms account for 50 per cent of surface area in cereals and for 60 per cent of production; 15 per cent of dairy farms produce 50 per cent of milk in the Community; 10 per cent of beef farms have 50 per cent of beef cattle (p. 9).
7 Ibid.; the per capita purchasing power of those engaged in agriculture improved very little over the period 1975 to 1989, but at the same time

216

the active agricultural population fell by 35 per cent (and farm support expenditure doubled in real terms).

8 In the essay 'Pour une Nouvelle Politique Agricole Commune', published in the 1993 *Revue des débats Européens* by the Groupe des Belles Feuilles (Paris).

9 Figures from the Commission publication *A Community of Twelve: Key Figures* (1991: 19).

8   EXTERNAL RELATIONS

1 Commission publication *Europe: World Partner* (1991: 19).

2 World Bank/OECD estimates on the benefits arising from the Uruguay Round, quoted in the *Financial Times*, 16 December 1993.

3 *Europe: World Partner*, p. 10.

4 *Progress Report Number One on EC/US Relations*, p. 5.

5 Ibid., p.2.

6 Letter to the author from M. Jean Guyot, a close associate of Monnet (who in 1954, according to Monnet, conducted a 'brilliant negotiation' when raising the first loan from the US on behalf of the High Authority of the Coal and Steel Community).

7 *Europe: World Partner*, p. 23.

8 Figures from a speech by Mr Nobuo Matsunaga, President of the Japan Institute of International Affairs, in London in 1992.

9 Ibid.

10 All quotes from EFTA Secretariat document *The EEA Agreement* (1992).

9   THE COLLAPSE OF COMMUNISM

1 'We are not building a coalition of states, but a union of peoples' (a speech by Monnet in 1952, used as the motto to Monnet 1976: 7).

2 These, and some other statistics in this chapter, are from the Economic Review *Current Economic Issues* by the European Bank for Reconstruction and Development (1993).

3 Statistics from OECD *Economic Survey of Germany* (1993: 78).

4 Statistics from the paper *The Threat of Managed Trade to Transforming Economies* by Sylvia Ostry (published by the EBRD in 1993).

5 *Current Economic Issues*, p. 17.

6 Figures in this paragraph from the Commission paper *Towards a Closer Association with the Countries of Central and Eastern Europe*, presented to the Copenhagen European Council in June 1993.

7 *Economic Survey of Germany*, p. 79.

8 Quoted in *Le Monde*, 10–11 October 1993. A similar theme can be found in the article by Czech Prime Minister Vaclav Klaus at p. 33 of *The Economist*, 10 September 1994: 'But let the European institutions resist any temptation to favour the division of Europe into two parts, a luckier one and a less lucky one, as in the days of the cold war.'

10 WHAT IS EUROPEAN INTEGRATION?

1 What Churchill suggested in his 1946 Zurich speech was the following:

> The structure of the United States of Europe, if well and truly built, will be such as to make the material strength of a single state less important. Small nations will count as much as large ones and gain their honour by their contribution to the common cause. The ancient states and principalities of Germany, freely joined together for mutual convenience in a federal system, might each take their individual place among the United States of Europe.
>
> (Cannadine 1989: 313).

2 Some quotations from the contribution by the Commission to the inter-governmental conferences which resulted in the Maastricht Treaty (*Bulletin of the European Communities: Supplement 2/91*) give a flavour of this historicism (emphasis mine throughout):

> [The Community] will not be able to put these plans into effect unless at the same time it reinforces the credibility of the objectives of the Single Act and lays the foundations of the *new system of international relations in which history has reserved for it, if it has the will and the means,* an important role alongside the other great world powers.
>
> *The march towards economic and monetary union.*
>
> [T]his will foreshadow the role the Parliament *will play when the building of the Community is complete,* that is to say when European union has been achieved.
>
> (pps 15, 34 and 36)

3 See for example the essay 'Constitutional Reform in the United Kingdom' by Frank Vibert in the 1991 Institute of Economic Affairs publication *Britain's Constitutional Future.*

4 From *Le Monde,* 8 November 1993.

5 *Theory of Right.* (Popper quotes this at Chapter Six, note 4 of Vol. I of the *Open Society.*) The birthplace (Konigsberg) of Kant, the philosopher of pure reason and author of *Perpetual Peace,* was one of the most bombarded pieces of European territory during the last war. It is currently the Russian military enclave known as Kaliningrad (named after the Soviet head of state appointed by Stalin). Its history is as vivid an illustration of departure from the conditions for general liberty in Europe as one might wish to find.

6 Popper's quotations from Pericles come from Book II of Thucydides' *History of the Peloponnesian War* (see Chapter Ten, notes 10, 15, 31 of the *Open Society*), and from Democritus from the fragments of his work in Diels, *Vorsokratiker* (see Chapter Ten, note 29 of Vol. I of the *Open Society*). More generally, Popper has developed in several places the idea that the fundamentals of European democratic civilisation and

politics can be traced back to Greece, and specifically to Athens of the sixth and fifth centuries BC. This is a basic theme of the *Open Society* but see also for example the essay 'Back to the Presocratics' in his *Conjectures and Refutations* (1991), and 'Books and Thoughts – Europe's First Publication' in *In Search of a Better World* (1992). Popper suggests in the latter work (purely as a hypothesis) that it may have been the development of the Athenian book market which triggered the astonishing rise of Athenian civilisation. It would be an interesting project to trace the relationship between the development of the open society on an ever expanding basis in Europe (from small city state to continent) and the expansion of the underlying market economy. If it is true, as A.N. Whitehead once remarked, that all western philosophy consists of footnotes to Plato, perhaps it is also true that most of what we think of as European civilisation can be traced back to the Athenian Agora (which doubled up as place of assembly *and* market).

7 I give the last word to Havel, whose great speech of 1990 (Havel 1991: 390) is the epitaph on totalitarianism in his country. It opens with the words:

> My dear fellow citizens,
> For forty years you heard from my predecessors on this day different variations of the same theme: how our country flourished, how many million tons of steel we produced, how happy we all were, how we trusted our government, and what bright perspectives were unfolding in front of us.
> I assume you did not propose me for this office so that I, too, would lie to you . . .

BIBLIOGRAPHY

GENERAL WORKS REFERRED TO IN THE TEXT

Bagehot, W. (1983) *The English Constitution*, London, Fontana.
Basic Law for the Federal Republic of Germany (1991) Bonn, Press and Information Office, Federal Government.
Brittan, L. (1994) *Europe: The Europe We Need*, London, Hamish Hamilton.
Burgess, S. and Edwards, G. (1988) 'The Six plus One: British Policy-making and the Question of European Economic Integration, 1955', *International Affairs*, London, Royal Institute of International Affairs.
Cannadine, D. (ed) (1989) *Speeches of Winston Churchill*, London, Penguin.
Carrère d'Encausse, Hélène (1992) *Victorieuse Russie*, Paris, Fayard.
Cecchini, P. (1988) *The European Challenge: 1992*, UK, Wildwood House.
Churchill, W.S. (1965) *The Second World War*, Vol. I, London, Cassell.
Colchester, N. and Buchan, D. (1990) *Europe Relaunched: Truths and Illusions on the Way to 1992*, London, Hutchinson Business Books.
Constitution de la République Française (1958) Paris, La documentation française.
Donaldson, P. (1973) *Guide to the British Economy*, London, Pelican.
Goodman, S.F. (1990) *The European Community*, London, Macmillan.
Havel, V. (1991) *Open Letters: Selected Prose*, London, Faber & Faber.
International Organisation and Integration (1983) The Hague, Martinus Nijhoff.
Lawson, N. (1992) *The View From No 11*, London, Bantam Press.
Maritain, J. (1954) *Man and The State*, London, Hollis and Carter.
Massigli, R. (1978) *Une comédie des erreurs 1943–1956*, Paris, Plon.
Mattera, A. (1990) *Le marché unique Européen: ses règles, son fonctionnement*, Paris, Jupiter.
Monnet, J. (1976) *Mémoires*, Paris, Fayard.
Popper, K.R. (1971) *The Open Society and Its Enemies*, Vol. I, Princeton, NJ, Princeton University Press.
Popper, K.R. (1990) *The Open Society and Its Enemies*, Vol. II, London, Routledge.
Popper, K.R. (1991) *Conjectures and Refutations*, London, Routledge.
Popper, K.R. (1992) *In Search of a Better World*, London, Routledge.

Reich, R.B. (1991) *The Work of Nations*, New York, Vintage Books.

Spaak, P.-H. (1971) *The Continuing Battle: Memoirs of a European 1936–66*, translated by H. Fox, London, Weidenfeld & Nicolson.

Taylor, A.J.P. (1975) *English History 1914–1945* (2nd edn), London, Pelican.

Témoignages à la mémoire de Jean Monnet (1989) special limited edition published by the Fondation Jean Monnet pour l'Europe, Lausanne, with prefaces by Hirsch, Uri, Delouvrier, Fontaine and Rieben.

Thompson, J. (1992) *Justice and World Order*, London, Routledge.

Urwin, D.W. (1991) *The Community of Europe: A History of European Integration Since 1945*, London, Longman.

Young, J.W. (1984) *Britain, France and the Unity of Europe 1945–1951*, Leicester, Leicester University Press.

EC DOCUMENTS

There are three main categories of document relevant to this book:

1 Treaties

The ECSC Treaty, the EC Treaty, the Euratom Treaty and the SEA are published together by the Office for Official Publications of the European Communities, L-2985 Luxembourg, in an abridged text dated 1987 (Treaties of the European Communities).

The Maastricht Treaty is published separately by the same office (text dated 1992).

2 Major policy reports (which led to later Treaty change)

Rapport des chefs de délégation aux ministres des affaires etrangères (1956) (known as the 'Spaak Report'). This report, produced under the rubric 'Comité Intergouvernemental Créé par la Conférence de Messine' and produced in Brussels on 21 April 1956 (Reference Mae 120 f/56 (corrigé)) is, as far as I know, unavailable in English. My own copy came from the French government archives.

Report on Economic and Monetary Union in the European Community (1989) by the Committe for the Study of Economic and Monetary Union (known as the 'Delors Report').

White Paper on Completing the Internal Market (1985) by the European Commission, Brussels (referred to as the 'White Paper').

3 Miscellaneous documents by the Commission dealing with specific technical subjects

A Common Agricultural Policy for the 1990s (1989), periodical 5/1989 in the European Documentation series of pamphlets.

A Community of Twelve: Key Figures (1991), Document 6–7/1991 in the European File series.

The Development and Future of the Common Agricultural Policy (1991), bulletin of the European Communities Supplement 5/91.

EEC Competition Policy in the Single Market (1989), periodical 1/1989 in the European Documentation series.

The European Economic Area (1992), pamphlet in the European File series.

Europe: World Partner (1991), in the European Documentation series.

Growth, Competitiveness, Employment (1993) White Paper published as bulletin of The European Communities Supplement 6/93.

Our Farming Future (1993), an updated pamphlet in the European Documentation series.

Guide to VAT in 1993 (1992), specialist guide intended for businesses and taxation experts issued by the Commissioner in charge of taxation, Mme Scrivener.

Intergovernmental Conferences: Contributions by the Commission (1991), bulletin of the European Communities Supplement 2/91.

Progress Report on EC/US Relations (1993), first report in a special series by the Commission, dated July 1993.

Towards a Closer Association with the Countries of Central and Eastern Europe (1993), report by the Commission to the European Council.

Towards a Single Market in Financial Services (1992), document 3/1992 in the European File series.

Most of the above EC documents can be found either in the Information Offices of the European Commission, of which there is at least one in each member state (in the UK there are four: in London, Belfast, Cardiff and Edinburgh) or else in European Documentation Centres, located for the most part in university libraries. In the UK there are over fifty such centres.

INDEX

Acheson, Dean 155
Adenauer, Konrad 6–9, 15
African Caribbean and Pacific
  (ACP) countries 165
agriculture 129–30, 148–50; aims
  of CAP 203; CAP 48, 51, 55,
  129, 135–50, 163; cost of CAP
  144–5; EC public stocks 139; EC
  self-sufficiency 138; farm
  incomes 145–6; green currency
  system 141–4, 150; link with
  common market 130–5; milk
  quotas 144; price mechanism
  136–41; reforms 144, 146–8;
  results of CAP 144–6; set-aside
  schemes 149; Spaak Report 24,
  26–7; state aid 77; support price
  trends 140–1, 143; surpluses
  145; Treaty of Rome 31
Agriculture Council 140
Albania: Comecon 176; EU trade
  agreement 183
Atlantic Alliance 170, 171–88
Atomic Energy Community see
  Euratom
Austria: accession negotiations 38,
  160, 164, 188, 202; EEA, 164;
  EFTA 160, 161, 188; farm
  support system 149

Bagehot, Walter 196
balance of payments 28–9
banking 96–9; independent
  central banks 111, 116, 118;
  single licence 97

Bank of International Settlements
  97
Belgium, attitude to UK member-
  ship 18, see also Benelux
Benelux: Coal and Steel
  Community 7, 8, 12–13, 19;
  defence relations 170
Bevin, Ernest 18, 21
Blair House Agreement (1992) 157
Bodin, Jean 197
Bosnia 172
Bowie, Robert 9, 155
Bretton Woods exchange rate
  system 25, 94, 105, 116–17, 141
Britain see United Kingdom
British Commonwealth 20, 21, 33
British Supply Council 3
Brittan, Sir Leon 43, 100, 209
Brussels 14, 41, 210
Buchan, D. 61, 75
budget, EC 43, 50, 51, 78, 144
Bulgaria: Comecon 176; Europe
  Agreement 183; trade relations
  with EU 183–4
Burgess, S. 34

Cannadine, D. 6, 17, 167, 195
capital: free movement 25, 29, 30,
  69, 94; levels 97; national
  controls 94
Capital Adequacy Directive 100
Carrère d'Encausse, Hélène 180
'Cassis de Dijon' ruling 46, 57
Cecchini Report 29, 61–5, 90, 92
China 158

Churchill, Sir Winston: motto 190; on Franco–German relations 7, 17–18, 166–7; United States of Europe 6, 11, 20, 126, 195
citizenship 49, 163, 204, 210
Clearing House System 59, 72
coal industry, state aid 77; *see also* European Coal and Steel Community
co-decision procedure 42, 43, 44
Colchester, N. 61, 75
commissioners 40
Committee of the Regions 47, 49
Committees of Inquiry 44
Common Agricultural Policy (CAP) *see* agriculture
common commercial policy 48
common market: approach 22–30, 211; coal and steel 8; competition rules 74; definition 54; partial completion 31, 34, 106–7; UK attitude 33
communism, collapse of 36, 39, 176–8, 192–3, 212; global economy 173, 211; motor of growth 181–5; problem of method 188–91; re-inventing the state 178–81; rule of law 185–8; state subsidies 78; switch in trade 16, 78
competition policy 9, 27, 59, 74–5, 84–5, 90, 119
Conciliation Committee 44
Conference of Parliaments 209
consensus 53, 66
Copenhagen European Council 184, 188
Council for Mutual Economic Assistance (CMEA, Comecon) 16, 78, 176–8, 186, 200
Council of Ministers: administration 42; origins 13, 26; role 40–1; working methods 41
Court of Auditors 47, 143
Court of First Instance 47
Croatia 184
cross-border financial transfers 98, 127

CSFR, former: Europe Agreement 183; trade relations with EU 181–2, 184
currency: crises (1992, 1993) 113–15; single 29, 38, 108; snake 105; transfers 24
customs union 25, 30–1, 37, 55, 66, 163
Cyprus: application 38; EU agreement 165
Czechoslovakia: association agreement 38; Comecon 176; split 179, 180, 184
Czech Republic 184, 193

Decisions 42
defence 169
de Gaulle, Charles 3, 34, 156
Delors, Jacques 53, 107, 210
Delors Report 92, 107–10, 113, 115, 119–21, 122, 124, 127
democracy 207–10
Democritus 213
Denmark: accession 1, 37, 162; EFTA 161; Maastricht referenda 38, 114
developing countries, EU relations 164–5
Directives 42
Directorates-General: DG I (External Relations) 40; DG III (Internal Market) 16, 40; DG IV (Competition) 16, 40; DG VI (Agriculture) 40; DG VIII (Development) 40; DG XVI (Regional Policy) 40

EC–Japan Joint Declaration 158
Economic and Monetary Union (Emu) 104–7, 125–8, 203; analysis 122–5; crisis in the system 113–18; Delors Report 92, 107–10; economic union 118–21; EEA exclusion 163; Inter-Governmental Conference 38; Maastricht Treaty 92, 110–13
Economic and Social Committee 47

EC Treaty (European Economic Community Treaty 1957, Treaty of Rome) 30–2; barriers to aims 187; common agricultural policy 48, 130, 133–5; common market 54; common transport policy 48; competition rules 74; Council of Ministers 41; Court of Justice 46; EFTA 161; exchange rates and currency 104–5; external economic relations 152–4; harmonisation 86; Maastricht additions 110; monopolies 81; movement of capital 94–5; nationalised industries 79; objectives 106; service sector 55; Social Fund 48

Edwards, G. 34

employment: agricultural 150; free movement of employees 25, 58; industrial 150; self-employed 58; services 150; single market effects 61; unemployment 61, 123, 178

Erhard, Ludwig 32

Euratom 23, 32–3, 35, 40

Europe Agreements 183, 184

European Atomic Energy Community Treaty 1957 (Treaty of Rome) 32–3

European Central Bank 46, 47, 48, 109, 121, 125

European Coal and Steel Community 5–17; administration 26; creation 7, 34, 203; development 23; Franco–German reconciliation 5–10, 15, 17–18, 20–1, 23, 32; High Authority 9–16; UK attitude 18, 21–2, 33

European Coal and Steel Community Treaty 1951 (ECSC Treaty, Treaty of Paris) 3, 7–10, 12, 23, 37, 74, 155

European Commission: banking survey 98; Berlaymont building 210; 'college' of commissioners 40; Directorates-General 16, 40; farm prices 140; merger controls 76; origins 3, 16, 26; powers 35, 203; roles 40; single market 53; staff 40; state aid policy 78

European Community (EC): activities 205; budget 43, 50, 51, 78, 144; coal and steel 16; decision taking 53, 66; enlargement 203; institutions 40; intervention policies 30; members' expectations 22, 205–6; sovereignty issue 196–202; term xvi, 38; US relations xiii; see also European Union

European Council: Emu 104, 107, 113; origins 3, 12–13, 41; relationship with Parliament 44, 208; role 41–2, 43, 49; single currency decision 111–12; voting system 13

European Court of Justice: 'Cassis de Dijon' ruling 46, 57; economic law 187; insurance ruling 101; origins 12, 14, 26; powers 203; role 44–7; single market 54

European Currency Unit (Ecu) 108, 111, 127

European Defence Community 21, 22, 35, 169, 170

European Economic Area (EEA) 38, 91, 151, 152, 160–4, 185

European Economic Community Treaty 1957 (Treaty of Rome) see EC Treaty

European Free Trade Area (EFTA): creation 161–2; EEA creation 38, 91, 160, 162–4, 184, 185; members' accession to EU 51, 54, 188–9; trade relations with EC 152, 182, 184

European Investment Bank 31, 47, 165

European Investment Fund 30

European Monetary Institute (EMI) 47, 111

European Monetary System (EMS) 48, 105–6, 107–9, 113–17, 163; crises (1992–3) 113–16, 117, 122

European Parliament: co-decision procedure 43; Conference of Parliaments 209; origins 12, 14, 26; relationship with Council 44, 208; rights 43–4; role 43–4, 209

European Parliamentary Assembly 12, 14, 26, 26

European Social Fund 31, 48

European System of Central Banks (ESCB) 109, 110, 127, 203

European Union (EU): concept 49, 168; decision taking 42, 207; defence 170–1; democracy 207–10; external relations 151–2, 173–5; institutions 39–47; policies 47–52; term xvi, 38; *see also* European Community

Exchange Rate Mechanism (ERM) 106, 108–9, 113

exchange rates 25, 27, 29, 104–6, 113–18, 123–4, 127–8

expenditure policies 50

External Relations 151–2, 173–5; common foreign and security policy 163, 166–72; with developing countries 164–5; economic relations 152–4; European Economic Area 160–4; with Japan 157–60, 175; with US 154–7, 175

Falklands invasion 167

farming *see* agriculture

farm support mechanisms 136

federation 11

financial services sector 92–3, 101–3; banking 96–9; compartmentalisation 93; divided market 93–5; insurance 100–1; integration 95–6; mutual recognition 96; securities transactions 99–100; single licence 96

Finland: accession negotiations

38, 160, 164, 188, 202; EEA 164; EFTA 160, 188; farm support system 149

foreign currency transfers 24

foreign policy: co-operation 39, 40, 152; common 163, 166–72

France: agricultural production 140; Coal and Steel Community 7–17, 19, 32; constitution 194, 209; defence relations 170; farm support prices 141–2; financial market 95; franc 105–6, 141; Maastricht proposals 126; Maastricht referendum 115; monopolies 81; national central bank 111; nuclear energy programme 33; relations with Germany 5–10, 15, 17–18, 20–1, 23, 32; Renault aid 78; sovereignty 196; Spaak Report discussions 30; trade unions 88; UK entry vetoes 34, 37

freedom of movement 29, 30, 69, 95, 119, 162

free trade area 25, 26

French Constitutional Council 43

French Modernisation Commission 35

frontier controls 69, 70, 71

General Agreement on Tariffs and Trade (Gatt): agriculture 26; customs union 25, 132; EC representation 154; impact on EC 149, 153; rules 25, 132; Uruguay Round 129, 148, 153, 157, 159, 173, 174, 175

Generalised System of Preferences 165

Germany: abolition of capital movement restrictions 94; agricultural production 140; Bundesbank 108, 114, 115; Coal and Steel Community 7–17, 19; constitution 194, 209; DM 105, 106, 108, 113, 114, 115, 118, 123; EU development 126; farm support prices 141–2, 143; former East 16, 39, 43, 149, 171,

176, 179, 180, 181, 188–9;
Maastricht ratification 122–3;
Nato 170; nuclear energy
programme 33; post-war
economy 5, 32; rearmament
issue 21, 22, 170, 171; relations
with France 5–10, 15, 17–18,
20–1, 23, 32; sound money 108,
110, 115; sovereignty 196; trade
unions 88; Treuhand 179;
unification 39, 43, 114, 115, 123,
171, 179, 188, 195; WEU 170
global economy 173–4, 211
Greece: financial market 95; joins
EC 37
green currency system 141–4, 150
Greenland 39
G7 154

harmonisation 27–8, 57–8, 66, 86
Havel, Václav 190, 213
health and safety 58, 86
Hegel, Georg Wilhelm Friedrich
198, 200, 208
High Authority of the European
Coal and Steel Community:
creation 2, 9–11, 17, 21; develop-
ment of Euratom 23, 32, 35;
European Commission 16, 40;
first President 3; powers of
intervention 14; relationship with
member states 12–13, 35, 203;
siting 13–14; UK view 17, 21–2
High Contracting Parties 167–8
Hitler, Adolf 17
Hobbes, Thomas 198, 202
Hopkins, Harry xiii
Hungary: application 38, 188;
association agreement 38;
Comecon 176; trade relations
with EU 181–2, 184, 193

Iceland 160, 164
inflation 178
information, obtaining and
publishing 9–10
Insider Dealing Directive 100
insurance 68, 100–1
interest rates 27, 108, 112, 114

Inter-Governmental Conference
on Economic and Monetary
Union (1990) 38
Inter-Governmental Conference
on Political Union (1990) 38
Inter-Governmental Conference
to revise the Treaty of Rome
(1985) 38
internal market 38
International Monetary Fund
(IMF) 94, 105
International Steel Cartel 7, 15
Investment Services Directive
99–100
Investor Compensation Directive
100
Ireland: accession 1, 37
Israel: EU policy 172
Italy: agricultural production 140;
Coal and Steel Community 7, 8,
13, 19; financial market 95; lira
106, 113; state aid to industry
77; WEU 170

Japan: banks 97; economy 151,
152, 173; financial firms 102;
Gatt 173; power erosion 173;
relations with eastern Europe
182, 185, 192; relations with EU
157–60, 175

Kant, Immanuel 212
Kennedy, John F. 155–6
Keynes, John Maynard 3
Kissinger, Henry 2

law, EC: direct effect 45; primacy
over national law 45, 209;
proliferation of legislation 67;
value to eastern Europe 187
Lawson, Nigel 125–6, 127
League of Nations 3, 4, 7, 12
Liechtenstein 160, 164
Lomé Convention 165
Louis, J.V. 195
Luxembourg: compromise 37; ECJ
44; High Authority siting 14,
17; see also Benelux
Maastricht Treaty 1992 (Treaty on

European Union): agriculture 134; citizenship concept 49, 204, 210; common foreign and security policy 151–2, 167–72, 173, 204; Conference of Parliaments 209; Court of Justice 46–7; creation of institutions 47; EC activities 48; economic aspects 24, 39, 203, 204; EMS crises 113–14; Emu 47, 54, 92, 104, 107, 110–13, 121, 122–3, 127; European Council 42, 44; European Parliament 43, 44; European Union 49–50; German ratification 122; industrial cooperation 83–4; negotiations 126; 'pillars' 40, 152; Protocol on Social Policy 86–9; ratification xi; signing 38

Macmillan, Harold 19–20

macroeconomic issues 28–9, 64–5, 119, 120–1

MacSharry reforms 144–8

Malta: application 38; EU agreement 165

Mansholt, Sicco 149

Maritain, Jacques 197–9

market: economies 202–3; order 47–8; regulation 27; reinforcement measures 74; see also common market, single market

Marshall Plan xiii, 32, 155, 176, 192

Marx, Karl 200

Mattera, A. 46, 54, 195

Mayne, Richard 130, 210

Mayrisch, Emile 6–7

Mediterranean countries 165

Members of the European Parliament (MEPs) 43

Merger Control Regulation (1989) 76

mergers, large-scale company 76

Merger Treaty (1967) 16

Messina conference (1955) 23

Middle East, EU policy 172

Monetary Compensatory Amounts (MCAs) 142

Monnet, Jean 2–5; agriculture policy 129–30; background xii–xiv; Coal and Steel Community 6–15, 17; on Community 35, 177, 206, 210; on Free Trade Area 161; French economic modernisation 32; Japan relations 157–8; Messina conference 23; Provisional European Government 41; UK entry views 18–22; US relationship xiii, 154–6, 175; vision of Community 46, 189–90, 194–5; Werner Report 104

monopolies and monopoly practices 24, 27, 80–1, 186

mutual recognition 57–8, 96

national: capital controls 94; regulations 24, 25, 56–7, 66

nationalised industries 79

Netherlands, guilder 113; see also Benelux

North Atlantic Free Trade Area (NAFTA) 157, 160

North Atlantic Treaty Organisation (Nato) 21, 169, 170, 171, 172

Norway: accession negotiations 38, 160, 164, 188, 202; EEA 164; EFTA 160, 161, 188; farm support system 149

nuclear energy 23, 32, 33

OECD 154, 181–2, 185, 192

oil price shocks 53

Ombudsman 44

Opinions 42

'Partnership and Co-operation Agreements' 183

pension funds 102

petition, right of 44

'pillars' 40, 152

Plato 200

Plowden, Lord 2, 19

Poland: application 38, 188; association agreement 38; Comecon 176; economy 181; Europe Agreement 183;

government 180; trade relations with EU 181–2, 184, 193
Political Co-operation 38, 49, 172
Popper, Sir Karl vi, xii, 89, 128, 197–201, 209, 212
Portugal: accession 37, 165, 189; EFTA 161; financial market 95
posts and telecommunications 23
Presidency 42, 43
price mechanism, agricultural 136–41
protectionism 53
Protocol on Social Policy 86–8
Provisional European Government 41
public expenditure: programmes 51; subsidies 53, 77; *see also* state aid

qualifications, professional 58
quotas 24, 25, 144

recession 53, 118, 123
Recommendations 42
Regional Development Fund 48, 83
regional-level action 49
Regulations 42
Reich, Robert 159–60, 173–4, 175, 211
Research and Technological Development Programmes, Community 83
Retraining Fund 30
Romania: Comecon 176; Europe Agreement 183; trade relations with EU 183–4
Roosevelt, Franklin D. 3, 155
Rousseau, Jean-Jacques 198
Roussel, Eric xiii
Ruhr 5, 7, 9
Russian Federation: Bosnia engagement 172; capital flight 178; EU membership question 193; Europe Agreement 183

Saar 3, 5
Saint-Simon, Comte de 201
salaries 27, 28

Schuman Plan 3, 7, 19–20, 21, 155
Second Banking Coordination Directive (1988) 96–7, 99–100
securities transactions 99–100
service sector 24, 26, 53, 58–9
single currency 29, 38, 104, 110–13; economic criteria 112
Single European Act 1986 (SEA): agriculture 134; Court of First Instance 47; economic integration 39; Emu 104; EU policies 48; European Council 42; European Parliament 43; external relations 167; freedom of movement 69, 95, 162; research and development 83; signing and ratification 38, 55; single market legislation 41, 53–4, 55, 66–7; size 110; social issues 86
Single European Market: agreement to go forward 66–7; Delors Report 119; economic welfare gains 64; fiscal barriers 56, 59–60, 71–3; further market measures 74–81; incomplete 119; industrial co-operation 81–5; in practice 68–9, 90–1; medium-term macroeconomic effects 65; monetary union 123; origins 16; physical barriers 56, 69–70; principles 53–5; programme 31, 55–60; promise of growth 60–6; Social Europe 85–90; target date for completion 38, 60, 68; technical barriers 56–9, 70–1
single licence 96
Slovak Republic 184; *see also* Czechoslovakia
Slovenia 183
Smith, Adam 30
Social Charter (1989) 86–7
Social Europe 28, 85–90
social security costs 28, 51
Solemn Declaration on European Union 38
South Africa sanctions 167
sovereignty: Coal and Steel

Community 19, 34; fiscal issues 73; French Constitutional Council's view 43; Monnet's aims 35, 195; problem 196–202; term 36, 195–6, 205; UK attitude 22

Soviet Union, former: collapse in trade 16, 181; Comecon 176; fragmentation 179; hyper-inflation 178; invasion of Prague 31; Marshall Plan 176; opinion poll 180; resources 191; threat 18, 20–1, 22, 171

Spaak, Paul-Henri 18, 23, 30

Spaak Report: agriculture 130–5; common market benefits 66; free movement of capital 29, 94, 104, 116–17; harmonisation 27–8, 66, 85–6; influence on Treaties of Rome xiii, 31, 32, 33, 54, 130, 160–1; monopolies 24, 27, 80, 186; single market objective 54–5, 90, 106, 211

Spain: accession 37, 165, 189; financial market 95

Stability Pact for Europe 172

Stalin, Josef 21

standards, differing national 53, 56–7

state aid to industry 27, 53, 59, 76–81, 184, 186

Statute for a European Company 83

steel production 5, 7, 16, 184

Strasbourg: European Parliament 43; High Authority siting proposal 14

subsidiarity, concept of 50

subsidies see state aid

supply-side economics 29–30, 64

Surveillance Authority 162

Sweden: accession negotiations 38, 160, 164, 188, 202; EEA 164; EFTA 160, 162, 188; farm support system 149

Switzerland: accession application 38; EEA vote 164; EFTA 160, 162

takeovers, company 82–3

taxation: Coal and Steel

Community arbitration 10; company 83; costs 28; differing practices 60, 72–3; fiscal barriers to single market 59–60; legislation 25; VAT see VAT

Taylor, A.J.P. 2

Thompson, Janna 197

Trade and Co-operation Agreements 183

trade unions 28, 86, 88

Transatlantic Declaration 156

Trans-European Networks 83

transition period 30, 34

transport: common policy creation 31; liberalisation 69; single market legislation 68; state aid 77; tariffs 24

Treaties of Rome see EC Treaty and European Atomic Energy Community Treaty

Treaty of Paris see European Coal and Steel Community Treaty

Treaty on European Union 1992 see Maastricht Treaty

Turkey: application 38; EU agreement 165

Ukraine 183

'Undertakings for Collective Investment in Transferable Securities' 99

unemployment 61, 123, 178

United Kingdom (UK): abolition of capital movement restric-tions 94; accession 17, 34, 37, 162; accession applications 34, 37; budgetary contribution problem 38; Coal and Steel Community 17–22; defence relations 170; EFTA 161–2; Emu 109, 113, 123; green currency system 142; House of Lords 209; implementation of Directives 42; interest in European movement 11, 17–18; Rover–British Aerospace deal 78; Social Policy opt-out 86; sovereignty 196; sterling 105–6, 113; trade unions 88;

Treaty of Rome 33–4; US alliance 20; US investment 91; *see also* British
United Nations (UN) 151, 154, 165
United States of America (US): banks 97; Bosnia policy 172; economy 151, 152; financial firms 102; investment in Europe 91; Monnet's relationship xiii, 154–5; nuclear technology 23; post-war Germany policies 5, 9, 21; power erosion 173; relations with eastern Europe 182, 185, 192; relations with EU 154–7, 171, 175; relations with UK 20, 91
United States of Europe xii, 6, 11, 20, 126, 195
unit trusts 99
Uri, Pierre 23
VAT 59–60, 72–3; Information Exchange System 72

Versailles Treaty 16
Voluntary Export Restraints 184
voting system: number of votes 43; qualified majority 13, 42–3; 66–7; simple majority 42; unanimous 41, 42

Walesa, Lech 190
Warsaw Pact 171
Werner Report 104, 105
Western European Union (WEU) 170–1
White Paper (1985) 53, 55–60, 69–71, 76, 78, 81–3, 95
White Paper (1993) 183
World Trade Organisation 174

Young, J.W. 21
Yugoslavia, former: EU relations 172, 188, 189; fragmentation 179–80; problems 172, 181, 189; trade 181, 184

THE ORGANISATION OF EUROPE

By examining the basic ideas behind the complexities of European economic and political integration, and by giving an overview both of today's problems and their historical background, *The Organisation of Europe* provides a key to understanding one of the most important economic and political developments in modern times.

David Harrison suggests that the heart of the process of integration has been the gradual development over the post-war period f a European market economic order, with its own institutions nd rules. This process is new, dynamic and open-ended, and is t easily explained in terms of traditional political models. The orporation of post-communist Europe provides its next major allenge.

n an examination of the main European policy problems rket building from the common market to the single market, nomic and monetary union, financial integration, agricultural licy, relations with the rest of the world and political union) to its conclusion, which contains an analysis of what is at stake in European integration (and a critical look at the widely accepted idea of transferring or retaining sovereignty), this volume is easily accessible and a valuable, jargon-free explanation of a nique economic and political experiment.

avid Harrison is a former British diplomat who has also orked as a consultant on the French financial markets and for e European Bank for Reconstruction and Development.